THE OFFICIAL PRICE GUIDE TO

DOLLS

BY
THE HOUSE OF COLLECTIBLES, INC.

We have compiled information herein through a *patented computerized process* which relies primarily on a nationwide sampling of information provided by noteworthy collectible experts, auction houses and specialized dealers. This sophisticated retrieval system enables us to provide the reader with the most current and accurate information available.

EDITOR
THOMAS E. HUDGEONS III

SECOND EDITION
THE HOUSE OF COLLECTIBLES, INC., ORLANDO, FLORIDA 32809

IMPORTANT NOTICE. The format of **THE OFFICIAL PRICE GUIDE SERIES**, published by **THE HOUSE OF COLLECTIBLES, INC.**, is based on the following proprietary features: **ALL FACTS AND PRICES ARE COMPILED THRU A COMPUTERIZED PROCESS** which relies on a nationwide sampling of information obtained from noteworthy collectibles experts, auction houses and specialized dealers. **DETAILED "INDEXED" FORMAT** enables quick retrieval of information for positive identification. **ENCAPSULATED HISTORIES** preceed each category to acquaint the collector with the specific traits that are peculiar to that area of collecting. **VALUABLE COLLECTING INFORMATION** is provided for both the novice as well as the seasoned collector: How to begin a collection; How to buy, sell, and trade; Care and storage techniques; Tips on restoration; Grading guidelines; Lists of periodicals, clubs, museums, auction houses, dealers, etc. **AN AVERAGE PRICE RANGE** takes geographic location and condition into consideration when reporting collector value. **A SPECIAL 3rd PRICE COLUMN** enables the collector to compare the current market values with the last's years average selling price . . . indicating which items have increased in value. **INVENTORY CHECKLISTS SYSTEM** is provided for cataloging a collection. **EACH TITLE IS ANNUALLY UP-DATED** to provide the most accurate information available in the rapidly changing collectors marketplace.

All of the information, including valuations, in this book has been compiled from the most reliable sources, and every effort has been made to eliminate errors and questionable data. Nevertheless the possibility of error, in a work of such immense scope, always exists. The publisher will not be held responsible for losses which may occur, in the purchase, sale, or other transaction of items, because of information contained herein. Readers who feel they have discovered errors are invited to WRITE and inform us, so they may be corrected in subsequent editions. Those seeking further information on the topics covered in this book, are advised to refer to the complete line of Official Price Guides published by The House of Collectibles.

© MCMLXXXIV The House of Collectibles, Inc.

All rights reserved. No part of this book may be reproduced or utilized in any form or by any means, electronic or mechanical, including photocopying, recording, or by any information storage and retrieval system, without permission in writing from the publisher.

Published by: The House of Collectibles, Inc.
Orlando Central Park
1900 Premier Row
Orlando, FL 32809
Phone: (305) 857-9095

Printed in the United States of America

Library of Congress Catalog Card Number: 82-84647

ISBN: 0-87637-434-8 / Paperback

TABLE OF CONTENTS

Market Review	1
Building A Doll Collection	3
Investing And Selling	8
Doll Repairs	12
Doll Fakes	14
Care, Storage, And Display	16
Glossary	22
Doll Manufacturers' Marks	31
Common Abbreviations	40
Books	41
Clubs	44
Museums	45
Recommended Reading	48
How To Use This Book	49
Alexander Doll Company, Inc.	51
American Character Doll Company	62
Arranbee Doll Company	68
Arrow Plastic	72
Aspen Productions	74
Averill Manufacturing Company	75
Baby Berry	76
Bantam	77
Belton	78
Bergmann	79
Ernst Bohne	81
Borden	82
George Borgfeldt	82
Bru	84
Buschow And Beck	87
Cameo	88
C.B.S.	90
Chad Valley Company	92
Martha Chase	93
Patti Chimera	94
Columbia Toy Products	95
Cosmopolitan	96
Dakin	97
Thomas Dam	99
Dee Cee	100
Dolly's Dolls	101
Dream Dolls	102
Cuno And Otto Dressel	104
Duchess	105
Eegee	107
Effanbee	110
Eppy	122
Excel	123
Fisher Price	125
Fleischaker	127
Fleisher Studios	128
Fun World	129
Fy	131
Gama	132
Gaultier	133
Gebruder Heubach	135
Gebruder Krauss	137
Gerber	138
William Goebel	139
Gorham	142
Greiner	143
Hallmark Cards	144
Heinrich Handwerck	145
Hazelle's	149
Heubach Kopplesdorf	150
Holiday Fair	154
Hollywood Doll Company	155
Hummel	156
Ideal	156
Imperial	180
Irwin	181
Japan	183
Jolly	184
Jumeau	186
Junel	195
Kenner	196
Kestner	199
King Features	202
Kathe Kruse	205
A. Lanternier	206
Lenci	208
Lesney	211
Limoges	213
Lovee	214
Armand Marseille	215
Mattel	219
Metti	229
Migliorati	230
Edward Moberly	231
Nancy Ann Storybook Doll Company	233
Nasco	239
Ruth E. Newton	240
Rose O'Neill	241
Adelaide Patti	243
Perfecta	244
Petite Portraits	244
Pierotti	245
Princess Christina	246
Grace Storey Putnam	246
Bernard Ravca	248
Otto Reinecke	249
Royal Doulton	250
Schmid	253
Schoenhut	254
Schulte	256
Skippy	257
Steiff	258
Terry Lee	260
Vanity	260
Vogue	261
Walt Disney Productions	264
Bergman Walterhausen	268
Norah Wellings	268
Paper Dolls	289

ACKNOWLEDGMENTS

We would like to thank the East Florida Doll Collector's Guild for allowing us photographic privileges at their January 1983 Doll Show. For their cooperation we would like to thank the following: Annabelle Hahn, Venice, FL 33595; Antique Appraisal, Bill and Mary New, Holiday, FL 33590; Jean Bayl, Maitland, FL 32751; Bobi's Doll Creations, Bobi Langkau, Portage, WI 53901; Cathie Clark, Springfield, OH 45505; Dolly's Dolls, Minnie Byrd and Dollie Robbins, Jacksonville, FL 32208; The Doll Shop, Joyce Imhoff, Richmond, IN 47374; Marcia Duggins, Melbourne, FL 32935; Everett Filder-Auctioneers, Orlando, FL 32817; The Ginny Doll Club, Lakeland, FL 33803; Olive Jolly, Delray Beach, FL 33444; Joyce's Dolls, Joyce Terry, St. Augustine, FL 32084; Lady Arden Dolls, Toledo, OH 43607; Lavonne McElroy, Great Falls, MT; Porcelain by Sonja, Bellbrook, OH 45305; Mabel C. Sousa, Punta Gorda, FL 38950; Suzanne Gibson Dolls, Auburn, NY 13021.

PHOTO RECOGNITION

COVER — Marc Hudgeons, Orlando, FL 32809.

BECOME AN "OFFICIAL" CONTRIBUTOR TO THE WORLD'S LEADING PRICE GUIDES

Are you an experienced collector with access to information not covered in this guide? Do you possess knowledge, data, or ideas that should be included?

If so, The House of Collectibles invites you to **GET INVOLVED**.

The House of Collectibles continuously seeks to improve, expand, and update the material in the **OFFICIAL PRICE GUIDE SERIES**. The assistance and cooperation of numerous collectors, auction houses and dealers has added immeasurably to the success of the books in this series. If you think you qualify as a contributor, our editors would like to offer your expertise to the readers of the **OFFICIAL PRICE GUIDE SERIES**.

As the publishers of the most popular and authoritative Price Guides, The House of Collectibles can provide a far-reaching audience for your collecting accomplishments. *Help the hobby grow* by letting others benefit from the knowledge that you have discovered while building your collection.

If your contribution appears in the next edition, you'll become an **"OFFICIAL"** member of the world's largest hobby-publishing team. Your name will appear on the acknowledgement page, *plus you will receive a free complimentary copy.* Send a full outline of the type of material you wish to contribute. Please include your phone number. Write to: **THE HOUSE OF COLLECTIBLES, INC.,** Editorial Department, 1900 Premier Row, Orlando, Florida, 32809.

NOTE TO READERS

All advertisements appearing in this book have been accepted in good faith, but the publisher assumes no responsibility in any transactions that occur between readers and advertisers.

MARKET REVIEW

Whether due to a stronger economy or not, experts agree that the doll market continues to get stronger, with rare dolls being the most sought after items. A rare French "A Marque" doll sold for $38,000 earlier this year, setting a world's record for a single doll sold at an auction. This alone tells much of the success the doll market has enjoyed in the past year.

Experts were often surprised with the selling prices of dolls since the sale price frequently was higher than expected estimates.

German bisque dolls are making an upward trend, as are German dolls with character faces. A bisque laughing faced child sold this year for more than $2,000; socket-headed dolls for close to $3,000; a socket-headed toddler around $1,000; and a character baby sold for about $1,100.

French bisque dolls are also popular. A French bisque child doll sold for more than $2,000; a five-inch French character doll went for $1,000; and swivel neck fashion dolls are selling at prices between $1,100 and $3,000. A swivel-headed child sold for close to $3,000.

According to experts, American dolls are receiving some good prices at auctions around the country. A Sheppard Baby, in excellent condition and dating near 1900, received close to $2,000 while a Shirley Temple doll, dating close to 1935, received $600. Madame Alexander dolls also did fairly well; in fact, they have become the number one doll to collect in the modern category.

American folk art dolls are starting to go for as much as $4,000. Experts believe that cloth dolls, and especially American primitives such as the Izannah Walker dolls are just beginning to come into their own.

Brus are not quite as popular as in past years — partly because they are not as rare as once thought. Though experts claim that rare Brus, and black and oriental Brus are coming to the forefront of their popularity.

In fact, there is more demand for black dolls, and predictions say that their rise in popularity is just beginning. A black bisque "Butler" doll house doll sold for more than $500, and some black dolls are selling for as much as $3,000 and $4,000.

The trend toward the rare dolls is certainly evident, and experts report cases of rarities going for all-time high prices. For example, a Britains Bahamas Police and Bandsmen sold at the highest price ever at an auction earlier this year. This particular item is especially rare since it was made only for one year and only for the Bahamas.

Lenci dolls, in good clean condition or rare ones in any condition, are also going at good prices. In recent months a Lenci golfer sold for close to $3,500; glass eyed girls and boys sold for more than $2,000; and a goose girl went for close to $950. The Gibson Girl dolls especially those by Kestner and Simon and Halbig may be on the brink of a rise in popularity. They have been selling at prices of more than $1,000.

And everybody's favorite rag dolls, Raggedy Ann and Andy, are still in demand. In fact, a recent popularity poll ranks these two in the top ten of favorite toys.

Very large and very small dolls don't appear to be quite as much in demand. China dolls, all-bisque dolls, and doll house dolls have dropped in popularity during recent years.

While rare dolls seem to have done the best this year with their sales soaring, remember that an outstanding example of anything always does well.

BUILDING A DOLL COLLECTION

If you become a doll collector you'll be in good and ever-growing company. Latest estimates place the doll collecting population in the U.S. at one million, easily ranking it as one of the most popular hobbies. The huge scope of doll collecting leads to many benefits for the hobbyists, such as special publications to receive and clubs to join. Doll collecting groups and societies are scattered all across the country.

Also, the heavy demand for dolls brings more and more specimens out into the market, at antiques shops, shows, garage sales, flea markets and other places. Collectors never need to wonder where to find dolls for sale. Instead they must think about how to specialize in one type of doll, since it would be impossible to buy everything .

Of course you can collect dolls strictly from retail shops — currently made dolls sold at the manufacturer's list prices. Hundreds of new dolls are available in different types including character, novelty, and traditional dolls. There's nothing wrong with buying dolls off the current commercial market, since some of them are bound to climb in value when they stop being produced. This is a way of "investing" along with collecting. However, most hobbyists find confining a collection to the currently marketed dolls unsatisfactory. There is a charm and appeal in the older dolls which, in the eyes of the average collector, is lacking from most new dolls. By adding older dolls to your collection, or concentrating on them exclusively, you can acquire many more different types. You can get unusual dolls and even, rarities. The older dolls are more historical and the quality of some — such as the chinas and bisques — surpass anything being manufactured today.

Fortunately the older dolls, even those more than 100 years old , are available to own and enjoy. Countless old dolls have perished through the years from breakage and other causes. But so many were manufactured, for so long a period of time, that an ample quantity has survived for today's collector. Most antiques shops have a few old dolls for sale. Some specialize in dolls and offer a selection of dozens or even hundreds. Then there are doll dealers (many of whom are collector/dealers) operating by mail, who issue lists and advertise in the hobbyist magazines. There are also collector auctions that feature dolls.

Yet even with all the old dolls passing through the market, going from the hands of dealers to collectors and vice-versa, there are still many awaiting discovery. America's attics continue to hold treasures untold. Most dolls on the market came out of attics, but the supply has been barely tapped. There are tens of thousands, possibly millions, more collectible dolls in attics right now. Either the owners are unaware of them, or do not know of their status. Most dolls found their way to the attic when the little lady of the house got too old to play with them — or received a new doll and lost interest in the old one. They were too nice to throw away, so they were sent to the attic . The idea morgin was that the grandchildren, could eventually inherit them. But often they were forgotten. Or they were out of style by then, so the grandkiddies received new dolls and those precious old ones just sat and sat, gathering cobwebs. Explore your attic, it could yield the beginnings of a doll collection!

Doll collecting has its rarities and its high-priced stellar attractions: dolls which cost hundreds of dollars and some that even go into the four-digit category. This is because of the large numbers of margin buyers competing for the better, scarcer specimens. If just 20 specimens of a particular doll are in existence and 5,000 collectors are anxious to own one, they will bid for it and boost the price up. Your local antiques shop may have an early china doll in the show window — a museum-type doll that passersby fall in love with, even if they have no interest in old dolls. The pricetag reads $300 or $400 and that sends a chill along your spine when you think of YOURSELF collecting dolls. How could the hobby be adaptable to a week-by-week budget? The answer is that this doll, or any other high priced specimens, is not representative of all collectible dolls. There are rarities and super-value items in the hobby, but the majority can be had for very moderate prices. Not all collectible dolls fall into the "antique" classification. Of those which DO, many are fairly reasonably priced. The doll which is OLD — SCARCE — BEAUTIFULLY MADE — and FINELY PRESERVED is the exception, not the rule. Hobbyists with unlimited cash to spend WISH dolls fitting that description came along regularly. They simply don't. For every $300 or $400 doll on the open market, there are dozens priced at $10, $20 and $30. In fact, you will often spend LESS on an old collectible doll than for a brand new doll in the toyshop. Chiefly, the higher priced specimens are china and bisque dolls. If you collect dolls of cloth, composition, celluloid, chalk, vinyl, plastic, rubber or other substances, you will not find many high prices. Avoid china and bisque and you can adapt doll collecting to just about any budget! Of course, even with china and bisque it is possible to collect on a tight budget, if you avoided "name" dolls and do some saving-up between purchases. It's all up to you!

A collection needs a focal point, a core to build around. Nobody just buys "old dolls"; each hobbyist has favorites, which he looks for and shuts his eyes to other kinds. There isn't much choice but to do this, since the range of collectible dolls is so enormous. So the first step in becoming a collector is to decide what kind of dolls to collect. The listings and pictures in this book should help, if you don't already have a fairly good idea. Even if you DO already lean toward one kind of doll, take a good look at the whole market and see what's available. Quite possibly there are some types of dolls available that you are not aware of.

The best kind of dolls for you to collect are those which interest you and fall into your budgetary range. Some dolls are more breakable than others, but this should not be a consideration when deciding on a group to collect. You'll be displaying your dolls and unless some accident occurs there should be no problem with breakage — even if you choose to collect chalks. ALL doll collections display excellently. The condition of the dolls is important for a pleasing display. Well-preserved dolls make a good display, and the more closely related they are, the better the display will be. The substance from which they're made does not matter. By the same token, a display of worn, broken, repainted or otherwise less-than-desirable dolls is not impressive, regardless of their material.

Another consideration, is *space.* Dolls take up more space than stamps or coins. They also display much better — a doll collection becomes a focal point in the home and adds to the interior decor. But if your display and/or storage area is limited, you may want to concentrate on small-size dolls — or buy rarities, which will give you a choice collection that does not increase too rapidly!

A beginner thinks in terms of *bargains.* Instead of going to the dealers who have the best selection he tries to figure out how to buy below the market. The beginner wants to buy where the dealers buy, and get his specimens for 40% or 50% of their "book" value. Sometimes you WILL get bargains in the doll hobby. If you browse around flea markets, garage sales and auctions, collectible dolls will turn up at very attractive prices — even less (sometimes) than the 40% or 50% "dealer buying price." Don't try to build a collection strictly from such buys. These "finds" do not occur often enough, and when they do occur it will usually be a doll that falls outside the scope of your collecting interest. You may go looking for Barbies and find a Marseille going for ⅓ the normal price. A Marseille at ⅓ the value is a terrific deal — but it's not going to fit into your Barbie collection. Often you will waste more in gas, money, time, and frustration looking for bargains, than the effort is worth. But don't avoid flea markets and other off-the-beaten-path sources. Visit them, and enjoy them. But realize that every worthwhile doll collection is built MAINLY from purchases in the antiques shops and from specialist dealers. Don't feel bad about paying the full retail values (as shown in this book). Most dolls continually rise in value. Today's full retail price becomes tomorrow's bargain.

INVESTING AND SELLING

Most hobbyists are into doll collecting for the sheer enjoyment of it. Shopping for dolls, setting up displays, researching dolls, and meeting other collectors is a source of enormous pleasure for them and they never think in terms of financial gain. That's fine. But along with the fun of collecting dolls there is also the opportunity — for those who want to seize it — to make money with dolls, too. There are various ways in which this can be done. You need not be a dealer to profit from dolls. Millions and millions of dollars are spent in the doll hobby every year. Anyone with a knowledge of dolls and their values, and of the market, can take part in selling. Many collectors do some selling as a sideline to their hobby, using the proceeds to buy dolls that they might not otherwise have been able to afford. Some do so well that they end up becoming dealers, even though they had no such intentions at the beginning! There is also the chance to profit from your own doll collection, when and if you ever decide to sell it.

The trend in doll values has been up — steadily and firmly — through the years. Nearly all doll collections increase in value while in the owner's possession, simply because the market prices go up constantly. There have been collectors who sold their dolls for twice or even three times as much as the collection cost. While there is no guarantee of profit in buying dolls, they've proven considerably better as investments than many other collectibles — better even than many stocks and bonds. Even if profit making is far from your thoughts, it's reassuring to know that the money spent on dolls is going into something with a future.

Whether you will profit from the eventual sale of your doll collection depends on several factors, some of which are under your control. A factor out of the hobbyist's control is the market itself. Values have to keep going up at a steady pace, to create a situation in which collectors can sell *today's purchases* at a profit *tomorrow*. There is no reason to suspect that this will fail to occur. The doll hobby is healthy and has been healthy for a long time. It's older than most other collecting hobbies and has a firm foundation. Antique and other fine dolls have been actively collected since the early 1900's and the number of new collectors coming into the hobby has been growing — mushrooming might be a better word — since then. They now total well over 1,000,000 individuals in the U.S. alone. This takes account only of those who buy out-of-production dolls and are collectors in the true sense of the term. If ALL doll owners were included — those who buy dolls at ordinary retail outlets — the figure would be ten times this high or more. Doll collectors' societies are at all-time highs in memberships, and the ranks of professional dealers are swelling. More and more new doll collectors' groups are starting up. And, very significantly,

10 / INVESTING AND SELLING

many more general antiques dealers are including dolls in their merchandise. There is unquestionably a doll collecting "boom" in the country. One of the MOST favorable signs is that the overall economic recession of 1982 had far less effect on doll collecting than on most other hobbies (including the two giant ones, coins and stamps). Why should this have been the case? Probably because the number of *non-collector investors* in doll collecting is much, much lower than in coins and stamps. Literally billions of dollars worth of collectible coins and stamps are purchased by individuals who are not hobbyists. They are strictly investors who buy with the intention of turning a profit. When economic storm clouds gather, these people suddenly stop buying and the market for coins and stamps feels the blow. In doll collecting, nearly everyone who buys is a hobbyist and a lover of dolls. Some are thinking in terms of profit but they still rank as collectors first and foremost. They continue buying regardless of what the national economy is doing or which political party occupies the White House.

Still, movements in the market are outside the collector's control, so he does need a certain amount of luck on his side in that respect. What he CAN control himself is the quality of his collection, which really counts even more. This means being attentive to condition. Dolls in the best grades of preservation rise in value faster than those in the "average" or lower classes. If the collector avoids space-fillers and seconds, he stands a much better chance of profiting from his collection when a sale is eventually made. The weight of numbers — and dollars — is definitely on the side of condition-conscious hobbyists. This is the case with the dealers, too, and we need not tell you that they exert an enormous influence over the market. Any dealer will buy collectible dolls in fine condition, because he has a demand for them from his customers. He may hesitate to buy defective specimens even if he can get them very, very cheaply. This is considered a gamble purchase by dealers, and dealers don't care to gamble.

Whether or not you profit from your collection may also depend, to some degree, on the type of dolls you buy. Any collectible doll in fine condition can be considered a potential "investment," but some groups do go up faster in value than others. This is not always entirely predictable because trends can develop in doll collecting, just as in any other collecting field. Dolls which are not among the most widely sought today could hit the top of the popularity list in five or ten years — or much sooner. However, the historic pattern in doll collecting, going all the way back before most of us were born, is for buying trends to surface gradually. There are very few "hotshots" in the doll hobby: groups that are popular one day and forgotten the next. Usually, when a trend develops it builds and builds over a long period of time and makes itself felt for decades. The major trend during the past 20 years of doll collecting has been bisque's emergence as the favorite among high quality molded-head dolls. This does not mean however that other groups will fail to gain in popularity.

If someone wanted to buy with profit in mind, as well as collecting enjoyment, the currently-made character dolls representing TODAY'S personalities might be an excellent choice. The trick here would be to concentrate on characters or personalities who seem certain of gathering a strong collector following. Any dolls related to the motion picture "Extra Terrestrial" would seem ideal for investment buying at the present time. All, or most, of the original E.T. dolls can still be bought at the manufacturer's price. In light of what happened to *Star Wars* and *Star Trek* memorabilia, all E.T. merchandise is almost sure to go up in value. With character dolls, especially those of this nature, you have very heavy competition to bring up the prices: not only doll enthusiasts will buy them, but collectors of nostalgia and memorabilia. Gene Autry dolls are bought by collectors of "western movie memorabilia." Laurel and Hardy dolls are bought by collectors of "silent film comedy memorabilia." And so on. The demand widens out and out, and each new group of collectors who seize onto these dolls helps to raise the values.

DOLL REPAIRS

Many collectible dolls in damaged condition have been damaged further, or utterly destroyed, through amateur repair attempts. Doll repair in its more advanced forms is an art and should be handled by professionals. There are many restorers specializing in dolls, in all parts of the country. You should be able to find one in the advertisements placed in hobby magazines, or possibly in your local area phone directory. If this does not avail, ask the local antique shops if there are doll restorers located nearby. Any museum or historical society which displays dolls among its collection will know of a competent restorer.

The fact that doll restoration is a thriving business shows that most serious collectors choose not to attempt their own repair work. Even an experienced collector who knows dolls from A to Z will usually not make any repair efforts except those of the simplest kind. One reason for this is that the professional has equipment and materials, including spare parts and matches for customes, which a collector would not be in a position to own. Also, a restorer can advise you on when repair work is apt to improve the value of the doll and when it is not, if this is of interest to you.

The types of damage found on dolls, particularly antique dolls, vary greatly. Whether restoration is worthwhile depends on the nature of the damage. There is no way that a worn or damaged doll can be made brand-new again, and the collector should not expect this. Old age in a doll is about as irreversible as old age in a human. There are many kinds of damage which should definitely be treated and which can be corrected. If, for example, you have all the parts to a strung doll and it needs restringing, it would be foolish not to have this operation performed. The doll will display much better when restrung, than as a heap of loose components! Parts that are hidden on a doll, either on the inside or hidden by clothing, are naturally more receptive to repair. On parts that show, especially the face, serious thought has to be given — will the repair accomplish the desired objective? For some forms of damage, such as chipping and flaking from the face of a painted doll, the cure is worse than the ailment. If a doll's head is sanded down and repainted, this might make it look better but the value as a collector's item will be totally lost. No attempts should be made to fill in cracks or chips. There is no way this can be done without interfering with the doll's desirability. Never repair, or even touch-up, and be sure that the person repairing your doll has these instructions. If the individual is a doll restoration specialist, he should already be aware of this principle. As we have stated elsewhere in this book, do not buy a defective doll in the belief that it can be fixed up good as new. If this was possible, the dealer would very likely have had the work done, and thereby given himself the chance to sell the doll at a much higher price.

DOLL FAKES

In terms of out-and-out fakes of antique dolls, there are virtually none. Fakers are stopped in their tracks by the difficulty of convincingly producing a fake. There would certainly be fakers turning out copies of old dolls, if this was within the realm of possibility. The problem (for them) is that most buyers of valuable dolls, in the $300 and up region, know what an old doll is supposed to look like. They make a close examination and would spot little details revealing the fake. Someone who does not know about antique dolls would perhaps miss the telltale signs of fakery, but such an individual is not apt to be spending $300, $500 or more for a doll. Also, there would be considerable work involved in producing the fakes, which cannot be just printed on a machine like fake postage stamps. Even if the faker could successfully sell his products as the genuine original, there may not be much profit in the activity!

We do not want to lull you into believing that fakes of antique dolls are absolutely non-existent. Fakes of everything turn up, now and then. On the American market they are certainly rare for the present.

While fakes designed to fool collectors are rare, some honest reproductions are made of antique dolls. These mainly come from France. They are exquisitely crafted and can easily be mistaken for an 1800's doll, if you do not notice the markings. These are called "honest reproductions" because there is no intention of defrauding anyone. These dolls (mostly bisque-head) are made in the spirit of yesteryear, for buyers who want the very best that the doll marker's art can produce. The approach is the same as that of the 1880's and 1890's bisque factories and the results are just about identical. These dolls are collectors' items as soon as they reach the market, and their prices are very high, understandably. They may rise in value just as fast as the antique specimens which inspired them, but this is hard to say. The absolutely "mint" appearance of these dolls should be a clue to their modern origin, as the usual age marks of a 100-year-old specimen are missing. No attempt is made to falsely age them, as is done to fakes. They are simply made to be beautiful dolls and this is exactly what they are. The collector should not hesitate to buy them, if he finds them appealing. He will not be accused of having "fakes" in his collection.

CARE, STORAGE AND DISPLAY

Care and storage are inter-related because proper display takes care and preservation into account. The first object of anyone who owns fine dolls is to preserve them in the condition in which they were acquired. If a display approach places a doll in potential danger, by (for example) exposing it to continuous direct sunlight or heat, it must be avoided. There are many ways of displaying and enjoying a doll collection while insuring the safety of its contents.

The approach to be taken in cleaning is determined to some extent by the nature of the doll and the condition. Some dolls are (to put it bluntly) a lot dirtier than others and need special, careful attention in cleaning. Then, too, the material from which the doll is made enters the picture, as some substances are more responsive to certain cleaning methods than others. There are some dolls which present real problems in cleaning because hardly anything can be done to them which would not harm the doll itself. Paper dolls fall into this group. Any attempt to wash paper dolls, even if by merely soaking them in water, runs the risk of bleaching out their colors and possibly leaving the doll with a stiff, unnatural appearance. Each case has to be judged individually. When the risk involved appears to be too great, there is not much choice but for the collector to forego cleaning and keep the doll "as is." This is why a knowledge of doll materials and their response to cleaning attempts is vital to the collector. It enables him to judge which dolls are a good buy and which ones fall into the questionable class. If a doll is not likely to respond well to cleaning efforts, it may be

CARE, STORAGE, AND DISPLAY / 17

wisest not to purchase such a doll unless it is not in need of cleaning.

It is important first of all to differentiate between the ruggedness of the doll and the ruggedness of its painted color. Some dolls are made of very hard materials, which can be washed without harming the material in any way. But their coloration is vulnerable to damage in cleaning. Chalk dolls are an example. If you had a white (unpainted) chalk doll or statuette, it could be safely washed in hot soapy water. The chalk would withstand this operation without any problem, and you could get the item perfectly clean. But when chalk dolls are painted, as they almost always are, the paint is far from permanently fixed on their surfaces. Because of the powdery surface of chalk, the paint does not fix very well on it. Any kind of strenuous rubbing, or immersing in water, can loosen some of the paint. You will be able to make a better judgement of this by examining the particular doll. If the surface has a powdery feel, and some small patches of color appear to already be missing, you can be quite sure this is a delicate specimen which has to be cleaned gingerly. If, on the other hand, the surface looks hard and shiny, and there is no powdery feel upon running your fingers across it, the color is probably fairly well fixed.

Before anything else is done, the doll needs to be undressed and dusted. Undressing is essential because the clothing is always dealt with separately. Do this cautiously. It is possible that there may be hidden pins or stitches, which would cause rips or holes if the clothing is taken off in a hurry.

Quite likely a good bit of the discoloration or faded appearance of the doll is being caused by nothing more than surface dust. In any event the doll must be thoroughly dusted before anything else can be accomplished. Lay the doll flat on a table, face up, and go over the whole surface with a clean feather-duster. If you have one with short, closely-set feathers it will do a better job. Then turn the doll on its stomach and repeat the process. There are still plenty of loose dust particles on the doll and they need to be removed next. You can do this with an artist's *camel-hair brush.* Don't wipe with a rag at this stage of the cleaning procedure — you will only push the dust around and accomplish nothing. A good art supply shop will have a *wide* camel hair brush. You will need one at least 1½" wide and preferably 2". Get the kind with long bristles if you have a choice. Before using it, run adhesive tape around the metal which connects the hairs to the handle — this could scratch the doll if it comes in contact with it. Then it is simply a matter of working over the whole surface area of the doll with this brush, going carefully into each crevice and detail. Wash the brush in warm soapy water afterwards, and rinse thoroughly. Hang it up to dry.

Some of the grime on an antique doll is fixed into the surface about as solidly as the paint, and you will not be successful in removing it. Anything which would cut through it will also remove the paint — and faced with that kind of choice you are wise to settle for living with the grime.

If the head is being cleaned separately from the rest of the doll, it is permissible to immerse the body in water. Some collectors also immerse the head (if it does not have sleep eyes), but this is a risky step which we do not recommend. Of course if the body contains any kind of mechanism, it cannot be immersed. Lukewarm water is used, without any cleaning agent. After soaking for a few minutes the body is removed and wiped over the whole surface with a cloth dipped in warm water (warmer than the soaking water). Then the body is soaked again, in fresh water. These steps can be repeated several times and the surface should get somewhat cleaner with each repetition, as the water and light rubbing breaks down the uppermost layers of grime. Don't scrub. Think of this as soaking a stamp from a piece of paper! Dry the body thereafter by patting with a dry cloth or cotton swabs and leave it in an airy place to dry further. The inside of the body (of a hollow-bodied doll) can be dried partially with a cotton swab on a stick. The remaining moisture will simply evaporate. Length of drying time will depend on how much humidity is in the air. It may range from an hour to a day or longer. Do not attempt to speed it up with a hair drier. Nature will take its course.

Instead of immersing the head, wipe it with a damp rag that has been dipped in warm water and thoroughly wrung out. This will need to be repeated several times at least. With each wiping you will dislodge some grime. The rag gets soiled quickly so it has to be rinsed out repeatedly. Be careful of the area around the eyes and the eyes themselves. In cleaning a wax or china doll you can place a few drops of household ammonia in the water, but ONLY a few drops (no more than the equivalent of one teaspoon of ammonia in a quart of water). Rubbing alcohol can also be used in the same proportion. Never use a strong solution of these substances, or any cleanser, as they could wash the paint right off the doll.

20 / CARE, STORAGE, AND DISPLAY

After washing and drying a wax or china head, you may want to apply a light coating of oil as a kind of "sealer." Oil (if not heavily applied) adds to the appearance and prevents dust particles, etc., from actually reaching the surface. The best kind of oil for this use is linseed oil. Soak a thin rag in it, then wirng out the rag thoroughly and wipe lightly over the whole surface. Oiling a doll's head in this manner is far preferable to lacquering, which used to be recommended by some doll "experts." Oil accomplishes about the same objectives as lacquer but can be easily removed at any time. Bisque dolls should not be oiled, as oil tends to give bisque an unnatural, harsh appearance and is disagreeable to most collectors. However it does not harm the doll in any way. The basic rule to follow is: if the doll is naturally glossy or shiny, oil it; if not, don't. In other words, go with the flow.

The clothing is washed separately from the doll itself. Each piece should be washed individually, not (of course) in a machine but by hand. You can use mild soap but don't rub too much. If the clothing is very old it may be quite fragile. You can soak it in soapy water first to make the job easier. Several washings may be necessary to get it really clean. If there are obstinate stains you may do better leaving them as they are.

Do not redress the doll until several days after cleaning, to make sure that both the doll and its costuming has thoroughly dried. If just the slightest bit damp when redressed, this will create a situation detrimental to the doll's preservation. Humidity will build up between the clothing and the doll's body, which can lead to mold formation.

CARE, STORAGE, AND DISPLAY / 21

The chief danger to any doll (except cloth!) is of course breakage. So when you plan a storage and display arrangement for your collection, the first objective is to keep your dolls safe from breakage. Your display arrangement must, then, be planned in consideration of your circumstances. If there are pets and youngsters in the house, some added precautions will need to be taken, but this should not cause any great inconvenience. The keynote is space. If you have wall space, the rest comes easy. In crowded, small areas, some improvising may be necessary. Do not hesitate to place shelving high up on walls, right near the ceiling, if space elsewhere is limited. Since dolls are large and bold, they can be easily viewed from a distance. There is no need to get them directly at eye level. This is one of the important advantages in displaying a doll collection. But do take into consideration the weight and strain sustained by each shelf. A shelf of dolls can be heavier than a shelf of books, if the dolls are large and positioned close together. In using long shelves, place a brace at the center to help bolster them. Also, examine the condition of your wall to determine if it will securely hold the shelf brackets. If there is any doubt, you may do better foregoing wall shelving and displaying your dolls in a standing case. A case with glass doors will provide protection against dust.

If a doll refuses to stand or sit, which is the case with some, a special prop can be used. This is an aluminum holder with two arms, which grasp the doll around its body and keep it standing. The holder is mounted on a vertical rod and fits into a pedestal base. They come in various sizes and can be purchased at the hobby shop and usually from doll dealers.

GLOSSARY

ACTION

Used to describe the mechanical (usually spring driven) action of a doll. The most common is walking, but action incorporated into dolls has taken numerous other forms over the years, such as raising one or both arms or creeping along the floor.

ANTIQUE

Strictly speaking, an "antique" is defined as any object 100 or more years old. Though this applies to dolls as well as to other manufactured items, collectors are loose in their interpretation of it. Any doll made before 1900 is regarded as antique by most collectors and dealers. Whether or not the designation can be properly applied, to any given doll, is not really a matter of much importance, since the value hinges on other factors.

BALL JOINT

Ball jointed dolls were introduced around 1885 and became almost instantly popular. The ball joints were applied at the junctures where the arms and legs met the body, and sometimes also at the knees and even the wrists. Elastic string secured the parts together, with the result that such dolls could be bent to take almost any pose. This principle had earlier been used — and was adapted from — the wooden mannequin dolls from the world of art instruction.

BLANK OPEN MOUTH

Doll whose open mouth is painted white to suggest teeth, but in which individual teeth are not indicated.

BRUSH MARKS

A painted-head doll in which traces of brush marks are visible. These can occur regardless of the material, as they were the fault of the paint being too thick or the use of a too-stiff brush.

CARNIVAL DOLL

Doll made to be given as a prize at a carnival or amusement park, either in games of chance or skill (such as knocking down metal bottles with a baseball). Usually made wholly of chalk. These date mainly from the 1930's and later and a large number are Japanese imports.

CENTER PART

Refers to the doll's hair being parted in the center.

CHARACTER DOLL

Doll designed in the likeness of a comic strip character, show business personality, or other specific model. The Shirley Temple and Charlie Chaplin types are examples.

CORK STUFFED

Shredded cork stuffing has sometimes been used in dolls, particularly those made in Germany in the early 1900's. It was inexpensive and believed to give the doll body a more lifelike appearance.

CRECHE DOLL

Figure not made as a doll but as a component in a nativity (creche) set. Modern creche figures are usually of chalk or hollow composition, with painted bodies, and do not interest doll collectors. However in the 18th and 19th centuries, particularly in Italy, some very elaborate ones were made, just as fine as the best dolls. These are highly sought collectors' items, even when they occur for sale individually (lacking other components of the set).

DOLL-WITHIN-DOLL

A doll modeled to represent a child holding a doll. These date mainly from the 1880's and 1890's. The smaller doll is often exquisitely designed. In many specimens it is, as would be expected, lacking, since the two were not joined together in any way (the larger doll simply cradled the small one in her arms).

FIVE PIECE BODY

A convenient way of saying that the doll's arms and legs are attached to the body, having been made separately.

FROZEN CHARLOTTE

A type of doll made entirely of one piece, like a statuette, usually of ceramic. They came in many sizes and poses and were popular in the late 1800's. The name derives from a New England folk tale, of a young lady who forgot to wear winter clothing on a snowy night and froze solid (the connection being, of course, that the dolls are likewise "frozen" — their bodily parts cannot be moved).

FULLY JOINTED

Doll whose body is jointed (moveable) at the shoulders, elbows, thighs, and knees.

GRANDMA DOLL

Doll representing an elderly woman. These are extremely unusual.

INSET EYES

Eyes set into the doll's head (from inside the skull), rather than being manufactured as part of the head. Inset eyes have always been considered desirable and a mark of quality, as they allow the use of a material different than that of the doll's head (usually glass) and achieve greater realism. Inset sets may be either stationery or of the sleep variety.

KEY WOUND

Doll containing a spring-driven motor, wound with a key. Though spring-wound motors were known from the early era of clock and watch making, hundreds of years ago, no attempt was made to incorporate them into playthings until the 1840's.

KID BODY

Doll body made of kidskin (skin of young goats), stuffed with material. The stuffing may be rag, cotton, shredded cork, etc. Kid bodies were made in two duplicate pieces sewn together along the edges. The stuffing was usually worked in as the sewing progressed.

LOWER LEGS

Used in reference to forelegs (that part of the leg from the knee to the foot).

MANNEQUIN

Figure (of an adult, child or infant) intended for the display of clothing merchandise in a shop. While not manufactured as dolls, mannakins are of interest to some doll collectors because of their close relationship to dolls. The possibilities of mannequin collecting have not yet been fully explored. The older and probably better specimens are mostly of European origin, and can be found in European antique shops.

MARY TODD LINCOLN

The controversy still rages, among doll experts, over whether manufacturers of the 1860's (the era of Lincoln's Presidency) modeled some of their dolls after Mrs. Lincoln (Mary Todd Lincoln). For many years it was conclusively believed that they did; but this belief has been seriously questioned. Though a resemblance exists in many dolls, to the facial features of Mrs. Lincoln, this could well be coincidental.

MECHANICAL

Any doll containing a mechanical mechanism. The majority are "walkers," and are operated by a spring-driven motor. Dolls featuring a voice-box are not technically referred to as mechanicals — only those in which a mechanism operates some bodily part to simulate human motion.

MISS FLAKED RICE

Lithographed cloth doll of the early 1900's, which served as an advertising vehicle for a brand of breakfast cereal manufactured at that time.

MOLDED HAIR

Doll hair which is not painted on, and not applied, but is an integral part of the head itself. The contour of the hair (hairdo) is included in the head mold, therefore the origin of the term "molded hair." Molded hair is usually painted as a finishing touch.

MOVING EYES (or MOVING EYEBALLS)

This feature is different than sleep eyes (doll eyes which open and close). Moving eyes move from side to side, as if following an object. They are usually found only on ventriloquist dummies and only on the more lavish specimens. The action is regulated by a string which, attached to a loop, fits over one of the operator's fingers and is worked from the back, out of view of the audience.

OPEN HEAD

The majority of bisque doll heads, on dolls made in Europe from the 1870's to the early 1900's, are of the "open" variety: there is a rather large hole at the crown. This of course would be hidden after applying the wig, but the question remains as to why it existed in the first place.

ORIGINAL BOX (M.I.B.)

Dolls still in their original manufacturer's box are always worth a premium value.

PEDLAR (or PEDDLER) DOLLS

A class of early dolls sold by itinerant street hawkers, mostly in England, Scotland and Ireland, but to some extent elsewhere as well, including the large towns of the eastern U.S. They were intended to represent the peddlers themselves, and came equipped with tote-boxes (hung over their shoulders by straps) containing miniature versions of peddler merchandise: scissors, combs, files, ribbons, bottles, yarn, etc. In good condition, with the original contents, they are highly prized.

PENNY WOODEN

Carved wooden dolls of small size, dating from the 18th and 19th centuries. Penny woodens were the most common sort of dolls in their time but, despite this, are by no means plentiful on today's doll collecting market.

PLAY DOLL

Doll intended to be used as a plaything by a child, as opposed to a "show" doll (for decoration). Of all dolls that have ever been manufactured, the play type are far in the majority.

PRESS ACTION

Dolls which, when pressed or squeezed, "do something." The action may consist of raising or lowering arms, turning head, etc., or they may simply emit a squeal. The squeal type, generally with a soft rubber body, is by far the most plentiful. Early versions of press action dolls contained a bellows in the body.

SANDERS JOINT

A type of ball and socket joint patened in 1880, used on many dolls made thereafter.

SHOULDER HEAD

Doll head which does not include merely head and neck but is continued down to the shoulders, which are of the same composition as the head and neck.

SHOW DOLL

Doll intended to be placed on a bed or otherwise displayed, rather than played with.

SLEEP EYES

Eyes which are open when the doll is upright, but close (turning into eyelids) when the doll is laid down.

STUMP DOLL

Very early group of dolls, made chiefly in Europe from about 1680 to the third quarter of the 18th century. Consisting of an upper body and head carved from a solid block of wood, stump dolls got their name because the body (hidden by the clothing) terminated in a flat stump, like a tree stump.

SWIVEL HEAD

Head which can be rotated from side to side and, when rotated, remains in the position to which it was moved (rather than snapping back by itself).

UNMARKED

About ¼ of all antique dolls, and a smaller percentage of those from the modern era, carry no identifying markings of any kind. There are various possible reasons for manufacturers to avoid marking their dolls, including the production of dolls that were very similar in design to those of an established patent holder.

VENTRILOQUIST MOUTH

Doll whose mouth can be opened and closed like that of a ventriloquist's dummy. The mechanism may be enclosed and operate simply by a string which hangs down through a hole at the back of the head or neck.

WALKER

Doll that walks as a result of mechanical action, usually a spring-driven motor. There are "independent" walkers and others which have an accessory of some kind attached, such as a baby carriage or a pet dog. The attachment helps in balancing the doll and makes its motions more fluid and natural; independent walkers tend to tremble and bounce.

WHEELED WALKERS

Doll on a platform set with wheels. The legs do not move; the doll is propelled entirely by the slow rotation of the wheels. A long gown on the doll, reaching to the ground, concealed the apparatus. These dolls did not fall down, but their movement had less appearance of real walking.

WOOD CHIP BODY

Doll body stuffed with wood shavings. This was done occasionally in the 19th century.

MANUFACTURERS' MARKS

Alt, Beck And Gottschalck

DANCING KEWPIE SAILOR

Louis Amberg And Son

KEWPIE

George Borgfeldt And Company

Bru

BRU J^{NE} R

BREVETE S.G.D.G.

Y 8 M

32 / DOLL MANUFACTURERS' MARKS

Cameo

Effanbee

Martha Chase

PAWTUCKET, R.I.
MADE IN U.S.A.

Franz Schimidt And Company

Danel et Cie

BÉBÉ FRANÇAIS

DOLL MANUFACTURERS' MARKS / 33

Gauthier

Gebruder Heubach

8192
Germany
Gebrüder Heubach
5/0 1/2
G   5/0 1/2 H

Goebel

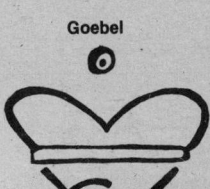

34 / DOLL MANUFACTURERS' MARKS

Heinrich Handwerck

H HANDWERCK

Hch 6/0 H.
Germany

Jumeau

DÉPOSÉ
TETE JUMEAU
B^{TE} SGDG
6

Max Handwerck

Germany

Kämmer And Reinhardt

K &✡& R

SIMON & HALBIG
122
32

Heubach Koppelsdorf

DOLL MANUFACTURERS' MARKS / 35

Kestner

Kley And Hahn

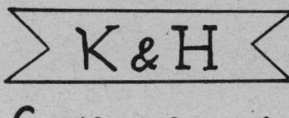

Kewpie

Käthe Kruse

Kewpie

Lanternier

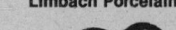

Limbach Porcelain

Lenci

Louis R. Kampes Studios

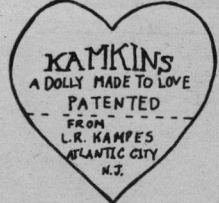

DOLL MANUFACTURERS' MARKS / 37

Armand Marseille

Armand Marseille
Germany.
390.
A 12/0x M.

Recknagez

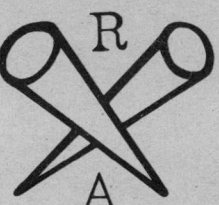

Morimura Brothers

Rhecinische Gummit And Celluioid Fabric

Marque de Fabrique

Pierotti

Pierotti

Bruno Schmidt

38 / DOLL MANUFACTURERS' MARKS

Schmitt

Simon And Halbig

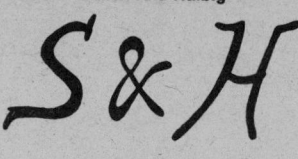

Schoenhut

SFBJ

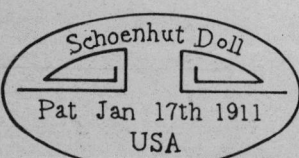

Steiff

Bouton dans l'oreille.

DOLL MANUFACTURERS' MARKS / 39

Herm Steiner

Herm Steiner

]S[

Germany

STEINER
.S.G.D.G.
PARIS
A11

|S|)S(

Superior

M & S
Superior

Jules Steiner

Unis France

COMMON ABBREVIATIONS

Alex — Madame Alexander
A.M. — Armand Marseille
Amer. Char. — American Character
BJ body — ball-jointed body
BK — bent knees
bl. — blue
bld. — blonde
br. — brown
c. — circumference
cell. — celluloid
cl — cloth
c/m or clm. — closed mouth
comp. — composition
dk. — dark
E.J. — Emile Jumeau
Fr. body — French body
gl. — glass
hd mk. — head mark
H.H. — human hair
hp. — hard plastic
JCB — jointed composition body
JDK — J.D. Kestner
Jtb. — jointed
l.t. — lower teeth
m. — mohair
M.I.B. — Mint In Box
mld hair — molded hair
ml — molded lash
o/c or o cl. m — open closed mouth
o.m. — open mouth
p — pierced
P. E. — painted eye

P. L. — painted lash
ptd. — painted
p.w. eyes — paperweight eyes
rep. — repair
repl. — replacement
S&H — Simon and Halbig
SFBJ — Socrete Francaise de Fabrication de Bebes et Jouets (group of French dollmakers)
sh.pl. — shoulder plate
sl. — sleeping
stat. — stationary
sw.n. — swivel neck

BOOKS

Anderton, Johanna Gast, *More Twentieth Century Dolls, Volume One*, Walace Homestead.

Anderton, Johanna Gast, *More Twentieth Century Dolls, Volume Two*, Wallace Homestead.

Anderton, Johanna Gast, *Sewing For Twentieth Century Dolls*, Wallace Homestead.

Anderton, Johanna Gast, *Twentieth Century Dolls*, Wallace Homestead.

Angione, Genevieve, and Judith Whorton, *All Dolls Are Collectible*, Crown Publishers, Inc.

Axe, John, *Collectible Black Dolls*, Hobby House Press, Inc.

Axe, John, *Collectible Boy Dolls*, Hobby House Press, Inc.

Axe, John, *Collectible Dolls In National Costumes*, Holly Hobby House, Inc.

Axe, John, *Collectible Patsy Dolls and Patsy-Types,* Hobby House Press, Inc.

Axe, John, *Collectible Sonja Henie,* Holly Hobby Press, Inc.

Axe, John, *Collecting Modern Dolls: How-To-Guidebook on Collecting Modern Dolls,* Hobby House Press, Inc.

Axe, John, *Encyclopedia of Celebrity Dolls,* Hobby House Press, Inc.

Axe, John, *Tammy And Dolls You Love To Dress,* Hobby House Press, Inc.

Buser, Elaine and Dan, *Guide To Schoenhut Dolls, Toys And Circus,* Collector Books.

Byfield, Magdalena, *In A Miniature Garden,* Hobby House Press, Inc.

Coleman, Dorothy S., Elizabeth A., and Evelyn J., *Collector's Encyclopedia of Dolls,* Crown Publishers, Inc.

Colton, Harold S., *Hopi Kachina Dolls,* University of New Mexico Press.

Doll Catalog, The, second edition, Hobby House Press, Inc.

Fawcett, Clara Hallard, *Dolls, A Guide For Collectors,* H.L. Lindquist Publications.

Fawcett, Clara Hallard, *Paper Dolls, A Guide To Costume,* H.L. Lindquist Publications.

Fawcett, Clara, *On Making, Mending And Dressing Dolls,* Hobby House Press, Inc.

Ferguson, Barbara, *Collecting Paper Dolls,* Wallace Homestead.

Foulke, Jan, *Focusing On Effanbee Composition Dolls,* Hobby House Press, Inc.

Foulke, Jan, *Focusing On Gebruder Heubach Dolls,* Hobby House Press, Inc.

Foulke, Jan, *Kestner, King of Dollmakers*, Hobby House Press, Inc.

Fraser, Antonia, *Dolls*, G.P. Putnam's Sons.

Haines, Frank and Elizabeth, *Early American Brides, A Study of Costume And Tradition*, Hobby House Press, Inc.

Herron, *Much Ado About Dolls*, Wallace Homestead.

Holtz, Loretta, *Developing Your Doll Collection: For Enjoyment And Investment*, Crown Publishers, Inc.

Holtz, Loretta, *The How To Book of International Dolls*, Crown Publishers, Inc.

Hoyer, Mary, *Mary Hoyer and Her Dolls*, Hobby House Press, Inc.

Jacobs, Flora Gill, *A History of Doll Houses*, Charles Scribner's Sons.

Johl, Janet Payter, *More About Dolls*, H.L. Lindquist Publications.

Jones, G.P., *An Easy To Make Godey Doll*, Dover Publications.

MacDowell, Robert and Karin, *Collector's Digest On German Character Dolls*, Hobby House Press, Inc.

Miller, Marjorie, *Nancy Ann Storybook Dolls*, Hobby House Press, Inc.

Revi, A. Christian, ed., *Spinning Wheel's Complete Book of Dolls*, Galahad Books.

Roth, Charlene, *Making Original Dolls of Composition, Bisque And Porcelain*, Crown Publishers, Inc.

Shea, Ralph A., *Doll Mark Clues*, published by the author, 489 Oak Street, Ridgefield, New Jersey 07657.

St. George, Eleanor, *The Dolls of Yesterday*, Charles Scribner's Sons.

Von Boehn, Max, *Dolls*, Dover Publications.

Waugh, Carol-Lynn Rossel, *Miniature Doll by Contemporary American Doll Artists,* Hobby House Press, Inc.

Westfall, Marty, *Handbook of Doll Repair And Restoration,* Crown Publishers, Inc.

Woodcock, Jean, *Paper Dolls of Famous Faces,* 5369 South Owasso, Tulsa, Oklahoma.

Whitton, Margaret, *The Jumeau Doll,* Dover Publications.

Young, Mary, *Paper Dolls and Their Artists,* 1040 Greenridge Drive., Kettering, Ohio.

CLUBS

Antique Toy Collectors of America
Route 2, Box 5A; Parkton, MD 21120

Doll Artisan Guild
35 Main Street; Oneonta, NY 13820; 607/432-4977
The Doll Artisan publishes bimonthly magazine for members.

Doll Collectors of America
14 Chestnut Road; Westford, MD 01886;
617/692-8392
Publishes a bimonthly bulletin for members.

Ginny Doll Club
305 West Beacon Road; Lakeland, FL 33803;
813/687-8015
Publishes the *Ginny Doll Club News,* an illustrated newsletter, for members.

International Barbie Doll Collectors Club
P.O. Box 79; Bronx, NY 10464; 212/885-2439
Publishes a monthly newsletter for members.

International Doll Makers' Association
3364 Pine Creek Drive; San Jose, CA 95132;
408/926-3077
Publishes *The Broadcaster* with membership news
every four months.

The International Rose O'Neill Club
P. O. Box 668; Branson, MO 65616; 417/334-3273
Publishes *The Kewpiesta Kourier* three or four
times a year for members.

Madame Alexander Fan Club
P. O. Box 146; New Lenox, IL 60451
Four fan club newsletters and ten issues of
Madame Alexander Shopper are published annually
for members.

National Institute of American Doll Artists
303 Riley Street; Falls Church, VA 22046
Publishes newsletter three times a year for
members.

Teddy Bear Club
P. O. Box 8361; Prairie Village, KS 66208

United Federation of Doll Clubs
Mrs. Edward Buchholz; Membership Chairman; 2814
Herron Lane; Glenshaw, PA 15116
Publishes a monthly newsletter, *Doll News* for
members.

MUSEUMS

Adirondack Center Museum; Elizabethtown, NY
12932

46 / MUSEUMS

Aunt Len's Doll And Toy House, Inc.; New York, NY 10031

Boothbay Railway Museum; Boothbay, ME 04537

Buccleuch Mansion; New Brunswick, NJ 08901

Burt County Museum; Tekamah, NE 68061

Chattanooga Museum of Regional History; Chattanooga, TN 37404

Cornwall Historical Society; Cornwall, CT 06753

Costume And Textile Study Center; Seattle, WA 98195

Eliza Cruce Hall Doll Museum; Ardmore, OK 73401

Enchanted World Doll Museum; Mitchell, SD 57301

Eugene Field Museum; St. Louis, MO 63102

Fort Seward Historical Society, Inc.; Jamestown, ND 58401

Gadsden Museum; Mesilla, NM 80046

Gay Nineties Button And Doll Museum; Eureka Springs, AR 72632

Geuther Doll Museum; Eureka Springs, AR 72632

The Historical Society of The Tarrytowns, Inc.; Tarrytown, NY 10591

Historical Society of The Town of East Bloomfield; East Bloomfield, NY 14443

House of A Thousand Dolls; Loma, MT 59460

Ledbetter Antique Car Museum; Custer, SD 57730

Mary Merritt's Doll Museum; Douglassville, PA 19518

MUSEUMS / 47

Milan Historical Museum, Inc.; Milan, OH 44846

Museum of Antique Dolls; Savannah, GA 31401

The New-York Historical Society; New York, NY 10024

Old Brown House Doll Museum; Gothenburg, NE 69138

Old Fort Museum; Fort Smith, AR 72901

Orchard Park Historical Society; Orchard Park, NY 14127

Patee House Museum; St. Joseph, MO 64502

Perelman Antique Toy Museum; Philadelphia, PA 19106

The Playhouse Museum of Dolls And Toys; Las Cruces, NM 88005

Raggedy Ann Antique Doll And Toy Museum; Flemington, NJ 08822

The Rockwell Museum; Corning, NY 14830

South Carolina Antique Toy Museum; Pendleton, SC 29670

Town of Bethlehem Historical Association; Selkirk, NY 12158

Town of Yorktown Museum; Yorktown Heights, NY 10598

Toy Train Museum of The Train Collector's Association; Strasburg, PA 17579

Union Mills Homestead; Westminster, MD 21157

United Counties Museum; Cornwall, ON CAN

Vent Haven Museum; Fort Mitchell, KY 41011

Recommended Reading . . .

The Official Price Guide to Dolls is designed as a basic introductory course for the beginning collector and flea market shopper, as well as a handy, tote-along reference book for the more seasoned hobbyist.

This guide offers the beginner a general overview of collecting techniques, tips, and prices for the collectibles most commonly bought and sold on the market today.

You can slip this price guide into a pocket or a purse and take along your own "official" expert on your next shopping excursion.

As your interest and your collection grows, you may want to start a reference library of your favorite areas. For the collector who needs a more extensive coverage of the collectibles market, The House of Collectibles publishes a complete line of comprehensive companion guides to the pocket-sized books. These larger price guides, which are itemized at the back of this book, contain full coverage on buying, selling, and caring of valuable articles, plus listings with thousands of prices for rare, unusual, and common antiques and collectibles.

$9.95-1st Edition, 576 pgs., Order #381-3

The House of Collectibles recommends **The Official Price Guide to Antiques and Modern Dolls**, first edition as the companion to this pocket book.

- **Over 100,000 Current Retail Values** for dolls in all price ranges representing over 300 manufacturers.
- **ANTIQUE DOLLS** — Irresistible 100 to 200 year old specimens made from wax, carved wood, and china are included for the connoisseur.
- **MODERN AND SEMI-MODERN** dolls in celluloid, chalk, plastic, composition, cloth, and other materials are featured with extensive listings of Shirley Temple dolls in all sizes and styles, comic character dolls, a Barbie reference guide, Walt Disney dolls, Peanuts, Kewpies, Super Heroes, and more.
- **MAJOR MANUFACTURERS** — Hundreds of U.S. and foreign manufacturers fully represented including American Character • Armand Marseille • Horsman • Gautier • Goebel • Handwerck • Jumeau • Kestner • S.F.B.J. • Schoenhut • Effanbee • Alexander • Mattel • Ideal • Kestner • Marx and more.
- **EXPERT TIPS** on starting and building a doll collection, where and how to buy from doll dealers, flea markets, auctions, antique shops, and more.
- **FULLY ILLUSTRATED**

Available from your local dealer or order direct from:
THE HOUSE OF COLLECTIBLES, see order blank

HOW TO USE THIS BOOK

All listings are arranged by manufacturers. for example, Barbie dolls, are listed under their manufacturer Mattel. And so on. Within each of the manufacturer groupings, all dolls are listed alphabetically. Following the doll's name is information to use in identifying it. This will include (usually) the material from which the doll is made, the manufacturer's markings (if any), and the size. Additional information is also provided for many of the listings. The mark will always be found on the body or head of the doll. If reference is made to a marking on a tag, clothing, or box, this will be mentioned. Keep in mind that the descriptions are for actual specimens. It is possible, in some cases, that a company made VARIATIONS of any given doll. Hence, if the description states BLONDE HAIR, this does not automatically mean a doll with BROWN HAIR, matching the description in all other respects, is a different doll. It could be — and probably is — the identical doll in a different version, and quite likely its value is the same as indicated. All the MEASUREMENTS are approximate, and a tolerance of at least ½" should be allowed. On very large dolls, it may be necessary to allow a greater tolerance. The CLOTHING on ANTIQUE DOLLS can vary from specimen to specimen, as it was a common practice in olden times for owners to make their own doll clothing. If the clothing on a specimen is obviously contemporary with it, and well preserved, it cannot hurt the doll's value, even if it cannot be classified as "original."

Values. In all cases, values are current selling figures from the secondary (used/secondhand/antique) market, and are present in the form of a range with a high and low price. The use of ranges allows for the inevitable differences in prices in different parts of the country, in sales made by specialist dealers as opposed to general dealers, etc. They show the average sums at the time of publication.

As a further aid, a third price column showing last year's average selling price is included. A comparison between the current prices and last year's price will, determine if a doll's value has increased, decreased or remained constant. It is apparent that many investors are buying dolls and this information should be useful to them — as well as to hobbyists.

ALEXANDER DOLL COMPANY, INC. / 51

ABORIGINALS	Current Price Range		P/Y AVG
☐ **Wednesday,** *cloth, unmarked, 1962, 23"*	65.00	80.00	62.00

EMMA AND MARIETTA ADAMS

☐ **Columbian Doll,** *all cloth, handpainted features, hair, bonnet, pioneer style clothing, stamped on back "Columbian Doll Emma E. Adams, Oswego, Centre, N.Y."*	550.00	650.00	550.00

ADVANCE DOLL AND TOY COMPANY

☐ **Wanda,** *walker, brown mohair wig, blue sleep eyes, pink dress, hat, 18", c. 1949*	175.00	225.00	185.00

ODETTE AIDEN

☐ **Mary Queen Of Scots,** *plastic, molded and painted features, dressed in reproduction of 16th century royal costume, jointed at the shoulders, unmarked, made in England in 1969, 8"*	49.00	58.00	47.00

ALEXANDER DOLLS CO., INC.

When Beatrice Behrman made her first portrait doll, a tribute to her little daughter, she had no idea of the empire that had just been born. Spurred by friends and acquaintances to market her talent, she founded the Alexander Company in 1923. By the age of twenty-eight, she was a successful business woman and designer. The eager public acceptance of her products continues to be a market phenomena.

Through the years the company has grown to 600 employees in the New York factory. Big business has never compromised the high quality standards set by Beatrice Behrman, A.K.A. Madame Alexander. The 130 doll models that have been produced since the 20's are grouped by theme:

52 / ALEXANDER DOLL COMPANY, INC.

historical figures, story book characters and ethnic dolls. Each doll is hand-painted, hand assembled and dressed in exquisite costumes.

Madam Alexander dolls are one of the few products that appreciate immediately over retail price. Department stores and gift shops have been known to limit the number a customer can buy on any given day.

This is an attempt to keep the dolls off the scalper's market, and it is only moderately successful. Now dolls quickly turn up at flea markets and antiques shops for resale at exorbitant prices.

The lifelike but whimsical dolls created by Madam Alexander are as much a part of American nostalgia as Norman Rockwell's characters. They both have captured the innocence and wisdom of children, and the adults who collect them are in love with these qualities.

	Current Price Range		P/Y AVG
☐ **Alexanderkin**, hard plastic, wears bathing suit, sandals, robe, square sunglasses, carries beach bag, 8"	70.00	90.00	65.00
☐ **Alice in Wonderland**, Madame Alexander, 12", c. 1983	65.00	75.00	65.00
☐ **Amy**, plastic, sleep eyes, blonde looped curls, 14"	95.00	110.00	80.00
Note: Amy was a character in Louisa May Alcott's Little Women.			
☐ **Bridesmaid**, vinyl head, composition body, vinyl wig, blue sleep eyes, high waisted gown with long bow and full sleeves, 15"	100.00	125.00	110.00
☐ **Brigetta**, from Sound of Music, mint in box, 11", c. 1972	200.00	250.00	225.00
☐ **Christening Baby**, infant, long white baby gown and bonnet, 13"	50.00	60.00	52.00
☐ **Cinderella**, blue outfit, c. 1983	70.00	80.00	75.00
☐ **Cinderella**, brown outfit, c. 1983	60.00	70.00	65.00
☐ **Cissette**, bent knees, handpainted, ballerina dress, 10"	130.00	150.00	135.00
☐ **Cissette**, blue taffeta dress, earrings, hat, 10"	100.00	120.00	110.00
☐ **Cissette**, hard plastic, sleep eyes, dressed in "Iceland" costume, 10½"	340.00	400.00	320.00
Note: Like many of the Alexander dolls, Cissette is found in a wide variety of costumes and these have some influence on the value.			
☐ **Cissy**, gray plush stole lined with pink	15.00	25.00	18.00

ALEXANDER DOLL COMPANY, INC. / 53

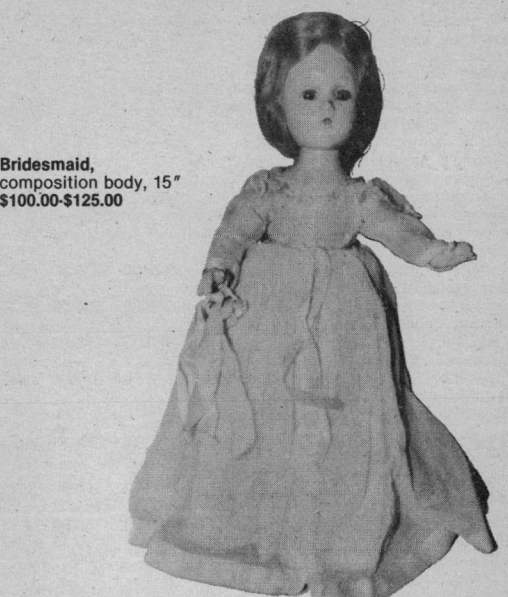

Bridesmaid, composition body, 15"
$100.00-$125.00

	Current Price Range		P/Y AVG
☐ **Cissy,** hard plastic, jointed at knees and elbows, long flowing yellow cape-style coat, sleep eyes, high heel open dress shoes, 21"	90.00	115.00	85.00
☐ **Cissy,** pink and yellow printed silk taffeta dress, earrings, straw hat, 20"	300.00	400.00	310.00
☐ **Composition,** blonde human hair wig, dimples, white satin dress, skates, cape, 15"	300.00	350.00	310.00
☐ **Composition,** head and jointed body, vinyl wig, blue sleep eyes, flared polka dot dress, velvet booties with bells, 14"	85.00	110.00	90.00

54 / ALEXANDER DOLL COMPANY, INC.

	Current Price Range		P/Y AVG
☐ **Dionne Baby,** composition head, yoke, arms, and lower legs, cloth torso and upper legs, marked "Dionne/Alexander," brown molded hair, brown sleep eyes with lashes, maroon and white linen dress, 17"	275.00	325.00	280.00
☐ **Dionne Quintuplets,** composition head, bent limb body, sleep eyes, wigs, original clothing, brass tags, 7"	1400.00	1600.00	1450.00
☐ **Dionne Quintuplets,** vinyl body, sleep eyes, together in terry cloth comforter, layette suits, signed by Madame Alexander	1000.00	1250.00	1050.00
☐ **Dionne Quint, Toddler,** auburn, mohair wig, print sunsuit, marked Alexander	240.00	280.00	245.00
☐ **Dionne Quint, Toddler,** molded body, pink bonnet, dress, marked Alexander	220.00	275.00	225.00
☐ **Dionne Toddler,** composition, original lilac wool coat, hat, leggings, tag, 17"	325.00	375.00	350.00
☐ **Ecuador Girl,** bent knees, dark pigtails, blue sleep eyes, coin earrings, straw hat, 8", c. 1960's	250.00	350.00	265.00
☐ **Edith,** "The Lonely Doll," vinyl head, rubber body, blue sleep eyes, pouty mouth, party dress, c. 1950	250.00	300.00	225.00
☐ **Elise Ballerina,** 12", c. 1983	130.00	160.00	135.00
☐ **Elise Bride,** 12", c. 1983	130.00	160.00	135.00
☐ **Elise Bridesmaid,** 12", c. 1983	130.00	160.00	135.00
☐ **Elise,** character, vinyl, jointed at elbows, knees, ankles, brown rooted hairs, blue sleep eyes, closed mouth, pink and white checked dress, white straw bonnet with flower trim, hose, high heels, 16", c. 1952	215.00	235.00	220.00
☐ **Elise,** hard plastic head, vinyl, long brown page boy, blue sleep eyes, dressed as bridesmaid, long chintz gown, wide brimmed hat, 17", c. 1952	150.00	200.00	175.00
☐ **First Ladies,** Series II: Angelica Van Buren, Julia Tyler, Sarah Jackson, Sara Polk, each	115.00	145.00	125.00
☐ **Gibson Girl,** the Cissette doll in "Gibson Girl" costume, long-sleeve white shirt, floor-length full skirt, boater style hat with trim, fancy belt	340.00	400.00	320.00
☐ **Goldilocks,** c. 1983	60.00	70.00	65.00

ALEXANDER DOLL COMPANY, INC. / 55

	Current Price Range		P/Y AVG
☐ **Gone With The Wind,** c. 1983	90.00	100.00	95.00
☐ **Goya,** portrait series, 21", c. 1983	300.00	350.00	310.00
☐ **India,** marked Alex, 8"	80.00	90.00	85.00
☐ **Irish,** doll, marked Alex, 8"	80.00	90.00	85.00
☐ **Israeli,** doll, composition head and body, bent knee walker, intricate costume, 7"	185.00	200.00	190.00
☐ **Israeli,** doll, knee bends, 8", c. 1965	60.00	70.00	65.00
☐ **Jacqueline,** brown eyes and hair, blue suit and pill box hat, black heels, stockings, pearl necklace, diamond ring, 21"	625.00	675.00	640.00
☐ **Jeannie Walker,** composition head and body, blue sleep eyes, sundress and straw hat, 12", c. 1941	500.00	600.00	550.00
☐ **Kathy,** character, vinyl, blond rooted hair, brown sleep eyes, pink dress, matching bonnet, pacifier on ribbon around neck, wrist tag, 17", c. 1956	220.00	235.00	220.00
☐ **Kathy,** molded hair, pretty eyes, 24"	8.00	12.00	10.00
☐ **Kathy Cry Dolly,** vinyl, sleep eyes, rooted hair, blond or reddish blond, wears infant smock, white, frilled bonnet, holds pacifier attached to neck with elastic band, 12"	50.00	65.00	45.00
☐ **Katie Greenaway,** hard plastic head, jointed body, brown human hair wig, fringed sleep eyes, white gown with wide green velvet band, matching cap, 12"	900.00	1000.00	950.00
☐ **Katie,** hard plastic, original costume, with wooden rocking horse labeled "100 Years In Toys, 1862-1962, commemorative doll for 100th Anniversary of F.A.O. Schwartz Toy Co., 11", rare	1000.00	2000.00	1100.00
☐ **Kelly,** character, vinyl, blond rooted hair, blue sleep eyes, closed mouth, pink dress with tiers of white lace, matching bonnet, original mint, no box, wrist tag, 15", c. 1956	185.00	210.00	185.00
☐ **Laurie,** vinyl head, sleep eyes, sad, long eyelashes, black hair, wears double-breasted jacket, plaid trousers, 12"	15.00	22.00	14.00

Note: Laurie was a character in Louisa May Alcott's Little Women.

56 / ALEXANDER DOLL COMPANY, INC.

	Current Price Range		P/Y AVG
☐ **Leslie Bauirje,** composition head and jointed body, black face, brown long wig, white frilly dress with flower headband, slippers, 14"	300.00	400.00	350.00
☐ **Lissy,** auburn hair, red dress, flowery white hat, navy coat	80.00	120.00	85.00
☐ **Lissy,** hard plastic, sleep eyes (straight-ahead staring), brown hair, long dress with waist sash, colonial style bonnet, 12"	230.00	280.00	200.00

Note: This is a scarce costume and accounts for much of the value. "Lissy" in one of the more common costumes sells in the $75.00 to $95.00 range.

☐ **Little Cherub,** vinyl head, latex body, molded head, wide sleep eyes, angel suit with wings and halo, 8½"	350.00	400.00	375.00
☐ **Little Colonel,** composition, green sleeping eyes, lashes, blonde mohair wig with long curls, yellow and white cotton dress and bonnet, pantaloons, snap shoes, 13½"	475.00	525.00	490.00
☐ **Little Genius,** caracul wig, 8"	90.00	100.00	95.00
☐ **Little Genius,** hard plastic and vinyl, skin wig, blue-gray eyes, open mouth, white gown with lace and ribbon trim, new booties, 8"	90.00	120.00	98.00
☐ **Little Red Riding Hood,** holds basket of fruit, marked Alex, 8"	80.00	90.00	85.00
☐ **Little Shaver,** vinyl, pink checked dress, 12"	130.00	150.00	140.00
☐ **Little Tiny Billie Toddler,** hard plastic, sleep eyes, long eyelashes, movable arms, wears diaper fastened by safety pin, 8"	100.00	125.00	90.00
☐ **Lord Fauntleroy,** 12", c. 1983	65.00	75.00	70.00
☐ **Lucinda,** pink outfit, c. 1983	80.00	100.00	85.00
☐ **Madelian Dubain,** vinyl construction, blue sleep eyes, jointed body, 11", c. 1948	500.00	700.00	550.00
☐ **Maggie,** blonde hair, pink clothes, straw hat, 21"	100.00	160.00	110.00

ALEXANDER DOLL COMPANY, INC. / 57

	Current Price Range		P/Y AVG
☐ **Maggie Walker,** *hard plastic, sleep eyes, flared printed skirt, carries suitcase with accessories inside (comb and brush, etc.) 18"*	85.00	110.00	75.00

Note: Price is for a complete specimen showing light wear only. For a Maggie Walker with suitcase but lacking the suitcase accessories, $75.00 to $95.00. For one without the suitcase, $60.00 to $80.00

☐ **Marc Antony and Cleopatra,** *12", pair, c. 1983*	125.00	175.00	135.00
☐ **Margaret O'Brien,** *hard plastic, mohair wig in looped braids tied with silk ribbons, hat, calf-length socks, black shoes, 17"*	215.00	250.00	185.00

Note: Margaret O'Brien was a child actress in motion pictures in the early 1940's.

☐ **Margot,** *hard plastic, sleep eyes, long eyelashes, long evening gown with shoulder straps, 9¼"*	125.00	155.00	110.00
☐ **Margot Ballerina,** *plastic, blonde, blue eyes, turquoise costume, satin slippers, # 1841, c. 1955*	150.00	200.00	156.00
☐ **Marlo Thomas,** *vinyl, sleep eyes, black hair, wears knee-length wool dress, strand of graduated pearls, textured stockings, boots, 16½"*	420.00	470.00	385.00

Note: A scarce doll, inspired by the TV show "That Girl" starring Marlo Thomas (daughter of Danny Thomas). It was produced only in 1967. Though Marlo and the show were hits, the doll was not — apparently because Marlo's role on the show was too "grown up" to appeal to little girls.

☐ **Marme,** *bent knee, walks, marked Alex, 8"*	90.00	110.00	95.00
☐ **Marybel,** *vinyl construction, blonde vinyl wig with bangs, sleep eyes, swivel waist, in box with hospital accessories, in coat with booties, 14"*	175.00	225.00	200.00
☐ **Mary Sunshine**	90.00	110.00	95.00

58 / ALEXANDER DOLL COMPANY, INC.

Margaret O'Brien,
hard plastic, c. 1948
$215.00-$250.00

	Current Price Range		P/Y AVG
☐ **McGuffey Ana,** *composition, brown sleeping eyes, lashes, open mouth, blonde human hair braids and bangs, plaid dress, white pinafore, red high button shoes, 15"*	245.00	285.00	260.00
☐ **McGuffey Ana,** *composition, blonde mohair braids and curly bangs, painted blue eyes, closed mouth, red and white checkered dress with organdy pinafore, black shoes, 9"*	175.00	225.00	190.00
☐ **McGuffey Ana,** *c. 1983*	60.00	70.00	65.00
☐ **McGuffy Awake,** *sleep eyes, braided hair*	200.00	220.00	180.00

ALEXANDER DOLL COMPANY, INC. / 59

	Current Price Range		P/Y AVG
☐ **Mike,** *bisque head, puppet body with bisque hands, mohair wigs, painted eyes, long wool robe with rope trim, c. 1932*	175.00	250.00	200.00
☐ **Napoleon and Josephine,** *12", pair, c. 1983*	125.00	175.00	135.00
☐ **Netherlands,** *wears wooden shoes, marked Alex, 8"*	80.00	90.00	85.00
☐ **Pamela,** *hard plastic, sleep eyes, dressed in national costume of Poland with multi-layered, boldly printed skirt, white ruffled blouse, 12"*	140.00	170.00	125.00
☐ **Pierrott,** *Wendykins, hard plastic, jointed, wig, sleep eyes, closed mouth, satin clown suit, dog on leash, mint in box, 8"*	1800.00	2200.00	1850.00
☐ **Polly Pigtails,** *hard plastic, sleep eyes, wide-brimmed straw hat, white dress with puff sleeves, white cotton stockings, black shoes, 13⅞"*	110.00	140.00	100.00
☐ **Portrait Queen,** *white brocade dress, mint in box, # 1186, 11", c. 1972*	300.00	400.00	310.00
☐ **President Ladies,** *set #2*	850.00	900.00	875.00
☐ **Presidents Ladies,** *set # 3*	950.00	1000.00	925.00
☐ **Princess Elizabeth,** *composition, sleep brown eyes, blonde wig, bridal dress and veil, 14"*	225.00	275.00	240.00
☐ **Puddin,** *dark hair and eyes, checkered dress in pink and white, made in 1976, 14"*	45.00	55.00	48.00
☐ **Pussy Cat,** *black, portrait series, 21", c. 1983*	300.00	400.00	320.00
☐ **Rebecca,** *c. 1983*	60.00	70.00	65.00
☐ **Red Boy,** *jointed knees, # 740, 8", c. 1972*	120.00	130.00	125.00
☐ **Renoir ,** *c. 1983*	60.00	70.00	65.00
☐ **Romeo,** *12", c. 1983*	65.00	75.00	70.00
☐ **Scarlett,** *portrait series, 21", c. 1983*	300.00	400.00	325.00
☐ **Scarlet O'Hara,** *composition head and body, black human hair wig, blue sleep eyes, green taffeta dress, 17"*	450.00	550.00	475.00

60 / ALEXANDER DOLL COMPANY, INC.

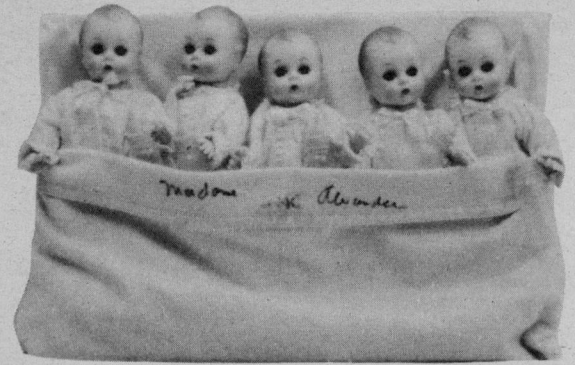

Quintuplets, vinyl, autographed .... $1000.00-$1100.00

	Current Price Range		P/Y AVG
☐ **Scarlett O'Hara**, *vinyl, sleep eyes, long black glossy hair, satin gown with trimming, satin bonnet, wears cameo on a chain at the neck, marked Alexander 1961, 21"*	110.00	140.00	90.00
Note: *Scarlett O'Hara was a character in Margaret Mitchell's "Gone With The Wind," made into a motion picture in 1939.*			
☐ **Sleeping Beauty**, *Disney special edition, 1959, 9"*	200.00	500.00	180.00
☐ **M.I.B.**	450.00	500.00	400.00
☐ **Sleeping Beauty**, *c. 1983*	70.00	80.00	75.00
☐ **Smarty**, *11"*	80.00	90.00	85.00
☐ **Sonja Henie**, *composition body, blonde mohair wig, sleep eyes, short lavender skating dress, ice skates, 14", c. 1950* .	200.00	220.00	215.00
☐ **Southern Belle**, *ribbon trimmed white gown, with box, 11", c. 1968*	350.00	450.00	400.00
☐ **Spanish Girl**, *knee bends, lacy tiered gown, labeled, 8"*	70.00	80.00	75.00

	Current Price Range		P/Y AVG
☐ **Toddler,** *composition head and arms, cloth body, molded hair, brown sleep eyes, open mouth, baby clothes and bonnet, 21"*	425.00	475.00	450.00
☐ **Tommy,** *hard plastic head, jointed body, short blonde human hair wig, brown sleep eyes, school boy suit with striped socks, straw hat, 12"*	900.00	1000.00	950.00
☐ **Tyrolean,** *bent knee, boy, girl, marked Alex, 8", pair*	240.00	280.00	250.00
☐ **Tyrolean Girl,** *bent knees, mint in box, # 798, 8"*	100.00	150.00	120.00
☐ **Tyrolean Boy and Girl,** *vinyl, jointed bent knee, original, 8"*	285.00	325.00	295.00
☐ **Waac Doll,** *composition, green eyes, red hair, 14"*	375.00	425.00	395.00
☐ **Wave Doll,** *composition, blue eyes, blonde hair, 14"*	375.00	425.00	395.00
☐ **Wendy,** *hard plastic, sleep eyes, dressed as tennis player with racquet, skirt, open-toe shoes, 8"*	90.00	115.00	80.00
☐ **Wendy Ann,** *hard plastic, sleep eyes, puffy cheeks, blond hair, wears jacket and skirt of matching style, two buttons on jacket, 8"*	70.00	90.00	62.00
☐ **Wendy Bride,** *plastic, sleep blue eyes, blonde hair, white satin dress, rhinestones, veil, 21", c. 1950's*	225.00	275.00	240.00

ALLIED

☐ **Bonnie Buttons,** *marked 39AE-1-A, 10"*	8.00	10.00	8.00
☐ **Susan,** *marked #2112, box marked Susan, 1967, made in Hong Hong*	1.50	2.25	1.50
☐ **Wendy,** *marked Allied Grand Doll Manufacturing Co., Inc., 1958, 9⅞"*	4.75	6.00	4.00

AMERICAN CHARACTER DOLL COMPANY

The American Character Doll Company ran from the turn of the century to 1968 when it was sold and disbanded. From their offices and factory in New York City, the company manufactured composition, rubber and later hard plastic dolls. They also operated an import division that distributed dolls from France and Italy to the American market.

The early founder, S.D. Hoffman, is credited with the "Can't Break It" process that improved composition to the point that it was more practical and cheaper than bisque for doll manufacturing. This process was later sold to the Horsman Doll and Toy Company who revolutionized the industry with it.

American Character Dolls typically have a distinct charm, whether composition or plastic, baby doll or ingenue, imported or from the New York factory. The company had a great impact on doll production in this country and their dolls enjoy avid collector interest.

	Current Price Range		P/Y AVG
☐ **American Beauty,** plastic, blonde hair (rooted), sleep eyes (blue), unmarked, made in 1955, 21½"	55.00	68.00	50.00
☐ **Astronut,** vinyl, molded and painted features, rooted hair (green!), marked Amer. Doll & Toy Co., made in 1960, 18½"	37.00	46.00	34.00
Note: It was no spelling error: "astronaut" was intentionally spelled "astronut" for the name of this doll. In 1960, when Astronut was marketed, America had not yet sent a man into space.			
☐ **Baby Lou,** plastic, molded and painted hair (reddish), open mouth, marked Amer. Char., made in 1950, 8"	9.00	12.00	8.00
☐ **Baby Sandy,** composition head, rubber body, rubber arms and legs, sleep eyes (metallic), molded hair, open mouth, wears vest and bow tie, marked Petite, 18"	140.00	170.00	130.00
☐ **Baby Tiny Tears,** nurser, plastic head, rubber body, rubber arms and legs, sleep eyes, marked Pat. No. 2675644, American Character, 1950, 13"	15.00	19.00	14.00
☐ **Barbara Sue,** vinyl head and body, vinyl arms and legs, disc jointed arms, mouth closed, reddish hair with a flower at			

AMERICAN CHARACTER DOLL COMPANY / 63

	Current Price Range		P/Y AVG
each side, frilly white dress, white stockings, marked Amer. Char. Doll, 15⅞"	40.00	55.00	34.00
☐ **Betsy McCall,** *long gown, 14"*	90.00	100.00	94.00
☐ **Betsy McCall,** *plastic, 8"*	60.00	70.00	65.00
☐ **Bride,** *plastic/vinyl, blonde hair (rooted), sleep eyes, marked Amer. Char. Doll, 1955, 18"*	47.00	58.00	42.00
☐ **Butterball,** *vinyl, rooted hair (sandy blonde), sleep eyes (blue), marked 1961, American Doll & Toy Co., 18½"*	41.00	50.00	37.00
☐ **Chuckles,** *marked Amer. Doll & Toy Co., 1961, 23¼"*	50.00	65.00	45.00
☐ **Dandy,** *composition head and body, molded hair, marked AC, made in 1942, 11½"*	16.00	21.00	15.00
☐ **Darlin Dollface,** *vinyl head and body, vinyl arms and legs, sleep eyes, partially opened mouth with pursed lips, rooted hair, print dress, 11"*	16.00	20.00	15.00
☐ **Graduate,** *vinyl, tufted hair, painted eyes, marked Amer. Doll & Toy Co., 1960, 21"*	37.00	46.00	35.00
Note: *A youth wearing a mortar board and scholar's gown. No connection with the Dustin Hoffman film.*			
☐ **Hedda Get Betta,** *vinyl, molded and painted features, novelty doll with three-faced head (operated by button on top of head), representing sleep, discomfort, and comfort, marked American Doll & Toy Corp., 1961, 21"*	39.00	48.00	35.00
☐ **Little Joe Cartwright,** *vinyl, molded and painted features, molded hair, painted clothing, made in Portugal, 8"*	47.00	60.00	42.00
Note: *This doll represents a character from the TV program "Bonanza," and dates probably from the early 1960's, when the show was at its height.*			
☐ **Little Love,** *composition head, cloth body, composition limbs, wig attached with adhesive, marked Amer. Char. Doll, 1942, 17⅞"*	43.00	54.00	40.00
☐ **Marie Ann,** *marked American Character, 1966, 13"*	26.00	31.00	25.00

64 / AMERICAN CHARACTER DOLL COMPANY

	Current Price Range		P/Y AVG
☐ **Marie Lee,** marked 3, American Character, 1966, 13"	26.00	31.00	25.00
☐ **Miss Chicadee,** plastic, molded and painted hair, painted eyes, unmarked, made c. 1949, 8"	25.00	30.00	23.00
☐ **Peek-A-Boo Toodles,** vinyl, brown hair (rooted), sleep eyes (blue), rosy red cheeks, marked American Char. Doll, 1956, 22½"	23.00	29.00	20.00
☐ **Polly Pretend,** combination vinyl and plastic, long hair, fixed eyes, partially open mouth, designed to represent a young girl dressed in her mother's or big sister's clothing, with hair roller, oversized shoes, etc. marketed in both black and white, marked A.M.S.C.O. 1974, 13½"			
Black version:	18.00	23.00	17.00
White version:	14.00	19.00	14.00
☐ **Poppi,** plastic head, plastic body and limbs, adult doll, wears flowered skirt, white blouse, fixed eyes, called Poppi because the doll "pops" apart at the waist and chest, 11½"	10.00	15.00	10.00
☐ **Pouty Miss Marie,** marked Amer. Char. Inc., 1965, 13"	25.00	29.00	24.00
☐ **Pretty Penny,** hard plastic head and body, puffy cheeks, sleep eyes with deep-set pupils that appear to follow the viewer, arms can be posed, long black silky hair, ribbon in hair, short dress, cotton ribbed stockings, 19"	50.00	65.00	48.00
☐ **Ricky Ricardo,** rubber doll, 15", 1959	45.00	52.00	40.00
☐ **Sunny Boy,** vinyl head, vinyl arms and legs, cloth body, fixed eyes (blue), molded hair, open mouth, wears high collar and large western-style necktie, 21"	50.00	65.00	47.00
☐ **Sweet Sue,** bride dress, 18"	80.00	90.00	84.00
☐ **Sweet Sue,** plastic/vinyl, brown hair (rooted), sleep eyes, unmarked, made in 1955, 19"	41.00	49.00	40.00

AMERICAN CHARACTER DOLL COMPANY / 65

	Current Price Range		P/Y AVG
☐ **Sweet Sue,** *hard plastic, sleep eyes, long eyelashes, closed mouth with puckered lips, dark red lips, honey blond hair, wears straw bonnet, 15"* ...	40.00	55.00	38.00
☐ **Teeny Betsy McCall,** *plastic, brown hair (rooted), sleep eyes (blue), marked McCall Corp., made in 1958, 8"* ...	23.00	28.00	22.00

Ricky Ricardo,
rubber, c. 1955, 15"
$45.00-$52.00

66 / AMERICAN CHARACTER DOLL COMPANY

Sweet Sue,
hard plastic, 17"
$41.00-$49.00

	Current Price Range		P/Y AVG
☐ **Terry Talks,** *composition, blonde saran wig, sleep eyes, white eyelet playdress, 22", c. 1950*	60.00	70.00	62.50
☐ **Tiny Tears,** *composition head, rubber body, molded hair, sleep eyes with tear ducts, layette suit, 12", c. 1950*	75.00	85.00	77.50
☐ **Tiny Tears,** *rubber, molded hair, sleep eyes with tear ducts, layette suit, 12", c. 1950*	75.00	85.00	77.50
☐ **Tisket -N- Basket,** *separate cloth doll in green and yellow basket with handle, green and yellow outfit, 10"*	8.00	15.00	10.00
☐ **Toodle-Loo,** *vinyl, rooted hair (blonde), painted eyes, infant doll, marked 1961, American Doll & Toy Co., 18½"*	44.00	55.00	40.00

AMERICAN CHARACTER DOLL COMPANY / 67

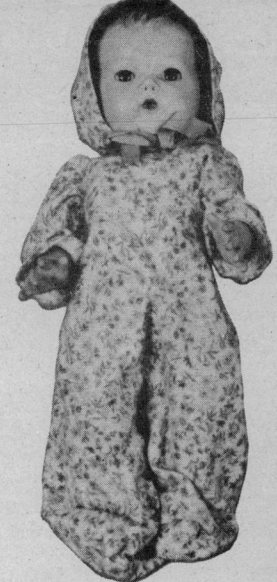

Tiny Tears, composition and rubber, c. 1950, 12"
$75.00-$85.00

	Current Price Range		P/Y AVG
☐ **Tressy,** plastic/vinyl, blonde hair (rooted), with growing-hair action, operated by knob at back of body, marked American Doll & Toy Corp., 1963, 11½"	10.00	14.00	10.00
☐ **Wee Girl,** marked Noen, 1940, 9¾"	25.00	29.00	23.00
☐ **Whimsie,** vinyl, painted eyes, rooted hair (blonde), upturned eyes with angelic expression, puffy cheeks, marked Amer. Doll & Toy Co., 1960, 21"	38.00	46.00	35.00
☐ **Whimsie,** as a monk, plastic, brown felt habit, 21"	25.00	35.00	30.00

AMSCO

	Current Price Range		P/Y AVG
☐ **Buffy**, marked 1971, Amsco Ind., Inc., 12¼"	42.00	51.00	40.00
☐ **Gramma**, cloth (stuffed), painted features, yarn hair (grey), painted eyeglasses, sold originally with a tag reading Amsco Toys, made in Hong Kong, made in 1971, 19"	11.00	14.00	11.00

APEX

☐ **Baby Wendy**, vinyl head, cloth body, vinyl limbs, sleep eyes (blue), bright red lips, wears baby bonnet, marked APEX, made in 1952, 18½"	27.00	36.00	25.00

ARLESFORD

☐ **Hilary**, porcelain, 24", c. 1979	125.00	175.00	130.00
☐ **Jane**, bisque porcelain, soft body, wigs, blown glass eyes, 24", c. 1979	100.00	150.00	110.00
☐ **Katherine**, bisque, porcelain, soft body, wigs, blown glass eyes, 24", c. 1979	100.00	150.00	110.00
☐ **Lisa**, bisque, porcelain, soft body, wigs, blown glass eyes, 24", c. 1979	100.00	150.00	110.00
☐ **William**, porcelain, 22", c. 1979	100.00	150.00	110.00

ARRANBEE DOLL COMPANY

Arranbee Dolls, an American company, was started in the early 1920's and produced highly collectable dolls until it was absorbed by Vogue Doll Company in 1960. In the early years of the company, bisque heads were imported from major German and French manufacturers and assembled on American made soft bodies. When World War I disrupted trade with Europe, especially Germany, Arranbee, like most of the other doll companies turned to making their own composition heads, and their quality became famous in the industry. In the early 1950's, hard plastic replaced composition for construction and Arranbee reached its pinnacle of success. The Nancy Lee Series produced during this time is one of the most sought after collectibles in the hobby. Vogue Dolls used Arranbee's

ARRANBEE DOLL COMPANY / 69

molds for the Itinial Ginny doll issues before disbanding the company and discontinuing the use of their marks.

Nanette, hard plastic, c. 1950, 14″ **$46.00-$55.00**

	Current Price Range		P/Y AVG
☐ **Angeline,** *plastic, blonde wig attached by adhesive, sleep eyes (blue), marked R & B, made in 1952, 17½″*	48.00	59.00	45.00
☐ **Army Boy,** *composition head and limbs, body stuffed with excelsior, molded hair, painted eyes, wears U.S. soldier's uniform of post-World War I era, featuring reproductions (in reduced size) of Lincoln cents for jacket buttons, 15″*	75.00	95.00	70.00

ARRANBEE DOLL COMPANY

	Current Price Range		P/Y AVG
Note: The uniform style would suggest a dating of c. 1920-25, but it is believed Army Boy was made slightly later than this.			
☐ **Baby Marie,** vinyl head, vinyl arms and legs, plastic body, sleep eyes, molded hair, partially open mouth, shaped for insertion of nursing bottle, wears diaper, quilt jacket, 8¼"	5.00	7.00	5.00
☐ **Debu-Teen,** composition body, cloth body, composition arms and legs, turnable head, brunette wig, attached by adhesive, sleep eyes, marked R & B, made in 1940, 18"	43.00	52.00	40.00
☐ **Dream Bride,** plastic, sandy blonde wig attached by adhesive, sleep eyes (blue), wears bridal gown, marked R & B, also carrying the mold mark 210, made in 1954, 21"	43.00	55.00	40.00
☐ **Francine,** plastic, blonde hair attached by adhesive, sleep eyes (blue), marked R & B, made in 1955, 17"	48.00	59.00	44.00
☐ **Judy,** plastic, blonde wig attached by adhesive, the wig formed into an elaborate hairdo of tightly wound braids curled into a ram's-horn and pinned against the head, sleep eyes (blue), marked with the mold number 210 and the patent number 2,537,598, made in 1951, 19"	62.00	75.00	58.00
☐ **Littlest Angel,** plastic, brown hair attached by adhesive, sleep eyes (blue), swivel head, jointed at the knees, marked R & B, made in 1956, 10"	12.00	16.00	11.00
☐ **Nancy Lee,** hard plastic head, hard plastic arms, legs and body, saran wig, deep flesh toned skin, short silk dress with floral pattern, tied with waist ribbon, white shoes, silk stockings, 17"	50.00	65.00	47.00
☐ **Nanette,** brown hair, blue sleep eyes, lashes, yellow blouse, floral print jumper, 15"	55.00	65.00	60.00
☐ **Nanette,** plastic, blonde mohair wig, blue sleep eyes, lashes, velvet gown, lamb jacket	70.00	80.00	75.00

ARRANBEE DOLL COMPANY / 71

	Current Price Range		P/Y AVG
☐ **Nanette,** plastic, brown wig, attached by adhesive, sleep eyes (blue), marked R & B, made in 1953, 14"	46.00	55.00	45.00
☐ **New Happytot,** vinyl head and body, sleep eyes (blue), marked Arranbee, made in 1955, 16"	24.00	30.00	23.00
☐ **Peachy,** plastic, molded hair (brown), painted eyes, unmarked, made c. 1950, 10"	11.00	14.00	10.00
☐ **Princess Betty Rose,** composition head, composition arms, legs and body, sleep eyes, closed mouth with dark lipstick, full, medium-length wig, wears long dress with lace trimming, marked R & B, 17½"	75.00	95.00	70.00
Note: Princess Betty Rose was released in the late 1930's, undoubtedly inspired by the American popularity of Britian's Princess Elizabeth.			
☐ **Prom Queen,** walker, plastic/vinyl, brunette hair (rooted), sleep eyes (blue), marked R & B, made in 1957, 17"	47.00	59.00	45.00
☐ **Rosie,** composition head (swivel), composition arms and legs, cloth body, sleep eyes, molded blond hair swept down in front, long at sides, doleful expression, partially open mouth, wears long white gown, marked Arranbee, 18½"	30.00	38.00	27.00
Note: Rosie was originally placed on the market in 1935. It was one of the better sellers among the Arranbee line.			
☐ **Scarlet,** composition head, composition arms, legs and body, sleep eyes (green), long eyelashes, closed mouth, wears long ball gown of U.S. Civil War era and large bonnet, gown is trimmed with silk ribbons, marked R & B, 15"	50.00	65.00	48.00
Note: Scarlet was inspired by the motion picture, "Gone With The Wind," released in 1939, and represents the character Scarlet O'Hara. It is believed that the doll went on sale in 1940. Public reaction to "Gone With The Wind" brought about a great deal of related			

72 / ARROW NOVELTY COMPANY

	Current Price Range		P/Y AVG

merchandise — including quite a few Scarlet O'Hara dolls by various manufacturers.

☐ **Skater Doll**, *bisque, blue skirt, plaid hood, jacket, skates* 150.00 200.00 175.00

☐ **Snuggle Doll**, *composition head, stuffed body, stuffed arms and legs, blonde wig attached by adhesive, fixed eyes (blue), unmarked, made in 1941, 17"* 53.00 65.00 50.00

☐ **Sonja Henie**, *composition head and body, brunette wig attached by adhesive, sleep eyes (brown), marked R & B, made in 1945, 21¼"* 49.00 58.00 47.00
Note: *Sonja Henie was an Olympic ice-skating champion and, later, motion picture personality.*

☐ **Taffy**, *plastic, sleep eyes (green), marked R & B, made in 1954, 16½"* 55.00 67.00 52.00

ARROW NOVELTY CO.

☐ **Skookum (Indian)**, *plastic, marked Trademark Registered, Skookum Indian, U.S.A., Patented 1950, 21"* 68.00 82.00 65.00
Note: *This doll was actually in production well before 1950 in various early versions, but was either not patented until 1950 or (perhaps) the patent was renewed in that year. It can also be found in a number of different sizes and facial expressions. The hair is always a coarse black wig, sometimes loose, sometimes braided, but always quite long.*

ARROW PLASTICS

☐ **Baby Doo**, *vinyl, molded and painted features, molded and painted hair, (blonde), bright red lips, marked with the Arrow symbol of an arrow piercing a diamond, made in 1957, 8½"* 7.00 10.00 7.00

	Current Price Range		P/Y AVG
☐ **Bye-Bye Baby,** vinyl, blonde hair (rooted), sleep eyes (blue), marked Arrow Plastics 18, made in 1957, 17¼".	25.00	30.00	23.00
☐ **Candy,** vinyl, molded and painted features, molded and painted hair, marked The Edward Moberly Co., 1958, 8"	4.00	6.00	4.00
☐ **Cindy,** vinyl, molded and painted features, molded and painted hair, marked 22 The Edward Moberly Co., made in 1962, 8"	6.00	8.00	6.00
☐ **Marlene,** vinyl, sleep eyes (blue), adult body, marked with an arrow inside a lozenge and the number 55, 24"	40.00	48.00	38.00
☐ **My Friend,** vinyl, molded and painted features, molded and painted hair, diapered toddler clutching a Teddy Bear, marked The Edward Moberly Co., 1964, 8"	4.00	6.00	4.00
☐ **Playful,** rubber, molded and painted features, marked 42, made in 1941, 11"	21.00	27.00	20.00
☐ **Pretty Lady,** vinyl, blonde hair (rooted), sleep eyes (blue), marked with the Arrow symbol of an arrow piercing a diamond, and additionally marked with the mold number 52, made in 1958, 31".	27.00	36.00	25.00
☐ **Stunning,** vinyl, sleep eyes (blue), adult body, marked with an arrow inside a lozenge and the number 55, 24"	40.00	48.00	38.00
☐ **Sweet Judy,** vinyl, sleep eyes (blue), adult body, marked with an arrow inside a lozenge and the number 55, 24"	40.00	48.00	38.00

ART FABRIC MILLS

☐ **Cloth,** lithographed face, cloth body, marked Art Fabric Mills, New York, patented February 13, 1900, 26"	170.00	210.00	165.00
☐ **Merrie Marie,** lithographed cloth face, cloth body, marked Art Fabric Mills, New York, 25"	190.00	235.00	180.00

ARTISAN NOVELTY

	Current Price Range		P/Y AVG
☐ **Little Miss Gadabout**, walker, plastic, sleep eyes (blue), unmarked, made in 1950, 18"	31.00	39.00	30.00
☐ **Lov You**, vinyl head, cloth body, vinyl arms and legs, unmarked, made in 1951, 22"	33.00	39.00	30.00
☐ **Raving Beauty**, plastic, red wig attached by adhesive, sleep eyes (brown), unmarked, made in 1953, 18½"	45.00	55.00	42.00

ASPEN PRODUCTIONS

☐ **Alan Alda of "M.A.S.H.,"** vinyl head, vinyl body, molded hair, has push-button in back which operates arms — putting this doll on the borderline of the puppet category, 8½"	5.00	7.00	3.00

Note: At the same time a companion doll was made, to represent Loretta Swit. Value is about the same, but as a set they would probably bring a slight premium. Both dolls wear molded combat boots.

AUNT SARAH

☐ **Aunt Sarah**, lithographed cloth, representing a grandmotherly woman holding bowl of pancake batter (trademark of Aunt Sarah's House of Pancakes), 18"	4.00	6.00	3.00

AURORA

☐ **Mary Many Face (Spanish National Costume doll)**, cloth, sponsored by UNECEFF, unmarked, sold originally with a tag reading Mary Many Face, Aurora Products Corp., 17"	15.00	19.00	14.00

AVERILL MANUFACTURING COMPANY

	Current Price Range		P/Y AVG
☐ **Baby,** bisque head, cloth body, celluloid arms and legs, sleep eyes, open mouth, two teeth, tongue, voice box, #1005/3652/4, #1386/47, 16"	800.00	1000.00	825.00
☐ **Baby Sweets,** by Maude Tousey Fangel, all cloth, printed features which include blue eyes with long lashes, curly blond hair, pug nose, sweet smile, white gauze dress trimmed in lace, matching hat, 14"	240.00	255.00	225.00
☐ **Bonnie Babe,** bisque head, cloth body with composition arms and legs, detailed molded head, blue sleep eyes, lovely gown, rare large size, 20" body length, 13½" head circumference	1000.00	1250.00	1000.00
☐ **Character,** composition head and arms, cloth body and legs, painted face, wig, original clothes, tagged, 10"	85.00	125.00	55.00
☐ **Chocolate Drop,** black all cloth doll, painted face, three black yarn pigtails, designed by Grace G. Drayton, 11"	195.00	220.00	195.00
☐ **Dolly Dingle,** all cloth, jointed arms and legs, painted features, designed by Grace G. Dayton,	185.00	210.00	175.00
☐ **Dutch Girl,** cloth, pigtailed mohair wig, regional costume, 13"	40.00	50.00	45.00
☐ **Indian Boy,** painted eyes, molded hair, green felt shirt, gray felt pants, green and red moccasins, 13"	60.00	70.00	62.00
☐ **Infant,** bisque head, cloth body, molded hair, blue sleep eyes, open mouth, two lower teeth, white baby dress with bonnet, 18"	1500.00	1750.00	1600.00
☐ **Italian Girl,** cloth, yarn hair, grown eyes, print dress, white apron, 14"	70.00	100.00	80.00
☐ **Minnehaha,** character, cloth molded, masked face, cloth body, long black yarn pigtails, brown eyes with real eyelashes, painted features, brown skinned, colorful outfit of orange yellow, green, white mocacsins, original wrist tag "Minnehaha," c. 1940's, mint, 13½"	80.00	90.00	80.00

AZARK

	Current Price Range		P/Y AVG
☐ **Calamity Jane,** *posable legs, marked Azark-Hamway, 12"*	4.00	6.00	4.00
☐ **Kit Carson,** *plastic body, plastic legs, vinyl head and arms, representing the gunfighter of the Old West, who wears a moustache, plaid shirt, striped vest, striped trousers, and tall boots, he carries a six-shooter, marked Hong Kong, c. 1974, 12"*	4.00	6.00	4.00

BABY BERRY

☐ **Christopher Robin,** *cloth body, cloth limbs, vinyl head, molded and painted hair (red), unmarked, age of manufacture unknown, representing a character from the writings of A.A. Milne*	37.00	45.00	35.00
☐ **Lil Abner,** *vinyl head, vinyl arms, legs and body, plaid shirt, pants patched at knees, dated 1957, 13"*	90.00	115.00	85.00

Note: Al Capp's "Lil Abner" was made into a stage play at about this time (1957), inspiring a wave of related merchandise. The character had been introduced into comic strips in the 1930's. Baby Berry also made a matching "Daisy Mae" doll, whose market value is about the same.

☐ **Mammy Yokum,** *vinyl head, cloth body, yarn wig, bulbous nose, square chin, large staring eyes, smokes corncob pipe, based on the character from the comic strip "Lil Abner" by Al Capp, 21"*	125.00	150.00	115.00

Note: Baby Berry also made a smaller version of Mammy Yokum, about 13", in a different style.

	Current Price Range	P/Y AVG

CONSTANCE BANNISTER

☐ **Bannister Baby,** *vinyl, molded and painted hair, sleep eyes (blue), nursing mouth, marked Constance Bannister, New York, date of manufacture unknown, presumably c. 1952, 17"* 70.00 88.00 65.00

Note: Constance Bannister was a professional photographer whose photos of babies were collected into several best selling books during the 1950's.

BANTAM

☐ **Sleepyhead,** *vinyl mask face, plush body, plush arms and legs, molded and painted features, molded and painted hair (blonde), sold originally with a tag reading Bantam U.S. Toys, made in 1962, 9⅞"* 5.00 7.00 5.00

BAUER & BLACK

☐ **Miss Curity,** *composition with sleep eyes, 1946, 21"* 43.00 54.00 40.00

BELLE

☐ **Baby Gem,** *vinyl, sleep eyes (blue), unmarked, believed to have been made in 1958, 8"* 6.00 8.00 6.00
☐ **Ballerina Belle,** *plastic/vinyl, brown hair (rooted), sleep eyes (blue), marked 16VW, made in 1956, 18½"* 7.00 9.00 6.00
☐ **Ballerina Belle,** *walker, marked AE 200-21, 1956, 18½"* 11.00 14.00 10.00
☐ **Belle-Lee,** *vinyl, blonde hair (rooted), sleep eyes (blue), unmarked, made in 1958, 10"* 4.00 6.00 4.00

78 / BELTON

	Current Price Range		P/Y AVG
☐ **Jackie**, vinyl head, stuffed arms and legs, stuffed body, short molded hair swept down in front, sleep eyes with medium-length lashes, wears corduroy overalls, mold number 14 on head, 14".	16.00	20.00	15.00
☐ **Little Miss Margie**, hard vinyl head, hard vinyl arms, legs and body, sleep eyes, long reddish-blond hair, pearl earrings, wears print dress with white collar and cuffs, no stockings, marked with P within circle, 10"	7.00	9.00	7.00
☐ **Melinda**, plastic/vinyl, unmarked, 1961, 14"	7.00	9.00	7.00
☐ **Miss B**, vinyl, brown hair (rooted), sleep eyes (blue), unmarked, made in 1954, 11½"	5.00	7.00	5.00
☐ **Perfect Companion**, walker, marked AE 553, sold in 1953, 22"	11.00	14.00	10.00
☐ **Twixie The Twisting Pixie**, jointed waist, marked P-16, 1958, 19"	26.00	31.00	25.00

BELTON

Beltons are among the aristocrats of the doll world. All specimens of this manufacturer rank as antiques, since the firm went out of business in 1855. Not only are they antiques, but the quality is quite high — and so, too, is the value. However, the scarcity factor with Beltons is not as extreme as with some other dolls of this general era, therefore keeping the values within more or less tolerable bounds. Some Beltons can be had for as little as $300 or $350, even in well-preserved condition: which is really saying something, for dolls of this kind of age, reputation, and visual appeal.

Belton was a French firm and was partially responsible for the worldwide acclaim achieved by French dolls in the mid 1800's. In that era, everyone acknowledged that the French were the supreme doll manufacturers. Though export into the U.S. was not nearly as heavy as it became later, well-to-do families tried to get French dolls for their children or (even more often) for display. When the Germans gradually overtook the French in doll manufacturing, they were careful to model most of their dolls along classical French lines — which meant the standard set by firms such as Belton.

Originally Belton was in partnership with Jumeau. Their company was founded at Paris in 1842. Jumeau then went off on his own and Belton carried on alone, until his death in the early 1850's, For several years thereafter his widow maintained the factory but sold out in 1855. Hence the whole history of Belton spanned only about a dozen years. None of the Belton dolls was made in large quantities, mainly because the export market was not, in the 1840's and 1850's, what it became in the 1880's and 1890's.

Belton dolls customarily bear a mold or model number but no other markings, and, in some cases, no markings whatsoever.

	Current Price Range		P/Y AVG
☐ **Bisque,** *jointed composition body, blue paperweight eyes, closed mouth, 18"*	1400.00	2200.00	1750.00
☐ **Bisque head,** *wood body, papier mache arms and legs, fixed eyes (very large, dark), painted lashes on upper and lower eyelids, partially open mouth with no teeth showing, thin face, pug nose, pierced ears, representing an adult woman, marked with the mold number 3, date of manufacture not known, 12"*	580.00	700.00	550.00

BENDEE

☐ **French Gendarme (policeman),** *wire encased in foam, fully posable, molded and painted features and clothing, representing a French gendarme of the 1890's, marked Bendee, date of manufacture unknown, made in England, 8¾"*	7.00	10.00	7.00

BERGMANN

Bergmann, a German firm, was a rather prolific doll producer during the early 1900's. Collectors should take note of the fact that Bergmann did not manufacture doll heads. It was strictly a maker of doll bodies and an assembler of dolls for distribution to the wholesale and export markets: that is, it bought doll heads made by other firms and attached them to its bodies. This was not, of course, a unique situation, as many other firms operated in a similar way; but companies which did not manufacture doll heads lack some of the status and glamor of firms

BERMAN AND ANDERSON

which did. The full name of the organization was Charles M. Bergmann and Co. It was set up in 1889, when the German doll industry was rolling in high gear. Bergmann dolls are found with heads by Armand Marseille, Halbig and others. They are certainly not inferior dolls if one judges them as a whole, and the market values show that hobbyists are not exactly taking them lightly. The costumes can be very exquisite.

Bergmann did a flourishing export business, which seems to have increased steadily in the years from 1900 until the opening of World War I. The full company name usually appeared on its dolls, rather than initials, and sometimes a date as well. The name of the manufacturer of the doll's head is often indicated, too. With virtually no exceptions, the Bergmann dolls have bisque heads, sleep eyes (usually with lashes) and handsome wigs.

	Current Price Range		P/Y AVG
☐ **Bisque,** *blue set paperweight eyes, long blonde curls, open mouth, white dress with red sash, red hair bow, 25"*	425.00	475.00	440.00
☐ **Bisque,** *brown eyes, blonde wig, white and pink cotton dress, 23"*	150.00	200.00	170.00
☐ **Bisque,** *brown sleep eyes, blonde mohair wig, open mouth, long green dress embroidered in white, 32"*	725.00	750.00	740.00
☐ **Composition Head,** *jointed body, blonde human hair, blue paperweight eyes, red velvet dress and hat, c. 1910, 25"*	550.00	600.00	575.00
☐ **Girl,** *jointed composition body, gray-blue eyes, white and blue cotton dress, blue satin belt, blue ribbon in hair, 23"*	325.00	375.00	340.00

BERMAN & ANDERSON

☐ **Oliver Hardy,** *vinyl head, vinyl arms, legs and body, painted features, designed to represent the motion picture comedy actor Oliver Hardy (of Laurel and Hardy), dates from the 1970's, 11"*	9.00	12.00	9.00
☐ **Stan Laurel,** *vinyl head, vinyl arms, legs and body, painted features, designed to represent the motion picture comedy actor Stan Laurel (of Laurel and Hardy), dates from the 1970's, 10¼"*	9.00	12.00	9.00

BLUMBERG

	Current Price Range		P/Y AVG
☐ **Baby's First Doll**, vinyl, molded and painted hair, sleep eyes (blue), marked 2F-3, made in 1960, 13¼"	5.00	7.00	5.00
☐ **Jimmy**, vinyl head, latex body, molded and painted hair, sleep eyes (blue), unmarked, made in 1955, 15½"	7.00	10.00	6.00
☐ **Perky Bright**, vinyl, molded and painted hair, sleep eyes (blue), unmarked, made in 1952, 12"	10.00	14.00	9.00
☐ **Rockabye Baby**, vinyl, molded and painted hair, fixed eyes, unmarked, made in 1963, 14"	6.00	8.00	5.00
☐ **Sally**, vinyl, marked 26 AE, 1958, 15"	8.00	11.00	7.00
☐ **Timmy**, vinyl head, latex body, molded and painted hair, fixed eyes (blue), unmarked, made in 1954, 15"	5.00	7.00	5.00

ERNST BOHNE

☐ **Porcelain**, half doll, beautiful molded porcelain head and torso with arms, elaborate coiffure wreathed with flowers, molded clothing on torso, 21"	900.00	1000.00	675.00

BOMBOLE FRANCA

☐ **Bed Doll**, plastic head, plastic arms, legs and body, sleep eyes, wig attached by adhesive, with ribbon in hair, closed mouth with quizzical facial expression, marked Made in Italy by Bombole Franca Co., 1959, 14"	7.00	9.00	7.00

Note: Called "bed doll" as it was designed to decorate a bed during daytime, a custom more prevalent in Europe than in the U.S.

BONOMI

	Current Price Range		P/Y AVG
☐ **Handora,** *plastic, sleep eyes (blue), jointed waist, marked Bonomi, Italy, made in the early 1960's, 22"*	33.00	39.00	30.00
☐ **Lizabetta,** *plastic, jointed waist, sleep eyes (green), strung, marked Bonomi, Italy, 19"*	37.00	47.00	35.00

BORDEN

☐ **Elsie, Borden's Cow,** *vinyl head, stuffed plush body, makes mooing sound, a premium of the Borden's Milk Co., made in 1958, 14"*	9.00	12.00	8.00

GEORGE BORGFELDT

☐ **Gladdie,** *ceramic head, fully molded and painted, composition limbs, cloth body, sleep blue eyes, original clothes and trunk with more clothes, 17"*	875.00	975.00	880.00
☐ **Gladdie,** *designed by Helen W. Jensen, ceramic head, composition legs and arms, cloth body, blue glass eyes, molded blond hair, laughing with open mouth, white bonnet with wide ruffle, white dress, shoes and socks, 20"*	825.00	875.00	800.00
☐ **Happifats,** *all bisque, jointed arms, painted black curl in middle of forehead, painted eyes with excited surprised expression, open smiling mouth, two teeth, molded clothes, 4"*	175.00	225.00	175.00

BROCK CANDY COMPANY / 83

Charlie McCarthy,
composition and cloth
$250.00-$300.00

	Current Price Range		P/Y AVG
MADAME ETNA BOUCHER			
☐ **Child,** *bisque head, ball jointed composition body, light brown long curls, stationary blue eyes, closed mouth, rare,* 10"	725.00	800.00	725.00
BROCK CANDY CO.			
☐ **Sam The Scarecrow,** *cloth (printed), date of manufacture unknown, probably mid 1960's, apparently given as a premium or promotional item in connection with the purchase of Brock candy products,* 17"	13.00	17.00	12.00

BROOKGLAD

	Current Price Range		P/Y AVG
☐ **Poor Pitiful Pearl,** *vinyl, rooted hair (blonde), sleep eyes (blue), marked A Brookglad Creation, made in 1957, 13"*	25.00	30.00	23.00
☐ **Rusty,** *vinyl, molded and painted hair (red), fixed eyes (blue), marked Rusty, made in 1958, 16"*	22.00	28.00	20.00

BROUSE

☐ **Abraham Lincoln Doll,** *bisque, original clothes, 17"*	250.00	275.00	225.00

BRU

The shortest name in the doll industry, Bru, belonged to a Parisian firm of the 1800's. It survived into the 20th century, though its most collectible and valuable dolls date to the earlier period. Though this was a long-established company, its output was apparently very small, to judge by the small number of specimens that have crossed the American market (and there does not seem to be any greater quantity available in Europe, either). Standards of quality at Bru were exceptionally high. To judge from the finished results, painstaking work went into modeling of the molds. Today the Bru dolls rank among the most valuable of all antique dolls, with prices nearly always in the four-digit category for well preserved specimens.

Founder of the firm was Leon Casimir Bru, in 1867. In 1883 it was sold to a man named Chevot, who continued to operate it as Bru since the name had won considerable recognition by then. It was sold again 1890, but these changes of ownership had, surprisingly, no effect on the product's quality. The usual Bru mark consists of a dot within a circle, sometimes in a half-circle. The mark *Bru Jne,* which appears on some of the company's dolls, stands for Bru Jeune (Bru, Junior and Company — the name by which the firm was known for a while).

Fashion,
bisque and kid,
c. 1875, 18″
$2000.00-$3000.00

	Current Price Range		P/Y AVG
☐ **Bébé**, bisque head, hands, kid body, blue paperweight eyes, blushed lids, brown human hair wig, closed mouth, pierced ears, original rose silk dress, mark: "Bebe Brevete S.G.D.G., Paris", 14″	5000.00	6500.00	4500.00
☐ **Bebe**, bisque head, kid body with jointed wood arms and legs, long black ringlet wig, blue paperweight eyes, ivory lace gown, leather shoes	8000.00	9000.00	8500.00

86 / BRUCKNER

	Current Price Range		P/Y AVG
☐ **Bébé,** *bisque head, kid body with bisque arms and legs, human hair wig, blue paperweight eyes, pierced ears, closed mouth, green and ivory silk gown and shoes, 11½"*	5000.00	6000.00	5500.00
☐ **Bébé Teteur,** *bisque head, kid body with bisque hands, curly blonde wig, blue paperweight eyes, painted eyebrows, nursing mouth, nightgown and cap, 13"*	5000.00	6000.00	5500.00
☐ **Bisque Head,** *French ball jointed body, human hair wig, paperweight eyes, pierced ears, closed mouth, red gown*	3000.00	4000.00	3250.00
☐ **Bisque Head,** *jointed composition body, blonde wig, blue sleep eyes, open mouth with upper teeth, pierced ears, original clothes, mark: "Bru Jne R 9", 22"*	5000.00	6000.00	5000.00
☐ **Bisque,** *swivel head, kidskin body with bisque forearms, fixed eyes (large, staring), partially open mouth, pierced ears, marked Bebe/Brevette Paris, 20"*	3800.00	4650.00	3750.00

BRUCKNER

☐ **Black Rag Doll,** *all cloth, stiffened mask face, 11"*	120.00	130.00	125.00
☐ **Rag Doll,** *printed face, original blue jumper with trimmed blouse and underwear, marked "Pat'd July 9, 1901", 12"*	60.00	70.00	60.00
☐ **Topsy-Turvy Rag Doll,** *all cloth with treated lithographed mask faces, two dolls in one, one face is white, the back side is black, cotton dress, 12"*	200.00	375.00	225.00

M. H. BUELL

☐ **Little Lulu,** *doll with mask face, height 14", c. 1944*	75.00	95.00	85.00

BUSCHOW & BECK

This German manufacturer specialized in dolls with metal heads, which it chiefly exported to the American market. It was not the only company making metal-head dolls, but it seems to have far outdone the competition in quantity. Metal-head dolls were first introduced in the 1880's (by another firm). They were supposed to solve the durability porblem, since the pretty bisque heads were breakable. Metal-head dolls could be sold at a lower price than those of bisque, and held out the promise of surviving longer than their purchaser. Indeed, they were virtually indestructible — but the popularity envisioned for them, by their promoters, never came to pass. They were simply not as good-looking as the bisque-head dolls, and the inducement of long wear was not enough to win over the public.

Buschow & Beck was in business in the later years of the 1800's and the earlier years of the present century. It did not make metal-head dolls exclusively, but also those of celluloid. On most Buschow & Beck dolls found on the U.S. market you will encounter the MINERVA trademark, which consists of that word in a semi-circle positioned atop a classical-style helmet (Minerva was of course a Greek goddess). This trademark was not used on all the firm's wares but exclusively on those alloted for export to America. Hence, if you doll-shop in the European antiques outlets, the Buschow & Beck dolls found there are not likely to have the "Minerva" marking.

For the collector these are not expensive dolls; they're old, not really bad looking, and represent something definitely "different." So you might want to consider them for your collection. Some can be found for under $100. Of course, as with any metal-head dolls, chipped paint brings down the desirability.

	Current Price Range		P/Y AVG
☐ **Metal,** *shoulder head, black, set on sateen body, muslin forelegs, black shoes, molded hair, mouth closed, marked Minerva, 12"*	150.00	190.00	140.00
☐ **Metal,** *shoulder head, set on cloth body, bisque forearms, molded reddish hair, painted head, fixed eyes, open mouth showing three teeth and traces of others, marked Minerva, 18¾"*	100.00	130.00	95.00
Note: This is a model of a boy about ¾ years of age.			
☐ **Metal,** *shoulder head, set on cloth body with bisque forearms and cowhide feet, fixed eyes, open mouth showing two teeth, marked Minerva, 20"*	90.00	115.00	85.00
Note: Figure of a young girl.			

	Current Price Range		P/Y AVG
☐ **Minerva,** metal head, bisque forearms, cloth body, brown wig, blue glass eyes, open mouth, antique pale green satin dress with white lace trim, Victorian sleeves, matching bonnet, 18"	185.00	205.00	190.00

CAMAY

☐ **Liza,** plastic/vinyl, black hair (rooted), sleep eyes (brown), marked Made in Hong Kong, 1969, 14"	7.00	9.00	7.00
☐ **Tim,** plastic/vinyl, brown hair (rooted), painted eyes, marked Made in Hong Kong No. 7011, made in 1969, 10"	5.00	7.00	5.00
☐ **Trease,** marked Made in Taiwan 15-10, 1969, 14¼"	6.00	8.00	6.00

CAMEO

☐ **Baby Mine,** vinyl, marked Cameo, date of manufacture not known, 20"	65.00	80.00	60.00
☐ **Betty Boop,** wood and composition, painted black hair and goo-goo eyes, molded composition bathing suit, original design by J. L. Kallus, 12"	450.00	550.00	500.00
☐ **Bye-Lo Baby,** composition head, jointed composition body, sleep eyes, white cotton gown, 12", c. 1900	350.00	450.00	355.00
☐ **Bye-Lo Baby,** solid dome composition head with flange neck, blue sleep eyes, close mouth, cloth body with composition hands, lace trimmed organdy dress, marks: Grace Storey Putnam, 13"	275.00	375.00	250.00
☐ **Bye-Lo Baby,** solid dome composition head with flange neck, molded painted brown hair, blue sleep eyes, painted closed red lips, new cloth body with bisque hands, long white infant dress, marks: Grace Storey Putman, 15"	125.00	150.00	120.00

	Current Price Range		P/Y AVG
☐ **Dumbo,** composition figure, swiveling trunk and googlie eyes, height 9", c. 1941	100.00	150.00	125.00
☐ **Giggles,** composition head and body, head turns, molded hair swept downward in front, fixed eyes, 14"	200.00	245.00	190.00
☐ **Kewpie,** bisque, all bisque construction with jointed shoulders, head turned slightly to doll's left, felt clothing, 4"	85.00	110.00	80.00
☐ **Kewpie,** bisque, all bisque construction, wears Civil War-type soldier's cap, black belt (painted on), carries rifle and sabre, 4"	110.00	140.00	100.00
☐ **Kewpie,** bisque, all bisque construction with movable arms, wears felt "band leader" costume, 4"	80.00	105.00	80.00
☐ **Margie,** composition swivel head, jointed body, painted eyes, red dress, 10", c. 1940	225.00	250.00	230.00
☐ **Miss Peep,** crier, vinyl, molded and painted hair, painted eyes, marked Cameo, made in 1957, 18"	23.00	28.00	22.00
☐ **Newborn Miss Peep,** vinyl, molded and painted hair, fixed eyes, marked Cameo, made in 1962, 19½"	29.00	36.00	27.00
☐ **Plum,** vinyl head, latex body, arms and legs, molded and painted hair, sleep eyes (blue), with a pair of "squeekers," marked Cameo, sold originally in a box which was marked Plum, Designed and Copyrighted by JLK, specimens with the box bring a premium over the value indicated, made in 1952, 24¼"	60.00	75.00	55.00
☐ **Skootles,** composition head, composition arms, legs and body, molded hair, painted eyes, closed mouth in broad smile, wears overalls and bright short-sleeved shirt with pattern of trees and branches, 15"	160.00	190.00	150.00
Note: Skootles dates to the 1930's and, like many depression-era dolls, was apparently not made in very large quantities.			
☐ **Scootles,** molded wood composition head, jointed wood composition body, painted blue eyes, closed mouth, 12"	350.00	400.00	325.00

90 / CARLSON

	Current Price Range		P/Y AVG

☐ **Scootles,** *vinyl, molded and painted hair (red), sleep eyes (blue), smiling mouth, marked Cameo, sold originally with a tag reading Designed & Copyrighted by Rose O'Neill, made in 1964, 19"* 38.00 47.00 35.00

CARLSON

☐ **George Washington,** *hard plastic, representing the first American President with a child's face and platinum blonde hair, attired in 18th century formal dress, unmarked but sold originally with a diamond-shaped tag reading Carlson Dolls, A Collector's Item, date of manufacture not known (probably around the time of the bicentennial), 7½"* 6.00 8.00 6.00

CASCELLOID

☐ **Unnamed,** *celluloid head, cloth body, sleep eyes, molded and painted hair, representing an infant, an unusual and distinguishing feature of this doll is that it has rubber ears, whose texture does not match that of the head, bisque hands, marked Pat. #535611, made in 1939, 18"* 65.00 78.00 60.00

C.B.S.

☐ **Armosandra,** *black, rubber, molded and painted features, molded and painted hair, nursing mouth, Amosandra was a character on the "Amos 'n' Andy" radio program, marked Amosandra, Columbia Broadcasting System, Inc., Designed by Ruth E. Newton, Mfg. by The Sun Rubber*

CENTURY DOLL COMPANY / 91

	Current Price Range		P/Y AVG

Co., Barberton, U.S.A., also marked with the patent numbers 2,118,682 and 2,160,739, made in 1949, 10½" 20.00 26.00 18.00

☐ **My Fair Lady,** vinyl head, vinyl arms, legs and body, jointed at the waist, head does not swivel, sleep eyes, brown hair in elaborate coiffure, silk dress with print pattern, carries mold mark 14R, no other markings, the box in which this doll was sold is imprinted C.B.S., Inc. and is dated 1956, 19" 85.00 100.00 80.00

Note: Represents the character Eliza Doolittle from "My Fair Lady," which was playing on Broadway at the time this doll was manufactured.

CELTIC TOYS

☐ **Leprachaun,** plastic head, plastic arms, painted eyes, has long white beard, felt clothing including jacket with two buttons, represents a leprachaun (tribe of tiny people who, in Irish folklore, inhabited forests), marked Made in Republic of Ireland, dated 1973, 8" 11.00 15.00 11.00

Note: The Republic of Ireland is southern Ireland.

CENTURY DOLL COMPANY

☐ **Betty,** composition head and hands, cloth body stuffed with excelsior, pin jointed knees, molded blond hair, painted eyes, marked Century Doll Co., 16" 55.00 80.00 52.00

CEY

	Current Price Range		P/Y AVG
☐ **Sherri**, vinyl, black hair (rooted), sleep eyes (blue), nursing mouth, marked J. Cey 20, made in 1961, 20¼"	11.00	15.00	10.00
☐ **Unnamed**, figure of young girl, plastic/vinyl, sleep eyes (blue), marked J. Cey, date of manufacture unknown, probably 1950's, 27"	33.00	39.00	32.00

CHAD VALLEY COMPANY

☐ **Girl Doll**, cloth head and body, painted eyes, pink and floral print, c. 1970, 14"	20.00	25.00	22.50
☐ **Little Red Riding Hood**, character doll, all cloth, jointed neck, shoulders, hips, mohair wig, glass eyes, label, 11½"	325.00	375.00	300.00
☐ **Prince Charles**, Royal Children series, felt pressed head, jointed velvet body, painted features, mohair wig, original costume, 15"	550.00	650.00	600.00

CHADWICK-MILLER

☐ **Sad Eyes**, plastic/vinyl, blonde hair (rooted), painted eyes (brown), marked Made in Hong Kong, made in 1965, 8"	3.00	4.00	3.00

CHASE BAG CO.

☐ **Eskimo Pie Boy**, cloth (printed), foam stuffed, unmarked, made in 1962, used as a premium by the Eskimo Pie Dairy Products company, 14½"	5.00	7.00	5.00

MARTHA CHASE

	Current Price Range		P/Y AVG
☐ **Baby,** all cloth molded oil painted head, jointed cotton body, painted hair, brown eyes, mark: "Chase Stockinet Doll"	375.00	400.00	350.00
☐ **Baby,** cloth doll, molded stockinet head painted with oils, cloth body, painted facial features and hair, long gown, 16"	450.00	650.00	425.00
☐ **Boy,** of black rag doll, cloth, stockinet, molded painted head, painted body, short curly black wig, clothes, shoes, 17"	800.00	1000.00	850.00
☐ **Boy,** latex, sailor suit, 17"	150.00	200.00	170.00
☐ **Celluloid,** molded face set on cloth head, molded hair, very wide googly eyes, tiny eyebrows, closed smiling mouth, dimples at sides of mouth, 22". **Note: Dating from the World War II era.**	15.00	19.00	14.00
☐ **Girl,** molded, painted blonde hair, painted blue eyes, closed mouth, 25"	350.00	400.00	345.00
☐ **Lady,** all cloth, molded oil painted head, jointed cotton body, molded and painted blonde hair featuring a coiled braided bun at the nape of the neck, blue painted eyes, original dress, 15"	950.00	1200.00	850.00

CHICAGO TRIBUNE

	Current Price Range		P/Y AVG
☐ **Dondi,** vinyl, molded and painted features, molded and painted hair, jointed at the neck, Dondi is a character in a comic strip of the same name, created by Gus Edson and Irwin Hasen, marked 1960 Chicago Trib. NY News Syndicate, 11½"	70.00	90.00	68.00

CHILTERN

	Current Price Range		P/Y AVG
☐ **Tricia,** vinyl, sleep eyes (blue), marked Chiltern, Made in England, made for Marshall Fields of Chicago, in 1961, 11½"	8.00	11.00	8.00

PATTI CHIMERA

	Current Price Range		P/Y AVG
☐ **Peddlar Woman,** *bisque head with molded grey hair, pulled back into bun, bisque arms and legs, cloth body, painted features including blue eyes, modeled features, box with trinkets, basket with miniatures, floral printed dress, red cape, black bonnet, 8½"*	25.00	35.00	25.00

CHRYSLER

☐ **Mr. Fleet,** *one-piece vinyl, a doll-bank with slot (behind head) for coins, designed to represent an auto mechanic, holding wrench, marked Chrysler Corporation 1973, 9"*	5.00	7.00	5.00

Note: *Apparently made as a promotional give-away, to children of parents who visited Chrysler showrooms.*

EMMA CLEAR

☐ **Emma Clear Grape Lady,** *china shoulder head has molded black hair held with elaborate gold accented snood with grape cluster at crest, blue glass inset eyes, pierced ears, china arms and legs, cloth body, lavender brocade dress, antique lace shawl, amethyst necklace, marks: back of shoulder head -Clear, 19"*	500.00	600.00	525.00

CLODREY

☐ **Edmond,** *plastic/vinyl, sleep eyes (brown), marked Clodrey 2018-6926, made in France in the early 1970's, 16"*	27.00	34.00	25.00

	Current Price Range		P/Y AVG
COCHRAN			
☐ **Cindy,** *all latex, jointed, painted blue eyes, human hair wig, original costume, 15"*	650.00	725.00	625.00
COLEMAN			
☐ **Dolly Walker,** *composition head and forearms, wooden body, fixed eyes glancing to doll's left, ribbons in hair, marked Harry Coleman Walking Doll, 26¼"*	140.00	185.00	135.00
COLUMBIA TOY PRODUCTS			
☐ **Flip The Football Doll,** *vinyl head, rag body, vinyl hands, rag feet, molded and painted features, molded-on football helmet (with chin strap, no face-mask), marked 1961 Roko, also marked Manufactured by Columbia Toy Products, 15"*	10.00	14.00	10.00
☐ **Snuffy Smith,** *cloth/nylon, marked Copyright King Features Syndicate, Inc., 14¼"*	70.00	90.00	65.00
Note: *Snuffy Smith was a character in the comic strip "Barney Google and His Horse Sparkplug" by Billy DeBeck.*			
COMIC TOY MANUFACTURING COMPANY			
☐ **Daisy, Dagwood and Blondie's Dog,** *rubber doll, collar and tag, swivels at neck, height 12", c. 1940*	50.00	70.00	65.00

CONFETTI

	Current Price Range		P/Y AVG
☐ **Bride,** composition, red wig attached by adhesive, painted eyes (blue), unmarked, made in 1947, 11"	8.00	11.00	8.00
☐ **Cleaning Day,** composition, blonde wig attached by adhesive, painted eyes, bright red lips, marked Confetti Doll, made in the mid 1940's, 7"	6.00	8.00	6.00

CO-OPERATIVE MANUFACTURING COMPANY

☐ **Jointed Wooden Doll,** painted facial features and molded hair, metal hands and feet, dressed, 12"	650.00	800.00	650.00

COSMOPOLITAN

☐ **Emily,** plastic head, cloth body, blonde wig attached by adhesive, sleep eyes (blue), open mouth with teeth, bright red lips, unmarked, made in 1948, 24"	65.00	82.00	60.00
☐ **Gloria,** plastic head, cloth body, latex arms and legs, blonde wig attached by adhesive, turnable head, sleep eyes (blue), open mouth with teeth, unmarked, made in 1948, 29"	42.00	54.00	40.00
☐ **Japan Girl,** all vinyl with Japanese costume, black hair, 9"	6.00	8.00	6.00
☐ **Make-Up-Own,** walker, a doll kit, the doll to be assembled by the purchaser, with instructions sheet, sold in 1956, height of doll when assembled, 10"			
Kit intact as originally sold	18.00	23.00	17.00
Assembled doll	10.00	13.00	10.00
☐ **Merry,** plastic/vinyl, marked AE 1406-41, 14"	4.00	5.00	4.00
☐ **Mousketeer,** vinyl, a young girl dressed in Mousketeer garb (from the TV program "The Mickey Mouse Club"), late 1950's, 8"	10.00	14.00	10.00

	Current Price Range		P/Y AVG
☐ **Pam,** plastic head, cloth body, vinyl arms and legs, blonde wig attached by adhesive, sleep eyes (blue), marked CDC (Cosmopolitan Doll Company), made in 1956, 22"	28.00	35.00	25.00

CROWN DOLL COMPANY

☐ **Pinocchio,** composition, painted white gloves	75.00	85.00	80.00

DAKIN

☐ **Aloha Alice,** stuffed nylon, unmarked on doll, sold originally with a tag reading Dream Dolls, R. Dakin & Co., 1956, representing a girl wearing Hawaiian native dance costume, 15"	9.00	12.00	9.00
☐ **Elmer Fudd,** vinyl, molded and painted features, painted eyes, jointed at the shoulders and hips, wears one-button jacket, derby hat, Elmer Fudd is a character in the comic strip "Bugs Bunny," created by R. Schlesinger, marked Warner Brothers, 1968, made in Hong Kong, 7"	15.00	20.00	14.00
☐ **First Date,** vinyl/plastic, blonde hair (rooted), closed eyes, long lashes, ribbon in hair, marked R. Dakin & Co., Product of Hong Kong, made in 1970, 6½"	6.00	8.00	6.00
☐ **Mickey Mouse,** vinyl head, vinyl body, wears fabric clothing, medium-size ears, large smile on face, in addition to Dakin & Co., also bears mark of Walt Disney, made in Hong Kong, mid 1970's, 8"	4.00	6.00	4.00
☐ **Minnie Mouse,** vinyl head, plastic body, bow-tied ribbon on top of head, wears fabric clothing, including polka-dotted skirt, oversized shoes, in addition to Dakin's, also carries the Disney mark, almost certainly made in Hong Kong, 6"	4.00	5.00	4.00

98 / DAKIN

	Current Price Range		P/Y AVG
☐ **Pebbles,** *plastic/vinyl, marked R. Dakin Co., Product of Hong Kong, 1970, 8"* ... **Note:** *Representing a character from the comic strip "The Flintstones" created by Hanna and Barbera.*	4.00	5.00	3.00
☐ **Popeye and Olive Oil,** *all plastic, jointed*	17.00	22.00	15.00

Popeye and Olive, plastic .... $17.00-$22.00

THOMAS DAM ("DAM THINGS")

Thomas Dam of Denmark was the original manufacturer (in the mid 1960's) of the vinyl "Troll" dolls which took America by storm. They were the hottest selling dolls of the decade next to Barbies. We are not listing them individually because all are essentially the same basic doll with different hair and costuming, or with various props. Those made by Dam (all of which are marked on the back) have a current collector value in the $5.00 to $8.00 range. Imitations by other companies are of less value. Special items such as Dam's "Troll Bank" are worth a premium.

	Current Price Range		P/Y AVG
DANEL ET CIE			
☐ **Bisque,** socket head set on combination wood and composition body (fully jointed), sleep eyes, closed mouth, pierced ears, marked Paris Bebe Tete Depose 7, accompanied by Eiffel Tower mark, 16"	1100.00	1300.00	1000.00
DARROW MANUFACTURING COMPANY			
☐ **Rawhide,** cotton body, kid arms, painted surface, blue and white dress, red leather boots, 15"	325.00	375.00	348.00
☐ **Rawhide,** leather shoulder head, rawhide leather arms, cloth body, molded and painted black hair and facial features, original cotton dress, paper label, 18"	1000.00	1500.00	500.00
D'AUTREMONT			
☐ **Man,** china head, jointed kid body, blue painted eyes, brown mohair wig, navy suit, red tie, 13"	1300.00	1500.00	1200.00

DEE CEE

	Current Price Range		P/Y AVG

☐ **Dee Dee,** *plastic/vinyl, blonde hair (rooted), sleep eyes (blue), nursing mouth, marked Dee Cee, this was a Canadian manufacturer, the doll was made in 1961, 14"* 22.00 28.00 20.00

☐ **Jodi,** *plastic/vinyl, marked AE7, date of manufacture unknown, probably mid to late 1970's 15"* 4.00 6.00 4.00

DELL PUBLISHING COMPANY

☐ **Donald Duck,** *vinyl head, vinyl body, molded clothing, wide open mouth, hands held together as if about to dive from diving board, no movable parts, marked Dell, Walt Disney, 6"* 5.00 7.00 5.00
Note: *The contract signed by Walt Disney, to use the Disney characters in Dell's "Four Color Comics," stipulated that the name "DELL" appear on character merchandise.*

DELUXE TOPPER

☐ **Baby Bunny,** *vinyl head, plastic body, vinyl arms, plastic legs, platinum blonde hair (rooted), fixed eyes (blue), marked 51 Deluxe Topper 1969, 20"* 15.00 19.00 14.00

☐ **Baby Catch-A-Ball,** *plastic/vinyl, rooted hair (blonde), fixed eyes (blue), holds hands in front of body in ball-catching attitude, when child throws ball to doll, dolls's arms automatically flip ball back, an ingenious design, the "secret" is in a pair of bracelets worn by Baby Catch-A-Ball, which are actually switches to activate the battery-operated mechanism, marked PB2-28 Deluxe Topper, 1969, 18"* . 26.00 32.00 25.00

	Current Price Range		P/Y AVG

DENNISON

☐ **Crepe Paper,** *features printed in India ink, representing a young lady in sleeping gown and hood, 20"* 32.00 42.00 30.00

DeSOTO

☐ **Heartbeat Baby,** *plastic head, latex arms and legs, stuffed cloth body, sleep eyes, blonde hair, silk dress, equipped with a mechanism which produces the sound of a heartbeat when the doll is laid on its back, 23"* 29.00 36.00 27.00
Note: *An interesting novelty doll, but it probably led many children to believe that the human heart functions only when one is lying down.*

DISNEY, WALT
SEE WALT DISNEY

DOLIAC ET CIE

☐ **Bisque,** *socket head set on combination wood and composition body, fixed eyes, open mouth, pierced ears, marked LD DEP. 9.L., 22"* 385.00 440.00 375.00

DOLLY'S DOLLS

☐ **Howdy Dowdy,** *plastic head, cloth body, molded hair, painted wide eyes, wool plaid shirt, blue jeans, leather belt, 18"* 15.00 20.00 17.50

Howdy Dowdy,
cloth
$15.00-$20.00

DREAM DOLLS

	Current Price Range		P/Y AVG
☐ **Aloha Alice**, *stuffed bylon, unmarked on doll, sold originally with a tag reading Dream Dolls, R. Dakin & Co., 1956, representing a girl wearing Hawaiian native dance costume, 15"*	9.00	12.00	9.00
☐ **Baby Peek 'N' Play**, *plastic/vinyl, fixed eyes (blue), one of the many interesting novelty/action dolls manufactured by this company during the 1960's, Baby*			

	Current Price Range		P/Y AVG

Peek 'N' Play could "hear," she responded to sharp noises by raising her hands to her face, (battery operated,) marked 17EYE, New, M94, made in 1969, 18" **22.00 28.00 20.00**

☐ **Bikey**, *plastic/vinyl, blonde hair (rooted), painted eyes, arms outstretched and hands shaped as if holding the handlebars of a bike, marked Bikey, Deluxe Topper, 1968, made in Hong Kong, 11"* **10.00 14.00 9.00**

☐ **Little Miss Fussy**, *plastic/vinyl, blonde hair (rooted), fixed eyes (blue), marked K-39, Deluxe Topper, 1967, 18"* **16.00 21.00 15.00**
Note: The same trademark was used on Deluxe Topper's "Party Time" doll.

☐ **Party Time**, *plastic/vinyl, fixed eyes (blue), open mouth, "blower" action (can blow up small balloons, blow out candles on a cake, etc.), operates by battery, marked K-39, Deluxe Topper, 1967, 18"* **16.00 21.00 15.00**

☐ **Tickles**, *talker, plastic/vinyl, blonde hair (rooted), sleep eyes (blue), marked 1963 Deluxe Topper 38, 20"* **14.00 18.00 13.00**

DREAMLAND

☐ **To Market, To Market**, *composition, painted eyes, unmarked, date of manufacture unknown, 11"* **29.00 34.00 27.00**

DREAM WORLD

☐ **Bride**, *composition, date of manufacture unknown, 10½"* **30.00 36.00 28.00**
☐ **Cuba** *(national costume doll), composition, 11"* **28.00 33.00 27.00**
☐ **Florence Nightingale**, *composition, representing the English nurse who became famous for her care of wounded soldiers in the Crimean War, 11"* **29.00 34.00 27.00**

104 / CUNO AND OTTO DRESSEL

	Current Price Range		P/Y AVG
☐ **Flower Vendor,** *composition, unmarked on doll, sold originally with a tag reading Dream World Dolls Make Dreams Come True, 11"*	29.00	34.00	27.00
☐ **Spanish** *(national costume doll), composition, unmarked, date of manufacture unknown*	28.00	33.00	27.00

CUNO AND OTTO DRESSEL

This family owned firm began in Sonneberg, Thuringia, Germany in 1700, but the earliest record of their doll-making dates around 1863. At that time, Otto Dressel, Sr. and his sons, Otto Jr. and Cuno, were registered as doll-makers. Prior to 1863 they were known primarily as toy makers. (Indeed, the family continued to produce wooden, papier mache, and composition toys in their Nurnberg and Grunhainichen toy factories well into the 20th century.)

The Holz Masse mark was registered in 1875. The Dressels made dolls of bisque, papier mache, wax, and composition. They were known to have used doll heads from other firms such as Simon-Halbig and Armand Marseille. Composition was used to make dolls around the turn of the century, and in 1906 the "Jutta" trademark was registered, followed in 1909 by the "Bambina" mark. At this time they began manufacturing dolls with kid bodies. Dressel dolls with celluloid heads appeared in 1911.

	Current Price Range		P/Y AVG
☐ **Bisque,** *ball jointed body, set brown eyes, short blonde mohair wig, open mouth, flowered dress with lace trim, 25"*	425.00	475.00	445.00
☐ **Bisque,** *kid body, bisque arms, cotton lower legs, universal joints, brown sleep eyes, dark brows, long brown hair, white dress, black velvet in thread through lace, mold number 1776, 24"*	375.00	425.00	400.00
☐ **Jutta,** *composition ball jointed body, blue eyes, brown hair, marked "1349," 24"*	400.00	450.00	420.00
☐ **Papier Mache,** *brown paperweight eyes, brown wool challis dress, marked "Holz-Masse"*	200.00	225.00	210.00

	Current Price Range		P/Y AVG
☐ **Papier Mache,** *shoulder head, kid arms, cloth body, painted blue eyes, brown mohair wig, original cream lawn dress with lace trim, 14"*	325.00	400.00	325.00
☐ **Polar Bear,** *bisque facial mask set against plush head, plush body, one-piece construction, glass eyes with open mouth, representing a young lady in arctic attire, wholly covered in fur plush but for the face, 9"*	130.00	155.00	125.00

DUCHESS

☐ **Carmen,** *plastic, painted eyes, representing the character from the Bizet opera "Carmen," marked Duchess Doll Co., Design Copyright 1948, 7½"*	7.00	10.00	7.00
☐ **Cinderella,** *plastic, blonde hair attached by adhesive, sleep eyes (blue), marked Duchess Doll Co., Design Copyright 1948, 7½"*	4.00	6.00	4.00
☐ **Dale Evans,** *hard plastic, marked Duchess Doll Corp., 1948, representing the motion picture actress, wife of Roy Rogers, 7"*	7.00	10.00	7.00
☐ **Danny The Groom,** *plastic, molded and painted hair, painted eyes, unmarked, made in 1949, 7"*	6.00	8.00	6.00
☐ **Martha Washington,** *plastic, white hair attached by adhesive, sleep eyes (blue), representing the wife of George Washington, with a child's face, marked Duchess Doll Corp., Design Copyright 1948, 7½"*	4.00	6.00	4.00
☐ **Miss Hollywood 1949,** *plastic, brunette hair attached by adhesive, sleep eyes (blue), marked Duchess Doll Corp., Design Copyright 1949, 7¼"*	4.00	6.00	4.00
☐ **Scarlet,** *plastic, brunette hair attached by adhesive, painted eyes (blue), representing the character Scarlet O'Hara*			

	Current Price Range		P/Y AVG
from the novel "Gone With The Wind" by Margaret Mitchell, marked Duchess Doll Corp., Design Copyright 1948, 7½"	9.00	12.00	9.00
☐ **Scotch Miss,** plastic, blonde hair attached by adhesive, sleep eyes (blue), a national costume doll, marked Duchess Doll Corp., Design Copyright 1948, 7½"	4.00	6.00	4.00
☐ **Tinker Bell,** plastic, blonde hair attached by adhesive, sleep eyes (blue), marked Duchess Doll Corp., Design Copyright 1948, 7"	7.00	10.00	6.00

DUKKER

☐ **Lupin,** vinyl, sleep eyes, closed smiling mouth, freckled cheeks, dressed in Norwegian peasant costume, unmarked on doll, sold originally with a tag reading Grimstad Dukker, Grimstead, Norway, date of manufacture unknown, 12"	30.00	38.00	27.00

DURHAM

☐ **Billy The Kid,** plastic, representing the Old West desperado, holds six-shooter in right hand, raises and points gun when button on back of doll is pushed, marked D. Durham Ind. Inc., New York, N.Y. 10010, made in Hong Kong, 8"	3.00	4.00	3.00
☐ **Skinny Jimmy,** vinyl, marked #1500 Durham Industries, Inc., New York, N.Y. 10010, made in Taiwan, 11"	4.00	6.00	4.00
☐ **Wild Bill Hickok,** plastic, representing the legendary "gunslinger" of the Old West, holds six-shooter in right hand; raises and points gun when button on back of doll is pushed, marked D. Durham Ind. Inc., New York, N.Y. 10010, made in Hong Kong, 8"	3.00	4.00	3.00

	Current Price Range		P/Y AVG

☐ **Wyatt Earp,** *plastic, representing the legendary sheriff of Dodge City, Kansas, popularized in a TV program during the late 1950's, holds six-shooter in right hand, raises and points gun when button on back of doll is pushed, marked D. Durham Ind. Inc., New York, N.Y. 10010, made in Hong Kong, 8"* 3.00 4.00 3.00

Note: This doll is not contemporary with the Wyatt Earp TV program, but was manufactured at a much later date, in the middle 1970's.

EEGEE

☐ **Adorable,** *vinyl, blonde hair (rooted), painted eyes, nursing mouth, marked 35 Eegee Co., 1967, 12LTPE, 13"* 11.00 14.00 10.00
☐ **Andy,** *plastic/vinyl, molded and painted hair, painted eyes, dressed in military uniform, marked EG-1961, 12"* 7.00 9.00 7.00
☐ **Baby Luv,** *vinyl head, vinyl arms and legs, cloth body, blond hair, painted eyes, bearing the mold number 14BT and dates 1973, 12"* 30.00 37.00 29.00
☐ **Baby Softina,** *vinyl with dublon body, molded hair, fixed eyes, wears plush velvety child's clothing of the 1890's, marked 3-Eegee Co.-16V3, made in 1970* 7.00 9.00 7.00
☐ **Baby Susan,** *vinyl, molded and painted hair, sleep eyes (blue), marked Eegee, made in 1958, 10"* 9.00 12.00 9.00
☐ **Ballerina Sherry,** *vinyl, marked Eegee 8, 8"* 8.00 11.00 8.00
☐ **Bobby,** *vinyl, fixed eyes (blue), marked Eegee, made in 1955, 13"* 32.00 39.00 31.00
☐ **Bonnie Ballerina,** *plastic/vinyl, sleep eyes, marked Eegee 5, made in 1964, 31"* 24.00 29.00 23.00
☐ **Bundle Of Joy,** *vinyl head, cloth body, vinyl arms, plastic legs, brown hair (rooted), sleep eyes (blue), marked 19-4 Eegee Co., made in 1964, 19"* 8.00 11.00 8.00

EEGEE

	Current Price Range		P/Y AVG
☐ **Buster,** *plastic/vinyl, marked 1959 Eegee, 16½"*	10.00	13.00	9.00
☐ **Carol,** *plastic/vinyl, sleep eyes, marked Eegee Co., 15 PM, 1B, made in 1968, 21"*	11.00	14.00	10.00
☐ **Chikie,** *composition, sleep eyes (tin), chubby face, open mouth with teeth, unmarked on doll, sold originally with a tag reading Chikie, another Eegee Doll, date of manufacture unknown, 16"*	75.00	90.00	70.00
Note: *The name should have been spelled "Chickie," as this doll represented a little girl who liked to feed chicks.*			
☐ **Cuddlekins,** *plastic/vinyl, molded and painted hair, fixed eyes (blue), nursing mouth, marked Eegee Co., 13VS, made in 1970, 10"*	5.00	7.00	5.00
☐ **Darling Baby,** *plastic/vinyl, sleep eyes (blue), marked 25 10T Eegee, 10"*	4.00	6.00	4.00
☐ **Georgie,** *cloth body, vinyl head, sleep eyes (green), marked 17 RNG Eegee, 1971, 23"*	10.00	14.00	9.00
☐ **Gemette,** *plastic/vinyl, brown hair (rooted), sleep eyes (blue), marked 1963-11, 15"*	7.00	9.00	7.00
☐ **Gigi Perreaux,** *plastic/vinyl, brunette hair attached by adhesive, sleep eyes (brown), marked E.G., made in 1951, 16¾"*	50.00	64.00	47.00
☐ **Grace,** *vinyl head, latex body, latex arms and legs, blonde hair (rooted), sleep eyes (blue), marked 33H-Eegee, made in 1957, 17"*	26.00	33.00	25.00
☐ **Granny,** *plastic/vinyl, marked Eegee 3, 14"*	36.00	44.00	35.00
☐ **Howdy Doody,** *vinyl, soft body, 18"*	6.00	12.00	5.00
☐ **Kiss Me,** *plastic/vinyl, sleep eyes (blue), novelty doll whose lips performed a kissing motion when its left arm was raised and lowered, marked 14-16 Eegee, made in 1963, 17"*	7.00	10.00	7.00
☐ **Lil Susan,** *plastic/vinyl, black hair (rooted), sleep eyes (blue), marked Eegee, made in 1956, 10½"*	8.00	11.00	7.00

	Current Price Range		P/Y AVG

- ☐ **Little Debutante,** *plastic/vinyl, blonde hair (rooted), sleep eyes (blue), marked 20HH Eegee, made in 1958, 28"* 33.00 39.00 31.00
- ☐ **Little Debutante Ballerina,** *vinyl head, vinyl arms, plastic body, jointed at the waist, knees and ankles, sleep eyes, wears ballerina costume, carries the mold mark 14R* 18.00 23.00 17.00
- ☐ **Little Miss,** *plastic/vinyl, blonde hair (rooted), sleep eyes (blue), marked 15US, Eegee Co., made in 1962, 16"* 7.00 9.00 7.00
- ☐ **Luvable Baby,** *vinyl, sleep eyes (blue), marked Eegee, made in 1956, 15"* 8.00 11.00 8.00
- ☐ **Luvable Skin Doll,** *vinyl head and body, blonde hair (rooted), sleep eyes (blue), marked Eegee 1½-9, made in 1958, 12"* .. 12.00 16.00 12.00
- ☐ **Merry Stroller,** *vinyl head, plastic arms and legs, plastic body, ribbon in hair, wears long gown, sold in suitcase, with accessories (including a change of clothing and slippers), 13", with case and accessories* 30.00 37.00 29.00
  - Doll alone 17.00 22.00 17.00
- ☐ **Miss Charming,** *composition head and body, blonde hair attached by adhesive, sleep eyes (blue), bright red lips, marked E.G., made in 1936, 19"* 53.00 66.00 51.00
- ☐ **Musical Baby,** *music box, vinyl head, cloth body, vinyl arms, plastic legs, blonde hair (rooted), painted eyes, marked 15, Eegee Co., 16W, made in 1967, 17"* 8.00 11.00 8.00
- ☐ **My Fair Lady,** *vinyl head, vinyl arms, legs and body, jointed at the waist, head does not swivel, sleep eyes, brown hair in elaborate coiffure, silk dress with print pattern, carries mold mark 14R, no other markings on doll, the box in which this doll was sold is imprinted C.B.S., Inc., and is dated 1956, 19"* 85.00 100.00 80.00

Note: Represents the character Eliza Doolittle from "My Fair Lady," which was playing on Broadway at the time this doll was manufactured.

	Current Price Range		P/Y AVG
☐ **Newborn Baby Doll,** *vinyl head, sleep eyes, marked Eegee Co. 173, 1963, 16".* **Note: Despite the name, this doll was not designed to resemble a newborn baby but a toddler of several months.**	8.00	11.00	8.00
☐ **Nurse,** *vinyl head, vinyl arms, legs and body, painted eyes, wears white nursing cap with red cross, and fabric clothing, 4½"*	3.00	4.00	3.00
☐ **Pix-I-Posie,** *vinyl, blonde hair (rooted), sleep eyes (blue), marked Eegee Co., 1966, also marked with the patent number 3,319,370 / 24, 18"*	12.00	16.00	12.00
☐ **Playtime Susan,** *vinyl head, vinyl arms, legs and body, molded hair (short, combed down), open mouth designed to receive nursing bottle, 15"*	8.00	10.00	8.00
☐ **Posi Playmate,** *vinyl head, foam body, foam arms and legs, vinyl hands, posable, platinum blonde hair (rooted), painted eyes, marked 18LT 1/Eegee Co., made in 1969, 18"*	9.00	12.00	9.00
☐ **Robert,** *vinyl head, latex body, vinyl arms, latex legs, molded hair, sleep eyes (blue), marked Eegee, made in 1956, 21"*	43.00	52.00	41.00

EFFANBEE

The Effanbee Doll Company was begun by B.E. Fleischaker and H. Braun in 1910, and after various corporate shifts and takeovers, is still operated by the sons of one of the founders. The reputation of this company for quality construction has never been challenged and their dolls are quite collectible.

In the early days of the company, they typically used all composition to manufacture their jointed baby dolls, usually molding and painting the hair instead of fitting the doll with a wig. Later cloth bodies appeared and by 1955, vinyl and hard plastic was the standard material for construction.

The company is famous for the movability that the jointed dolls have achieved. They have made great strides in walker doll technology as well as multi-jointed dolls with flexible mobility. The delicacy of their newer dolls and the care taken to detail in the costumes has made them instantly collectible.

EFFANBEE / 111

	Current Price Range		P/Y AVG
☐ **Abraham Lincoln,** *black suit, stovepipe hat, limited issue, c. 1983*	70.00	80.00	73.00
☐ **Afternoon Tea,** *absolutely Abigail Collection, c. 1982, 13"*	40.00	50.00	42.00
☐ **Alice in Wonderland,** *soft body, Huggable Collection, c. 1982, 14"*	28.00	37.00	30.00
☐ **Allison,** *blue, white dress, Grandes Dames Collection, c. 1983*	50.00	62.00	52.00
☐ **Anne Shirley,** *bisque, brown human hair wig, lacy pink taffeta dress, heels, 21"*	175.00	225.00	180.00
☐ **Baby Cuddle-Up,** *vinyl, molded and painted hair, sleep eyes (blue), open mouth with teeth, marked Effanbee, made in 1953, 23"*	30.00	38.00	28.00
☐ **Baby Cupcake,** *plastic/vinyl, sleep eyes (blue), marked Effanbee, 1963, 12"*	7.00	10.00	7.00
☐ **Baby Dainty,** *cloth and composition, painted eyes, marked Effanbee, Baby Dainty, believed to have been made in the late 1930's, 15"*	65.00	80.00	62.00
☐ **Baby Face,** *plastic/vinyl, brown hair (rooted), sleep eyes (blue), marked Effanbee 1967-2600, 15"*	11.00	14.00	10.00
☐ **Baby Face,** *Granny's Corner Collection, c. 1983, 20"*	35.00	45.00	36.00
☐ **Babykin,** *vinyl, molded hair, sleep eyes (blue), nursing mouth, marked Effanbee 1964, 8½"*	6.00	8.00	6.00
☐ **Barbara Jean,** *from the American children series designed by Dewees Cochran, composition, marked Effanbee, Ann Shirley body, original reddish wig, clear sleep eyes, open mouth, 17"*	360.00	395.00	365.00
☐ **Betsy Ross,** *floral print dress, Women of the Ages Collection, c. 1983*	40.00	50.00	42.00
☐ **Billy Bum,** *by Faith Wick, c. 1982, 16"*	50.00	60.00	52.00
☐ **Bride,** *hard plastic, holds bouquet, 19"*	100.00	150.00	130.00
☐ **Bride,** *lacy wedding outfit, ribbon trim, flowers, Bridal Suite Collection, c. 1983, 13"*	35.00	45.00	37.00
☐ **Bride,** *lacy wedding outfit, ribbon trimmed, flowers, Bridal Suite Collection, c. 1983, 15"*	40.00	50.00	42.00

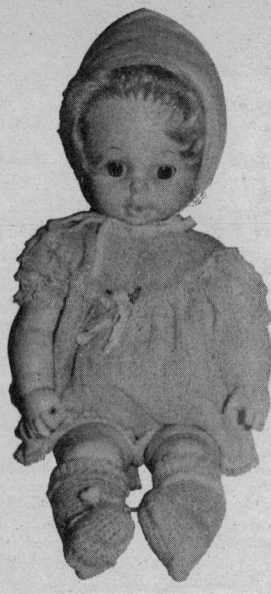

Baby,
rubber, c. 1973
$10.00-$12.00

	Current Price Range		P/Y AVG
☐ **Bridesmaid,** *lacy bridesmaid outfit, ribbon trim, flowers, Bridal Suite Collection, c. 1983, 13"*	35.00	40.00	37.00
☐ **Butterball,** *Granny's Corner Collection, c. 1983, 13"*	22.00	35.00	23.00
☐ **Butterball,** *with bunting, Crochet Classics Collection, c. 1982, 13"*	25.00	35.00	26.00
☐ **Butterball,** *with pillow, Heaven Sent Collection, c. 1982, 13"*	25.00	35.00	26.00
☐ **Buttercup,** *Granny's Corner Collection, c. 1983, 15"*	35.00	45.00	36.00
☐ **Buttercup,** *Heart to Heart Collection, c. 1982, 15"*	28.00	35.00	30.00

EFFANBEE / 113

	Current Price Range		P/Y AVG
☐ **Bubbles,** *composition and cloth body, 1910*	100.00	150.00	95.00
☐ **Button Nose,** *composition, molded hair, unmarked, date of manufacture unknown, believed to date from the World War II era, 8"*	45.00	58.00	42.00
☐ **Button Nose,** *vinyl head, cloth body, vinyl arms and legs, blonde hair (rooted), sleep eyes (blue), crier, marked 15-Effanbee-1968-9508, 16½"*	23.00	28.00	21.00
☐ **Canadian Doll,** *International Collection, c. 1982, 11"*	20.00	30.00	21.00
☐ **Candy Kid,** *composition, molded and painted hair, sleep eyes (blue), marked Effanbee, made in 1946, 12"*	47.00	59.00	45.00
☐ **Captain Kidd,** *c. 1983*	20.00	30.00	21.00
☐ **Carnegie Hall,** *Grandes Dames Collection, c. 1980, 18"*	50.00	55.00	52.00
☐ **Catherine,** *composition head, composition arms, legs and body, jointed at shoulders and thighs, molded hair, painted eyes, closed mouth, bright red lips, dark flesh-tone skin, 14"*	85.00	105.00	80.00
☐ **Charleston,** *Pride of the South Collection, c. 1982, 13"*	35.00	45.00	37.00
☐ **Charlie McCarthy,** *composition body, hands (with gloves) and feet (with shoes), cloth body, molded hair, painted features, tuxedo, monocle, 13½"*	465.00	520.00	475.00
☐ **Czechoslavakia,** *vinyl, jointed, International Collection, c. 1981*	15.00	25.00	16.00
☐ **Dallas,** *pink floral print dress, Pride of the South, c. 1983*	40.00	50.00	42.00
☐ **Danish Doll,** *International Collection, c. 1982, 11"*	20.00	30.00	21.00
☐ **Denmark,** *vinyl, jointed, International Collection, c. 1981*	15.00	25.00	16.00
☐ **Diane,** *red, pink dress, Grandes Dames Collection, c. 1983, 15"*	50.00	62.00	52.00
☐ **Dolly Dumpling,** *composition shoulder head, cork stuffed body, painted face and hair, cotton rompers, shoulder head marked "Effanbee", 15"*	150.00	200.00	150.00
☐ **Downing Square,** *Grandes Dames Collection, c. 1979, 15"*	35.00	45.00	37.00

114 / EFFANBEE

Composition Head and Body
$95.00-$100.00

	Current Price Range		P/Y AVG
☐ **Dutch Doll,** *International Collection, c. 1982, 11"*	20.00	30.00	21.00
☐ **Dy-Dee Doll,** *fur wig, 12 accessories*	125.00	175.00	140.00
☐ **Dy Dee Baby,** *plastic head, rubber body, molded and painted hair, sleep eyes (blue), nursing mouth, marked Effanbee, made in 1950, 11½"*	13.00	16.00	13.00
☐ **Dy Dee Doll,** *vinyl, jointed, sleep eyes, 20"*	40.00	50.00	42.00
☐ **Elisabeth,** *Grandes Dames Collection, c. 1982, 11"*	30.00	40.00	32.00

	Current Price Range		P/Y AVG
☐ Flapper, c. 1979, 15"	25.00	35.00	26.00
☐ Florence Nightingale, nursing outfit, Women of the Ages Collection, c. 1983	40.00	50.00	42.00
☐ Flossie, white eyelet dress, Bobbsey Twin, c. 1983	30.00	40.00	32.00
☐ Fluffy, black vinyl, jointed, sleep eyes, Girl Scout outfit, c. 1965	10.00	15.00	11.00
☐ Fluffy, vinyl, blonde hair (rooted), sleep eyes (blue), marked P-U, made in 1954, 10"	9.00	12.00	9.00

Note: Presumably, the letters P-U were the mold's identification. Usually, Effanbee placed its name in full on its dolls and if a mold number was to be recorded, it appeared directly alongside the company's name.

☐ Fortune Cookies, Just Friends, c. 1983	30.00	40.00	32.00
☐ Freddie, tweeds, hat, Bobbsey Twin, c. 1983	25.00	35.00	26.00
☐ French Doll, International Collection, c. 1982, 11"	20.00	30.00	21.00
☐ Frontier Woman, brown gingham, c. 1979, 15"	30.00	45.00	32.00
☐ Frontier Woman, gray cotton, c. 1978, 15"	30.00	45.00	32.00
☐ Gay Nineties, c. 1979, 15"	30.00	40.00	32.00
☐ Garden Party, absolutely Abigail Collection, c. 1983	40.00	50.00	42.00
☐ Gay Paree, lacy burgandy dress, Age of Elegance Collection, c. 1983	90.00	110.00	92.00
☐ George Washington, felt outfit, three cornered hat, limited issue, c. 1983	70.00	80.00	73.00
☐ German Doll, International Collection, c. 1982, 11"	20.00	30.00	21.00
☐ Gibson Girl, c. 1979, 15"	30.00	35.00	32.00
☐ Girl, Boy Skater Dolls, black vinyl, jointed, sleep eyes, blue velvet, silk outfits, silver skates	70.00	80.00	73.00
☐ Girl, composition, jointed, blonde human hair wig, blue sleep eyes, closed mouth, blue and white checked gingham dress, Anne Shirley on back, 16"	180.00	195.00	180.00
☐ Greek Doll, c. 1983	20.00	30.00	21.00
☐ Groucho Marx, Legend Series, with cigar, c. 1983	70.00	80.00	73.00

116 / EFFANBEE

	Current Price Range		P/Y AVG
☐ **Gumdrop,** plastic/vinyl, blonde hair (rooted), sleep eyes (blue), marked 1962 Effanbee, 16"	11.00	14.00	11.00
☐ **Half-Pint,** plastic/vinyl, blonde hair (rooted), fixed eyes, head twists, marked Effanbee 1966, 10"	8.00	11.00	8.00
☐ **Half Pint Boy,** Over the Rainbow Collection, c. 1981	15.00	20.00	16.00
☐ **Katie,** vinyl, molded and painted hair, sleep eyes (blue), marked Effanbee, made in 1957, 9"	23.00	29.00	21.00
☐ **Lil Darlin,** cloth body, vinyl head, cry box, marked Effanbee, 15¾"	19.00	24.00	18.00
☐ **Lil Sweetie,** vinyl, blonde hair (rooted), sleep eyes (blue), nursing mouth, wears bonnet, marked 5667 Effanbee, 1967, 15⅞"	15.00	19.00	15.00
Note: This mold (with different clothing) was used to represent several dolls in the Effanbee line during the mid to late 1960's.			
☐ **Magnolia,** lacy pink gown, matching bonnet, Grandes Dames Collection, 15"	35.00	45.00	38.00
☐ **Mark Twain,** white suit, limited issue, c. 1983	60.00	70.00	63.00
☐ **Martha Washington,** blue dress, Women of The Ages Collection, c. 1983	40.00	50.00	42.00
☐ **Mary Lee,** composition, sleep eyes, open mouth, bright red lips, teeth, glossy face, marked Mary Lee, date of manufacture unknown, but presumably c. 1935, 16" ..	95.00	115.00	90.00
☐ **Mary and Little Lamb,** vinyl, jointed, c. 1981, 11"	15.00	25.00	16.00
☐ **Mexican Doll,** International Collection, c. 1982, 11"	20.00	30.00	21.00
☐ **Mickey,** vinyl, molded and painted features, wears football helmet (old style, without facemask), marked Effanbee-10, made in 1956, 11"	8.00	11.00	8.00
☐ **Miss Black America,** International Collection, c. 1979, 11"	15.00	25.00	16.00
☐ **Miss Chips,** plastic/vinyl, black hair (rooted), sleep eyes (brown), wears bridal gown, marked Effanbee 1965-1700, 18" ..	22.00	28.00	21.00

EFFANBEE / 117

	Current Price Range		P/Y AVG

Note: Has dark skin but is usually classified as "suntanned white" rather than black.

Item	Low	High	P/Y AVG
☐ Mobile, *Pride of the South, c. 1982*	40.00	50.00	42.00
☐ Mommy's Baby, plastic head, cloth body, plastic arms and legs, sleep eyes (blue), marked Effanbee, made in 1952, 27"	33.00	39.00	31.00
☐ Mother Goose, vinyl, jointed, c. 1981, 11"	15.00	25.00	16.00
☐ Musketeer, c. 1983	20.00	30.00	21.00
☐ My Fair Baby, vinyl, sandy blonde hair (rooted), sleep eyes (blue), nursing mouth, bright red lips, marked Effanbee, made in 1958, 17½"	23.00	28.00	22.00
☐ My Precious Baby, vinyl head, cloth body, vinyl arms and legs, blonde hair (rooted), sleep eyes (blue), crier, marked 1960 Effanbee, 20"	14.00	19.00	14.00
☐ New Dy Dee Baby, vinyl, blonde hair (rooted), nurser, sleep eyes (blue), marked Effanbee 1969, 16½"	10.00	14.00	10.00
☐ New Orleans, *Pride of the South Collection, c. 1982, 13"*	35.00	45.00	38.00
☐ Night At The Opera, *Grandes Dames Collection, c. 1980, 18"*	50.00	60.00	52.00
☐ Norway, vinyl, jointed, *International Collection*	15.00	25.00	16.00
☐ Norweigan Doll, *International Collection, c. 1982, 11"*	20.00	30.00	21.00
☐ Olivia, *Grandes Dames Collection, c. 1982, 15"*	45.00	55.00	48.00
☐ Orange Blossom, by Joyce Stafford, c. 1982, 13"	40.00	45.00	42.00
☐ Patricia, composition, brown sleep eyes, blonde hair, closed mouth, blue pleated dress, marked, 14"	100.00	150.00	120.00
☐ Patricia, composition, red hair attached by adhesive, sleep eyes (brown), marked Effanbee-Patricia, mid 1930's, 13½"	68.00	83.00	65.00
☐ Patsy, all composition, painted blue eyes, molded hair, original clothes	125.00	150.00	125.00
☐ Patsy, composition, brown sleep eyes, real lashes, brown curly mohair wig, yellow dress with white collar, white leather shoes, 14"	175.00	215.00	185.00

/ EFFANBEE

	Current Price Range		P/Y AVG
☐ **Patsy**, *mold composition body, molded hair, painted eyes, original green dress, c. 1950, 10"*	225.00	250.00	235.00
☐ **Patsy**, *two piece snow suit in red, yellow, black and white, 13"*	80.00	90.00	82.00
☐ **Patsy Ann**, *blue sleep eyes, green print dress, white socks and shoes, 19"*	100.00	150.00	120.00
☐ **Patsy Ann**, *blue sleep eyes, painted hair, sweater and blue jeans, 19"*	90.00	100.00	92.00
☐ **Patsy Ann**, *composition, 20"*	100.00	150.00	120.00
☐ **Patsy Joan**, *composition, molded and painted hair (blonde), sleep eyes (green), marked Effanbee-Patsy Joan, also bearing (originally) a wrist tag carrying the same wording. Introduced in 1927 but taken off the market soon thereafter, reintroduced about 20 years later, most of those found today are the reintroductions, for which the stated value applies; the early specimens are of higher price, 16"*	50.00	68.00	47.00
☐ **Patsy Junior**, *composition head, composition arms, legs and body, composition hair, painted eyes, marked Effanbee Patsy Jr. Doll, placed on the market in 1930 or 1931, 11"*	80.00	100.00	77.00
☐ **Patsy Ruth**, *composition head, cloth body, composition arms and legs, sleep eyes (brown), marked Effanbee, Patsy Ruth, 1935, 27"*	200.00	250.00	190.00
☐ **Pavlova**, *Storybook Collection, c. 1979, 11"*	15.00	25.00	16.00
☐ **Peaches**, *vinyl head, cloth body, vinyl arms and legs, sleep eyes (blue), marked Effanbee 1965, 15"*	22.00	28.00	21.00
☐ **Peddler**, *by Faith Wick c. 1982, 16"*	75.00	85.00	79.00
☐ **Peter Pan**, *Storybook Collection, c. 1982, 11"*	20.00	30.00	21.00
☐ **Pinocchio**, *soft body, Huggable Collection, c. 1982, 14"*	28.00	37.00	29.00
☐ **Pinocchio**, *vinyl, jointed, molded nose, Storybook Series, c. 1981, 11"*	15.00	25.00	16.00
☐ **Polish Doll**, *International Collection, c. 1982, 11"*	20.00	30.00	21.00

EFFANBEE / 119

	Current Price Range		P/Y AVG

- ☐ **Polka Dotty**, *vinyl, molded and painted features, molded and painted hair, open mouth, pug nose, Polka Dotty was a character from the TV puppet program "Rootie Kazootie," a Saturday morning favorite in the days of live television, marked Polka Dotty-Rootie Kazootie-Effanbee, made in 1954, 19"* 65.00 85.00 60.00
- ☐ **Pollyana**, *c. 1983* 20.00 30.00 21.00
- ☐ **Precious Baby**, *character, vinyl head, vinyl hands, legs, cloth body, blond rooted hair, sleep eyes, c. 1957, 24"* ... 350.00 375.00 350.00
- ☐ **Precious Newborn**, *vinyl head, cloth body, vinyl arms and legs, blonde hair (rooted), painted eyes, marked Effanbee 1962, 14"* 25.00 31.00 23.00
- ☐ **Princess Di**, *mint in box, c. 1982* 145.00 155.00 149.00
- ☐ **Priscilla**, *light blue dress, Grandes Dames Collection, c. 1983, 11"* 35.00 45.00 39.00
- ☐ **Pun'kin**, *Granny's Corner Collection, c. 1983, 11"* 25.00 30.00 26.00
- ☐ **Pum'kin**, *vinyl, blonde hair (rooted), sleep eyes (blue), marked Effanbee 1966, 10"* 10.00 14.00 9.00
- ☐ **Queen Elizabeth**, *lacy white dress, Women of The Ages Collection, c. 1983* 45.00 55.00 49.00
- ☐ **Rebecca of Sunnybrook Farm**, *c. 1983* . 20.00 30.00 21.00
- ☐ **Recital Time**, *Abigail Collection, c. 1982, 13"* 40.00 50.00 42.00
- ☐ **Richmond**, *white and red gown, Pride of The South Collection, c. 1983* 40.00 50.00 42.00
- ☐ **Robyn**, *Grandes Dames Collection, c. 1982, 11"* 30.00 40.00 32.00
- ☐ **Roma**, *peach dress, hat, Age of Elegance Collection, c. 1983* 90.00 110.00 92.00
- ☐ **Romanian Doll**, *c. 1983* 20.00 30.00 21.00
- ☐ **Savannah**, *Pride of the South Collection, c. 1982, 13"* 35.00 45.00 37.00
- ☐ **Scarecrow**, *by Faith Wick, c. 1983, 18"* . 65.00 75.00 69.00
- ☐ **Scottish Doll**, *International Collection, c. 1982, 11"* 20.00 30.00 21.00
- ☐ **Skippy**, *composition head, cloth body, composition arms and legs, representing the comic strip character "Skippy" created by Percy Crosby, marked Skippy,*

120 / EFFANBEE

	Current Price Range		P/Y AVG
Effanbee, date of manufacture unknown but presumably c. 1935, 14"	75.00	95.00	70.00
☐ Spanish Doll, International Collection, c. 1982, 11"	20.00	30.00	21.00
☐ Spring, c. 1983	40.00	50.00	42.00
☐ Stephanie, gray, pink dress, Grandes Dames Collection, c. 1983, 15"	50.00	62.00	55.00
☐ Strolling in The Park, Abigail Collection, c. 1982, 13"	40.00	50.00	42.00
☐ Sugar Plum, Granny's Corner Collection, c. 1983, 20"	55.00	65.00	58.00
☐ Summer, Four Seasons Collection, c. 1982, 15"	35.00	45.00	39.00
☐ Summer, c. 1983	40.00	50.00	42.00
☐ Sunday Best, Abigail Collection, c. 1982, 13"	40.00	50.00	42.00
☐ Susan B. Anthony, mint in box, c. 1980	125.00	175.00	129.00
☐ Suzanne, all composition, jointed at neck, shoulder and hips, brown human hair wig, blue sleep eyes, rosebud mouth, Alice in Wonderland dress, white pinafore, wearing original Effanbee heart bracelet, head marked Effanbee Suzanne, 14"	145.00	155.00	145.00
☐ Suzanne, composition, blonde hair attached by adhesive, sleep eyes (brown), marked Suzanne-Effanbee, made in 1940, 13"	48.00	60.00	45.00
☐ Suzanne, pink, green ribbon trimmed dress, Grandes Dames Collection, c. 1983, 11"	35.00	45.00	39.00
☐ Suzie Sunshine, Granny's Corner Collection, c. 1983, 16"	38.00	45.00	40.00
☐ Suzie Sunshine, c. 1983, 18"	45.00	55.00	49.00
☐ Suzie Sunshine, plastic/vinyl, blonde hair (rooted), sleep eyes (blue), marked Effanbee 1961, 17"	11.00	14.00	10.00
☐ Swedish Doll, International Collection, c. 1982, 11"	20.00	30.00	21.00
☐ Sweetie Pie, composition, cloth, flirty eyes	125.00	175.00	129.00
☐ Sweetie Pie, Granny's Corner Collection, c. 1983, 18"	40.00	50.00	42.00
☐ Swiss Doll, International Collection, c. 1982, 11"	20.00	30.00	21.00

	Current Price Range		P/Y AVG
☐ **Thumkin,** vinyl head, cloth body, vinyl arms and legs, brown hair (rooted), sleep eyes (black), marked Effanbee 1965-9500U1, 18"	12.00	16.00	11.00
☐ **Tinker Bell,** c. 1983	20.00	30.00	21.00
☐ **Tiny Tubber,** black, Heart To Heart Collection, c. 1982, 11"	15.00	20.00	16.00
☐ **Tiny Tubber,** vinyl, blonde hair (rooted), sleep eyes (blue), nursing mouth, marked Effanbee, made in 1968, 10"	10.00	13.00	10.00
☐ **Tiny Tubber,** with pillow bunting, Crochet Classics Collection, c. 1981, 11"	20.00	25.00	21.00
☐ **Tintair,** plastic, platinum blonde hair attached by adhesive, sleep eyes (blue), marked Effanbee, made in 1951, 18"	62.00	78.00	60.00
☐ **The 70's Woman,** c. 1979, 15"	30.00	40.00	31.00
☐ **Twinkie,** vinyl, molded and painted hair (brown), sleep eyes (blue), nursing mouth, marked Effanbee 1959, 15"	11.00	14.00	10.00
☐ **U.S.A. Doll,** International Collection, c. 1982, 11"	20.00	30.00	21.00
☐ **Vicki,** Scottish outfit, Grandes Dames Collection, c. 1983, 11"	35.00	45.00	39.00
☐ **W. C. Fields,** vinyl, commemorative, c. 1980, 15"	50.00	60.00	55.00
☐ **Wee Patsy,** composition, believed to have been made around 1940, 5½"	110.00	135.00	100.00
☐ **Wicket Witch,** vinyl, soft body, sleep eyes, black, witch outfit, carries basket of apples	50.00	60.00	55.00
☐ **Winter,** Four Seasons Collection, c. 1982, 15"	35.00	45.00	39.00
☐ **Winter,** c. 1983	40.00	50.00	42.00

EINCO

☐ **Character Baby,** solid dome bisque socket head, five piece bent leg baby body, brushed stroked brown hair, blue intaglio eyes, open/ closed mouth, double chin, light blue linen romper suit,

122 / ELVIS PRESLEY ENTERPRISES

	Current Price Range		P/Y AVG
scalloped white collar, cuffs, marks: Einco 1½ Germany, 13"	600.00	750.00	600.00

ELVIS PRESLEY ENTERPRISES

☐ **Elvis Presley,** *plastic, molded and painted features, molded and painted hair, made in 1956 or 1957, wears plaid shirt and solid-color pants, has open mouth,* 18" 300.00 375.00   250.00

EPPY

☐ **Color Me,** *plastic, molded, jointed at the neck and upper arms, marked Eppy 1964, sold originally in a kit which also contained a set of crayons for coloring the doll (it could be washed and recolored at will),* 12" 6.00 8.00 6.00

ERB

☐ **Tarzan,** *plastic/vinyl, molded and painted features, fully jointed, Tarzan was created by Edgar Rice Burroughs, marked ERB Inc., 1972, (ERB, Inc., representing the estate and descendants of the late Edgar Rice Burroughs, licenses all Tarzan-related products),* 8" 5.00 7.00 5.00

EUGENE

☐ **Baby Missey,** *cloth body, vinyl head, vinyl limbs, sleep eyes (blue), marked 91/14, sold originally with a tag which*

	Current Price Range		P/Y AVG
read Eugene Doll Co., 91, made in Taiwan, date of manufacture unknown, probably 1970's, 9"	3.00	4.00	3.00
☐ **Baby Sarah Lee**, *black, plastic/vinyl, rooted hair, marked Eugene, 17⅞"*	6.00	8.00	6.00
☐ **Peepers**, *vinyl, jointed, flirt eyes, mint in box, 12"*	10.00	20.00	15.00

EUGENIA

☐ **Personality Playmate**, *plastic, brunette hair attached by adhesive, sleep eyes (brown), unmarked, made in this version in 1950, 17"*	39.00	48.00	37.00
☐ **Sandra**, *plastic, blonde hair attached by adhesive, sleep eyes (blue), unmarked, made in 1950, 15"*	38.00	47.00	35.00

Note: The actual manufacturer was Ideal, which did contracting for Eugenia.

EXCEL

☐ **Admiral William F. Halsey**, *plastic/vinyl, jointed, representing the U.S. naval commander of World War II, marked Excel Toy Corp., Hong Kong, made in the 1970's, 12"*	5.00	7.00	5.00
☐ **Annie Oakley**, *plastic/vinyl, jointed, representing the female trick-shot artist who performed with Buffalo Bill's Wild West Show, holds rifle, marked Excel Toy Corp., Hong Kong, made in the 1970's, 9½"*	3.00	5.00	3.00
☐ **Belle Starr**, *plastic/vinyl, jointed, representing the noted female desperado of the Old West, marked Excel Toy Corp., Hong Kong, made in the 1970's, 9½"*	3.00	5.00	3.00
☐ **Buffalo Bill Cody**, *plastic/vinyl, representing the Old West showman and story-teller, marked Excel Toy Corp., Hong Kong, made in the 1970's, 9½"*	3.00	5.00	3.00

	Current Price Range		P/Y AVG
☐ **Cochise**, *plastic/vinyl, representing the Indian chief popularized via a TV program during the 1960's, marked Excel Toy Corp., Hong Kong, made in the 1970's*	3.00	5.00	3.00
☐ **General George S. Patton**, *plastic/vinyl, jointed, representing the U.S. army general of World War II, marked Excel Toy Corp., Hong Kong, made in the 1970's, 12"*	5.00	7.00	5.00
☐ **General John J. Pershing**, *plastic/vinyl, representing the U.S. army officer who commanded allied forces in World War I, marked Excel Toy Corp., Hong Kong, made in the 1970's, 12"*	5.00	7.00	5.00
☐ **General Robert E. Lee**, *plastic/vinyl, jointed, representing the commander of Confederate forces in the Civil War, marked Excel Toy Corp., Hong Kong, made in the 1970's, 12"*	5.00	7.00	5.00
☐ **George Washington**, *plastic/vinyl, wears short jacket with brass buttons, sword, boots, tricorn hat, marked Excel Toy Corp., Hong Kong, made in the 1970's, 12"*	5.00	7.00	5.00
☐ **Jessie James**, *plastic/vinyl, jointed, representing the Old West bank robber, marked Excel Toy Corp., Hong Kong, made in the 1970's, 9"*	3.00	5.00	3.00
☐ **Lt. Col. Paul Revere**, *plastic/vinyl, representing the Boston silversmith who, according to popular legend, alerted townsfolk of a British invasion in the Revolutionary War, marked Excel Toy Corp., Hong Kong, made in the 1970's, 12"*	5.00	7.00	5.00
☐ **Lt. Col. Theodore Roosevelt**, *plastic/vinyl, representing President Roosevelt in his days as an officer in the Spanish-American War, wearing military dress with pistol in holster, marked Excel Toy Corp., Hong Kong, made in the 1970's, 12"*	5.00	7.00	5.00

	Current Price Range		P/Y AVG

- **Pochahontas,** *plastic/vinyl, jointed, representing the Indian princess of 17th century America who became well known through the writing of John Smith, the Virginia colonist, marked Excel Toy Corp., Hong Kong, made in the 1970's* 3.00 5.00 3.00
- **Ulysses S. Grant,** *plastic/vinyl, representing the Union Army general and U.S. President, wearing military dress with sword, marked Excel Toy Corp., Hong Kong, made in the 1970's, 12"* ... 5.00 7.00 5.00

MARK FARMER

- **Boy,** *bisque shoulder head, cloth body, bisque arms and legs, a modern doll made in 19th century style, date of manufacture unknown, presumably 1970's, 13"* 60.00 80.00 57.00

F.D.

- **Sissy,** *plastic/vinyl, brown hair (rooted), sleep eyes (blue), nursing mouth, marked F.D., made in 1963, 18"* 9.00 12.00 9.00
- **Winkin',** *vinyl, molded and painted features, molded and painted hair, representing the character in the Old English folk rhyme, "Winkin', Blinkin', and Nod," marked F.D., made in 1956, 8½"* . 6.00 8.00 6.00

FISHER PRICE

- **Audrey,** *vinyl head, cloth body, rooted hair, painted eyes, blouse with small heart pattern, marked 168240, 1973, Fisher Price Toys, 14"* 11.00 15.00 10.00

126 / FISHER PRICE

	Current Price Range		P/Y AVG
☐ **Baby Ann,** vinyl head, cloth body, rooted blond hair, painted eyes, floral print dress with large sash ribbon, marked 60, 188460, 1973, Fisher Price Toys, 13½"	10.00	14.00	9.00
☐ **Elizabeth,** black, vinyl head, cloth body, rooted hair, closed mouth in semi-smile, painted eyes, marked 18, 168630, 1973, Fisher Price Toys, 13½"	11.00	15.00	10.00
☐ **Honey**	6.00	10.00	5.00
☐ **Joey**	9.00	12.00	8.00
☐ **Mary,** vinyl head, cloth body, rooted hair, upturned eyes (painted), angelic facial expression, wears print dress and white apron, marked 168420, 1973, Fisher Price Toys, 14"	10.00	14.00	9.00
☐ **Mikey,** dark hair, bangs, freckles, pants, shirt, jacket, #205, My Friend	20.00	30.00	25.00
☐ **My Friend Becky,** vinyl, jointed brown rooted hair, blue eyes, painted features, green dress with white pinafore with floral print, white straw hat, white slippers	20.00	30.00	25.00
☐ **My Friend Jenny,** vinyl, jointed, dark brown rooted hair, brown sleep eyes, painted features, yellow and white gingham dress, white sleeves, white slippers, white straw hat, 17"	20.00	30.00	25.00
☐ **My Friend Mandy,** vinyl, jointed, blonde rooted hair, blue eyes, painted features, navy blue dress with white polka dots, red straw hat, red slippers, 17"	20.00	30.00	25.00
☐ **Natalie,** vinyl head, cloth body, rooted hair, upturned eyes (painted), grinning smile, marked 168320, 1973, Fisher Price Toys, 13½"	11.00	15.00	10.00
☐ **Susie Soft Sound,** open, shut eyes, electronic voice, 16"	40.00	50.00	45.00

HAM FISHER

	Current Price Range		P/Y AVG
☐ **Joan Palooka**, *vinyl head, latex body, sleep eyes, molded, painted hair, jointed arms, intended as a female counterpart of Joe Palooka, the heavyweight boxing champion of the comic strips, marked 1952, Ham Fisher, Ideal Doll, Ham Fisher was the creator of the Joe Palooka character, 14"*	20.00	25.00	18.00

FLAGG

☐ **Calypso Dancer**, *vinyl, unmarked, 7"* ..	10.00	13.00	9.00
☐ **Cowboy**, *vinyl, bendable, unmarked, 7"*	9.00	12.00	9.00
☐ **Cowgirl**, *vinyl, posable, unmarked, 6½"*.	9.00	12.00	9.00
☐ **Dancing Doll**, *posable, vinyl, rooted hair, believed to have been made between 1955 and 1960, sold in white and black versions, which differ in costuming and minor details, 7¼", White*	7.00	9.00	7.00
Black	8.00	11.00	8.00
☐ **Egyptian Girl** *(national costume doll), vinyl, bendable, 7"*	9.00	12.00	8.00
☐ **Flagg Dancer**, *vinyl, unmarked, 7"*	10.00	13.00	10.00
☐ **Frenchman**, *vinyl, unmarked, believed to date from the mid 1940's, 7"*	9.00	11.00	8.00

FLEISCHAKER

☐ **Bi Bye**, *vinyl head, vinyl arms and legs, stuffed cloth body, painted eyes, molded and painted hair, represents a one-week-old infant with mouth wide open, crying, originally came with a tag, dated 1949, made for the Fleischaker Novelty Co. by Lastic Plastic, 16"*	14.00	18.00	13.00
☐ **Little Girl Of Today**, *vinyl head, cloth body, vinyl arms and legs, sleep eyes (blue), marked Fleischaker Novelty Co. made in 1949, sold for several years thereafter, 23"*	160.00	190.00	150.00

128 / FLEISHER STUDIOS

	Current Price Range		P/Y AVG
☐ **Unnamed,** *plastic, stuffed, rooted hair, sleep eyes, partially open mouth, wears checkered dress (short) with puff sleeves, two buttons on dress, arms and legs wide apart, marked Copyright 1951 Lastic Plastic, 16½"*	18.00	23.00	17.00

Note: *This doll (unnamed) was manufactured by Lastic Plastic for the Fleischaker Novelty Co. The hairstyle is somewhat "afro."*

FLEISHER STUDIOS

☐ **Betty Boop,** *jointed wood doll, c. 1930, 12"*	75.00	100.00	80.00

FORTUNE TOYS

☐ **Pam,** *plastic, blonde hair attached with adhesive, sleep eyes (blue), unmarked, made in 1956, 7½"*	11.00	14.00	10.00

FREUNDLICH

☐ **Baby Sandy,** *composition, molded and painted hair, sleep eyes, open mouth, bright red lips, wears bonnet, unmarked, made in 1936, 11"*	115.00	135.00	110.00
☐ **Sandy Henville,** *composition, sleep eyes, open mouth, bright red lips, date of manufacture unknown, 16"*	100.00	120.00	95.00

FUN FARM

☐ **Funny,** *plastic/vinyl, brunette hair (rooted), painted eyes (brown), open mouth with one large tooth, marked*

	Current Price Range		P/Y AVG
1965 R. Dakin & Co., Product of Hong Kong, sold originally with a tag reading Fun Farm, San Francisco, 6"	5.00	7.00	5.00

FUN WORLD

	Current Price Range		P/Y AVG
☐ **Abe Lincoln**, *plastic, molded and painted features, molded and painted hair, holds hat in hand, stands on rectangular base, marked Hong Kong, made c. 1975, 8½"* .	11.00	14.00	10.00
☐ **George Washington**, *plastic, molded and painted features, molded and painted hair, arms hanging at sides, stands on rectangular base, marked Hong Kong, made c. 1975, 8½"*	11.00	14.00	10.00
☐ **Huggles**, *vinyl head, stuffed body, vinyl hands, rooted hair (reddish), painted eyes, marked Huggles by Fun World, made in 1971, 9"*	4.00	6.00	4.00
☐ **Sleepy Head**, *vinyl head, stuffed body, vinyl hands, rooted hair (brunette), painted eyes, marked Fun World, made in 1971, 11"*	6.00	8.00	6.00
☐ **Soul Sister**, *black, plastic/vinyl, rooted hair (black), painted eyes (brown), wears large hoop earrings, short dress, boots, marked Design No. 915-664, Made in Hong Kong, made in 1971, 8"*	9.00	12.00	9.00
☐ **Sparky**, *plastic head, plastic arms, legs and body, hair attached by adhesive, face painted as a clown, marked Made in Hong Kong, Fun World Inc., 1973, 7"* .	3.00	4.00	3.00

FURGA

	Current Price Range		P/Y AVG
☐ **Anna**, *brunette, dark sleep eyes, lashes, white, green velvet dress, pantaloons, pumps, holds hoop, Kent Collection, 18"*	35.00	45.00	40.00
☐ **Beatrix**, *blonde curls, hazel eyes, striped skirt, white blouse, pink bonnet, 18"*	45.00	55.00	50.00

FURGA

	Current Price Range		P/Y AVG
☐ **Chiara,** blonde hair, blue eyes, blue, white satin print dress, straw hat, c. 1983, 15"	40.00	50.00	45.00
☐ **Dame Louise,** plastic/vinyl, green eyes, pug nose, closed mouth, marked Furga, Italy, date of manufacture unknown, c. 1950's, 17"	15.00	20.00	14.00
☐ **Furina,** plastic/vinyl, brunette wig attached by adhesive, sleep eyes (blue), unmarked on doll, sold originally with a tag reading Furga, Made in Italy, made in 1955, 11"	100.00	130.00	95.00
☐ **Girl,** flowers in hair, blue sleep eyes, lashes, closed mouth, pink net, satin cape, gown	30.00	40.00	35.00
☐ **Mary, Mary,** plastic/vinyl, blue eyes, representing the storybook character "Mary, Mary Quite Contrary", marked Furga, Italy, made in 1974	18.00	25.00	17.00
☐ **Olympia,** white, green dress, matching hat, c. 1983	75.00	85.00	80.00
☐ **Pettrice,** frosted red hair, lacy green skirt, apron, beret, scarf, comes with artist's implements, c. 1983	75.00	85.00	80.00
☐ **Plastic,** red hair with long braids, white dress and bloomers, yellow boots, hula hoop, 14"	40.00	50.00	44.00
☐ **Plastic,** blue sleep eyes, silver blonde hair in large bun, pink velvet hoop dress, matching hat, white maribou trim, 16"	40.00	50.00	44.00
☐ **Plastic,** blue sleep eyes, short white hair, tan velvet hoop dress, white blouse, cape with hood trimmed in brown maribou, white boots, muff on gold chain, 14"	40.00	50.00	43.00
☐ **Plastic,** sleep blue eyes with long lashes, red hair wig, short white dress, pearl buttons, long white stockings, 22"	50.00	60.00	53.00
☐ **Snow White,** plastic/vinyl, blue eyes, marked Furga, Italy, made in 1974, 9"	18.00	25.00	17.00

FY

A Japanese firm which imported large quantities of dolls and/or doll heads into the U.S. and Western Europe shortly after World War I. The heads are bisque and of rather good quality. Some specimens have marked Oriental facial characteristics, and it can probably be presumed that these are the earlier ones, before the firm learned how to make a western-looking doll.

The word "Nippon," found in the marks of this manufacturer, was an Anglo-American word (now pretty well obsolete) meaning "Japan."

	Current Price Range		P/Y AVG
☐ **Bisque**, *infant head, usually found dressed as a toddler with a bonnet, sleep eyes (large for the head size), open mouth showing two well-formed teeth, wide nose, circular face, slightly arched eyebrows, marked Fy20-8-Nippon, date of manufacture unknown, probably early to mid 1920's, 10" (but the size will vary as this head is found on various bodies)*	90.00	120.00	85.00
☐ **Bisque**, *socket head with shoulder plate, fixed eyes (medium large), barest suggestion of lashes, almost horizontal brows, partially open mouth showing teeth, medium-dark lips, puffy cheeks, marked Fy9-Nippon-402, date of manufacture unknown, probably early to mid 1920's, 19½"*	180.00	215.00	170.00
☐ **Girl**, *composition ball jointed body, brown stationary glass eyes, open mouth, teeth, long brown curls, blue satin dress with lace trim, lace cap, white shoes with bows, 25"*	325.00	375.00	340.00
☐ **Girl**, *composition ball jointed body, long blonde human hair curls, turquoise-blue velvet dress with pink lace trim, matching hat, bonnet and purse, 23"*	270.00	340.00	300.00

GABRIEL

	Current Price Range		P/Y AVG

- ☐ **Dan Reid,** *plastic, molded and painted features, molded and painted hair, painted eyes, Dan Reid, a fictional character, was "the Lone Ranger's long-lost brother," marked 1975 Lone Ranger, made in Hong Kong for Gabriel Industries, Inc., 8"* 11.00 14.00   10.00
- ☐ **Timmy,** *molded and painted features, molded and painted hair, marked 1975 Gabriel Industries, Inc., made in Hong Kong, Timmy was a character on the "Lassie" TV program, 8½"* 11.00 14.00   10.00

GAMA

- ☐ **Florina,** *French, in a box, 9"* 45.00 55.00   45.00
- ☐ **Kate,** *French, in a box, 12"* 65.00 75.00   65.00
- ☐ **Stephanie,** *French, in a box, 7"* 25.00 30.00   20.00
- ☐ **Stephanie,** *French, with suitcase, 7"* .. 35.00 45.00   40.00

GANDA TOYS LTD.

- ☐ **Poland,** *plastic head, plastic arms, legs and body, blond wig attached by adhesive, sleep eyes, represents a young girl wearing national costuming of Poland, made in Hong Kong, 7"* 4.00 5.00   4.00
  Note: There were other "national costume" dolls in this Ganda series, all of which have the same value. The series was issued in 1973.

GANS AND SEYFARTH

- ☐ **Bisque,** *jointed composition body, brown eyes, lashes, multicolored pencil striped dress, organdy hat, 20"* 300.00 350.00   340.00

	Current Price Range		P/Y AVG
☐ **Country Girl,** *jointed composition body, brown eyes, lashes, brown wig, white dress, plaid hat, 24"*	350.00	400.00	370.00

GAULTIER

Parisian manufacturer active in the final quarter of the 19th century. Their dolls were of high quality and show considerable versatility in styling and materials. The heads were nearly always of bisque, but such components as wood, papier mache and composition were used for the bodies and limbs, sometimes all intermingled in the same doll. It is also likely that Gaultier sold bodiless heads to assembling companies. Dolls with Gaultier heads and cloth bodies were probably assembled elsewhere. A fine Gaultier in well preserved condition is a prize for the collector. They can be found in the U.S. but the prime hunting grounds are the antique shops of Paris — where they are more plentiful but VERY expensive.

☐ **Bebe,** *bisque head, jointed French composition and wood body, brown paperweight eyes, brown wig, pierced ears, closed mouth, lovely old brown velvet dress with lace trim and hat, mark: F.G. 7, 18"*	900.00	1300.00	850.00
☐ **Bebe,** *bisque head, shoulder plate, jointed French composition body, blue paperweight eyes, blond human hair wig, closed mouth, pierced ears, antique clothes, 20"*	2200.00	2500.00	2250.00
☐ **Bebe,** *bisque head, shoulder plate, jointed French composition body, blue paperweight glass eyes, blonde wig, pierced ears, closed mouth, antique dress, bonnet and undergarments, 18"*	3200.00	3800.00	3000.00
☐ **Bisque,** *socket head, fixed eyes, very large, almond-shaped, short painted lashes, heavy arching eyebrows, closed mouth, medium-dark lips, facial expression of contentment, marked with the initials F.G., and the mold number 10, date of manufacture unknown, estimated at c. 1880, 24½"*	1275.00	1550.00	1250.00

134 / GAULTIER

| | Current Price Range | P/Y AVG |

- ☐ **Fashion Lady,** *bisque head and shoulder plate, kid body, wired arms, kid covered fingers, blonde wig, paperweight grey eyes, closed mouth, pierced ears, beautiful wardrobe, marked F.G. on shoulder, 16"* .... 2500.00 2750.00 | 2500.00

Fashion, bisque, c. 1870, 22" $2500.00-$2700.00

- ☐ **Three Dolls,** *two children and one teacher, mechanical, bisque, wigs, closed mouth, two children turn and dance as music plays, teacher sits at piano, crank operated, base, original clothes, 12" x 8" x 2½"* .... 3100.00 3350.00 | 3150.00

GAY BOB TRADING COMPANY

	Current Price Range		P/Y AVG
☐ **Gay Bob,** *vinyl head, vinyl body, painted eyes, earrings, shirt, slacks and closet, c. 1982,*	8.00	12.00	10.00
☐ **Pirate,** *wax construction, brown curly wig and beard, painted brown eyes, velvet costume with high boots, three corner hat with skull and cross bones, 8½"*	150.00	200.00	175.00

GEBRÜDER HEUBACH

Gebruder Heubach ("The Heubach Brothers") operated at roughly the same time as Heubach (see below), and also in Germany, but was a different company. This was a large organization with agents and distributors virtually worldwide, and was known for ceramics of many different kinds. Today there are collectors of Gebruder Heubach who specialize in its plates, figurines, etc. While dolls did not comprise a major portion of the firm's business, it nevertheless turned out many of them, over a long period of time. Its dolls span the era from the American Civil War right up to the Depression, and various different kinds are included. Gebruder Heubach was one of the more innovative doll makers and designers, and for this have won a strong collector following. While most other firms were turning out dolls whose heads and facial expressions were virtual carbon copies of each other, Gebruder Heubach inaugurated many original types, which were well ahead of their time. In terms of grandeur these dolls are not the equal of French specimens of the same age, but their originality wins for them a high ranking — and high prices, in most cases.

☐ **Baby Doll,** *brown eyes, brown wig, 19"* .	300.00	350.00	340.00
☐ **Baby Doll,** *brown eyes, marked 300-20, 14"*	200.00	250.00	220.00
☐ **Baby Stuart,** *composition ball jointed body, intaglio eyes, closed pouty mouth, molded bonnet with pink rosebuds painted on, 12"*	900.00	1200.00	1050.00
☐ **Bisque,** *ball jointed body, set brown eyes, silver blonde human hair, open mouth, maroon dress with flowered pattern, lace trim, yellow straw hat, 17"* ...	150.00	200.00	172.00
☐ **Character Girl,** *jointed body, blonde wig, blue sleep eyes, blue cotton dress and hat, marked 8192, 16"*	475.00	500.00	485.00

136 / GEBRÜDER KNOCH

	Current Price Range		P/Y AVG
☐ **Child Character,** *bisque head, jointed composition body, blue intaglio eyes, molded hair with blue band, open-closed mouth, original white lawn dress with lace insets, 11"*	600.00	800.00	675.00
☐ **Child Character,** *bisque head, wood and composition body, molded hair, blue intaglio eyes, open mouth, lovely lace dress, 11"*	550.00	750.00	550.00
☐ **Christmas Children,** *child with sled, bisque face, cloth and wire bodies, 2½"*	100.00	150.00	120.00
☐ **Composition,** *head, ball jointed body, mohair wig, brown sleep eyes, green dress, 19"*	350.00	375.00	360.00
☐ **Composition,** *head and arms, cloth body, blonde human hair wig, brown sleep eyes, lacy hat and dress, 11"*	325.00	375.00	335.00
☐ **Polo Player,** *composition body and head, blond mohair wig, brown sleep eyes, red and white uniform, 16"*	400.00	425.00	410.00
☐ **Sailor Boy,** *bisque head, ball jointed composition body, molded blonde hair, blue intaglio eyes, closed mouth, navy suit and cap, marked No.6-6894, 19"*	750.00	800.00	775.00
☐ **Shoulder Head,** *blue eyes, black wig, 14½"*	125.00	175.00	140.00
☐ **Toddler,** *five-piece body, blue sleep eyes, brown human hair wig, open mouth, teeth, 14½"*	465.00	510.00	480.00
☐ **Toddler,** *jointed body, molded hair, open/closed mouth with laughing expression, molded teeth, 16"*	1000.00	1500.00	1220.00

GEBRÜDER KNOCH

☐ **Boy,** *character, bisque head, dome shaped with solid brush strokes, kid body with bisque forearms, intaglio eyes follow open-closed mouth, two teeth, small nose, old white shirt and knickers, incised symbol 143 plus "Made in Germany Gesch. 216 Gesch. 14/0, 13"*	260.00	290.00	270.00

	Current Price Range		P/Y AVG
☐ **Character Doll,** *baby, bisque head, cloth body, composition arms and legs, intaglio blue eyes, open/closed mouth, two lower teeth, painted blonde hair, long white baby dress, 10"*	475.00	525.00	495.00
☐ **Infant,** *bisque, wig, grey glass eyes, commercially dressed in 12" sheer cotton lace paneled and trimmed dress with layers of matching slips, chemise, and panties, original accessories, bottle holder etc., Gebruder Knoch incised, 8½"*	150.00	160.00	145.00

GEBRÜDER KRAUSS

☐ **Bisque,** *ball-jointed body, blue sleep eyes, black wig with long curls, red satin dress, 16½"*	165.00	200.00	180.00
☐ **Bisque,** *set blue eyes, feathered brows, pink dress with rose pattern, mold number 133-305, 26"*	425.00	475.00	440.00
☐ **Bisque,** *head, ball jointed composition body, human hair wig, brown sleep eyes, open mouth, pink and white dress, marked 165, 21"*	475.00	525.00	500.00
☐ **Bisque,** *socket head on fully jointed composition body, blue sleep eyes with real upper lashes, original blonde mohair wig, open mouth with four porcelain teeth, light blue sailor type dress with wide collar and lace trim, marks: 305 Gbr 165 K, 9 Germany, 26"*	275.00	350.00	300.00

GEM

☐ **Chubby Kid,** *composition, molded and painted features, molded and painted hair, unmarked, made in 1922, 12"*	70.00	90.00	65.00

GEM TOY COMPANY

	Current Price Range		P/Y AVG
☐ Girl, all composition, brown glued on wool wig, large painted side glancing eyes, looks like Buddy Lee except it is girl in pigtails, blue dotted dress, matching bonnet, lace trim, made in 1910 for Sears, 13"	65.00	80.00	65.00

GENERAL MILLS FUN GROUP

☐ Blythe, plastic/vinyl, rooted hair, blonde, large sad eyes which shift from side to side and change color when pullcord is pulled, wearing a bright print dress, marked Blythe TM, Kenner Products, 1972, also marked General Mills Fun Group (the Kenner Company was a subsidiary of General Mills), 12"	7.00	9.00	7.00

GEORGENE

☐ Little Lulu, cloth, unmarked, sold originally with a tag reading Georgene Novelties Inc., Copyright 1944, 15½"	58.00	70.00	55.00

Note: Little Lulu was a comic strip character created by Marjorie Buell.

GERBER

☐ Baby, says Mama, accessories, 17"	30.00	35.00	30.00
☐ Gerber Baby, rubber, molded and painted hair, fixed eyes, nursing mouth, bright red lips, wearing a bib marked "Gerber Baby" in script letters, marked on doll Mfg. by The Sun Rubber Co., Barberton, Ohio, made in 1956, 11"	14.00	18.00	13.00

Note: Used as a promotional item by the Gerber Foods Co., manufacturers of baby foods.

SUE GIBSON

	Current Price Range		P/Y AVG
☐ **Little Red Riding Hood,** *bisque head and arms, cloth body, long red hood, brown set eyes, elaborate costume with cape, carrying basket, 12½"*	450.00	550.00	475.00

A. C. GILBERT

☐ **Man from U.N.C.L.E., The,** *action figures, Napoleon Solo and Illya Kuryakin, c. 1965* 60.00 70.00 65.00

☐ **McDare,** *vinyl head, vinyl arms, plastic legs and body, molded, painted hair, painted eyes, represents an adult man wearing military style jumpsuit, zippered in front up to neck, false pockets, marked K53, K56, 11⅞"* 6.00 8.00 6.00

Note: *McDare was made in Hong Kong for the A. C. Gilbert Co., much better known for model railroad trains and Erector sets than dolls. The markings appear separately on each arm and represent the mold numbers for those components.*

GIRL'S WORLD

☐ **Emerald The Enchanting Witch,** *plastic/vinyl, violet colored skin, rooted hair, green, fixed eyes, wears black outfit with cone-shaped witch's hat, marked 1971, Girl's World, Pat Pend, made in Japan, 7"* 27.00 35.00 25.00

WILLIAM GOEBEL

The Goebel company, located in Germany, became internationally known in the 20th century for its Hummel figurines (which are not classified as dolls). In the 19th century this was a relatively small ceramics company which made wares of various kinds. It occasionally produced dolls, from the

WILLIAM GOEBEL

1800's up to the time it began turning out Hummels in the 1930's, and even (in fact) afterward. The basic difference is that its earlier dolls are not Hummel-oriented; they utilize themes which are not connected with the artwork of Sister Hummel. Nevertheless, many of the Goebel dolls are very distinctive and are instantly recognizable as Goebel, and they even have a slight suggestion of "Hummelness" about them.

	Current Price Range		P/Y AVG
☐ **Bisque,** ball jointed body, blue sleep eyes, reddish-gold human hair, open mouth, blue dress with rose pattern, lace trim, 14"	225.00	275.00	245.00
☐ **Bisque head,** ball jointed composition body, mohair wig, blue sleep eyes, open mouth, red hat and dress, 21"	375.00	400.00	385.00
☐ **Bisque,** head, papier mache body, molded and painted hair, sandy red, painted eyes, large looking to the left side of the doll, short painted lashes, tiny eyebrows placed high on the forehead, closed mouth with bright red lips, almost spherical head, fingers not well defined, chunky legs, representing a very young child, marked with the letter W surmounted by the wings of a bee, which later progressed into Goebel's "full bee" trademark, also marked with the mold number 12/0, date of manufacture unknown, probably first quarter of the 20th century, 6½"	125.00	145.00	120.00
☐ **Buster Brown,** porcelain head, human hair wig, blue sleep eyes, blue satin outfit, 18"	500.00	600.00	525.00
☐ **Chimney Sweep,** boy, based on the work by M.I. Hummel, soft vinyl, authentic German outfit, long black coat and pants, black brimmed hat, carries cleaning tool and undersized ladder, 11"	55.00	65.00	55.00
☐ **For Father,** boy based on the work of M.I. Hummel, soft vinyl, authentic German outfit, blonde molded hair, dark brown shorts with straps, white shirt, red kerchief at neck, green Tyrolean hat, holds oversized foaming mug and vegetables, 11"	55.00	65.00	55.00

	Current Price Range		P/Y AVG
☐ **Fratz,** *Redhead Dolls, soft vinyl, bright red hair, green eyes, freckles, red top with white polka dots, white baby pants, marked 1998, 9"*	45.00	55.00	45.00
☐ **Merry Wanderer,** *boy based on the work of M.I. Hummel, soft vinyl, authentic German outfit, black pants, mottled brown shirt, mottled green jacket, black brimmed*	55.00	65.00	55.00
☐ **On Secret Path,** *boy based on the work of M.I. Hummel, soft vinyl, authentic German outfit, blonde molded hair, white shirt, blue shorts with straps, red with black jacket, yellow plaid hat, carries walking stick, candles, and small bundle of sticks, 11"*	55.00	65.00	55.00
☐ **Raggedy Muffin,** *Redhead Dolls, soft vinyl, bright red hair, green eyes, freckles, green and white checkered dress, red pantaloons, red hankie pinned on front, marked 1991, 11"*	50.00	60.00	50.00
☐ **School Boy,** *boy based on the work of M.I. Hummel, soft vinyl, authentic German outfit, mottled green shorts with straps, white shirt, red kerchief at neck, bluish-gray Tyrolean hat, wears brown book bag on back, 11"*	55.00	65.00	55.00
☐ **School Girl,** *based on the work of M.I. Hummel, soft vinyl, authentic German outfit, mottled yellow dress with red bodice and white sleeves, carries book bag on her back, 11"*	55.00	65.00	55.00

GOODYEAR RUBBER COMPANY

☐ **Goodyear Baby,** *composition soft body, painted features, c. 1930, 13"*	75.00	85.00	78.00
☐ **Rubber Shoulder Head,** *cloth body, molded head with sausage curls, painted facial features and black hair, lovely clothes, mint, 13"*	750.00	1000.00	200.00

GORHAM

	Current Price Range		P/Y AVG
☐ **Alexandria**, bisque, blonde, light orange dress, green velvet coat, music box, c. 1983, 19"	250.00	300.00	260.00
☐ **Amy**, lacy blue satin, music box, c. 1983	200.00	250.00	220.00
☐ **Baby Doll**, blue dress, music box, c. 1983	125.00	175.00	130.00
☐ **Baby Doll**, light orange dress, music box, c. 1983	150.00	200.00	156.00
☐ **Baby Doll**, white lace, ribbon trim, music box, c. 1983	200.00	300.00	210.00
☐ **Benjamin and Ellice**, toddler twins, green, white outfits, music box, c. 1983	175.00	225.00	179.00
☐ **Beth**, lacy yellow dress, music box, Little Women series, c. 1983	250.00	275.00	260.00
☐ **Christina**, music box, c. 1983, 16"	200.00	250.00	210.00
☐ **Christopher**, bisque, velvet outfit, music box, c. 1983, 19"	250.00	300.00	260.00
☐ **Jeremy**, tweed outfit, music box, c. 1983, 23"	250.00	350.00	260.00
☐ **Jillian**, bisque, white lacy dress, music box, c. 1983, 16"	200.00	250.00	210.00
☐ **Jo**, lacy blue dress, music box, Little Women series, c. 1983	250.00	275.00	256.00
☐ **Melanie**, bisque, white satin dress, music box, c. 1983, 23"	250.00	350.00	260.00
☐ **Rosamond**, bisque, lace outfit, music box, c. 1983, 19"	225.00	300.00	230.00

GOTZ PUPPE

☐ **Gret**, vinyl, sleep eyes, brown, marked Gotz Puppe, "Gotz Dolls," made in Germany, 1968, 16"	15.00	19.00	14.00

GRANT'S

☐ **Bucky Bradford**, vinyl, squeeze toy, molded and painted features, molded and painted clothing, holds sign reading "It's Yum Yum Time," stands on platform base which reads "Bucky

	Current Price Range		P/Y AVG

Bradford," date of manufacture unknown, 8½" **5.00 7.00 4.00**
Note: Bucky Bradford was a symbol of the Grant restaurant chain.
☐ **Dress Me,** *plastic/vinyl, blonde hair attached by adhesive, painted eyes, marked 1963, Grant Plastics Co., 11½"* **6.00 8.00 6.00**

GREINER

☐ **Papier Mache,** *head, cloth body with leather arms, dark glass arms, original black and brown striped dress, original leather shoes, c. 1927, 21"* **800.00 950.00 875.00**
☐ **Papier Mache,** *shoulder head, cloth body, hair molded in sausage curls, painted blonde, painted blue eyes, brown plaid taffeta dress, red leather boots and gloves* **550.00 750.00 525.00**
☐ **Papier Mache,** *shoulder head, cloth body, leather arms, blonde molded elaborate curls over ears, painted blue eyes and facial features, original black wool dress, mark: "Greiner's Label' Patent Doll Heads No.7 Pat. Mar30'58, Ext. '72", 24"* **350.00 500.00 350.00**

GUND

☐ **Clown,** *vinyl mask face, rag body, stuffed, red hair, molded and painted features, marked Gund, made in 1964, 18"* **8.00 11.00 7.00**
☐ **Jiminy Cricket,** *vinyl and cloth hand puppet, in original box, c. 1960* **7.00 12.00 9.50**
☐ **Little Audrey,** *vinyl and cloth puppet in box, c. 1950* **12.00 19.00 14.00**

HALCO

	Current Price Range		P/Y AVG
☐ **Miss Fluffee,** plastic shoulder head, cloth body, vinyl arms, latex legs, sleep eyes, hair attached by adhesive, unmarked, The Halco Company was located in Pittsburgh, Pennsylvania, made in 1951, 29" .	33.00	39.00	32.00
☐ **Shirley Temple Look-Alike,** all composition doll, jointed neck, shoulders, hips, blonde mohair wig styled in ringlets, blue sleep eyes, open mouth, turquoise printed dress, matching bonnet, original Halco box, original paper label pinned to skirt, 16"	75.00	100.00	75.00

HALLMARK CARDS

☐ **Babe Ruth,** Famous American series, mint in box, c. 1979	10.00	15.00	10.00
☐ **Ben Franklin,** cloth, Bicentennial, mint in box, c. 1976	15.00	25.00	20.00
☐ **Beanbag Rabbit,** cotton and flannel, yarn hair, wears striped bowtie, marked Hallmark Cards, Inc., made in Taiwan, date of manufacture unknown, c. 1974, 9"	3.00	5.00	3.00
☐ **Betsy Clark,** vinyl head, cloth body, vinyl hands, molded and painted features, marked 1975 Hallmark Cards, Inc., K.T.C., made in Taiwan, 13"	3.00	5.00	3.00
☐ **Doll toy,** felt and cotton, stuffed, unmarked on doll, originally sold with a tag reading Hallmark Cards Inc., stock #200XDT, date of manufacture unknown, c. 1974, 6"	3.00	4.00	3.00
☐ **Drummer Boy,** cloth, Holiday series, with box, 7"	4.00	8.00	5.00
☐ **Indian Girl,** cloth, Holiday series, with box, 7"	4.00	8.00	5.00
☐ **Santa,** cloth, Holiday series, with box, 7"	4.00	8.00	5.00
☐ **Snowman,** terri, stuffed, figure of a snowman wearing a long scarf, unmarked on doll, originally sold with a tag reading Hallmark Cards, Inc., made in Taiwan, 200XDT, 6"	3.00	5.00	3.00

HALL SYNDICATE

	Current Price Range	P/Y AVG
☐ **Margaret,** *vinyl head, cloth body, molded and painted features, molded and painted hair, marked 1968 Hall Syndicate, Inc., 15"*	22.00 28.00	21.00

HEINRICH HANDWERCK

German firm, whose name translated to English would be "Heinrich's Handcrafts." It was founded in the 1870's in Thuringia, then a part of the Prussian Empire. Heinrich Handwerck was not only a manufacturer of doll heads, but an assembling factory which made dolls with the heads of other firms. For many years they were one of the principal customers of Simon and Halbig, a maker of bisque heads, and therefore many of the Heinrich Handwerck dolls are found with "S & H" heads. By the same token, dolls of other companies will be found with Heinrich Handwerck heads, but this does not occur as often. Though its dolls are highly collectible, and nicely made, it is obvious that the company strove usually for heavy output rather than meticulous workmanship. They were very much involved in the "import war" of the 1890's, in which a number of German doll makers poured dolls by the multi thousands into the U.S., hoping to win over the American market. (No single company succeeded in winning over the American market!) For the beginning collector and especially the lover of bisque who does not have limitless funds available, dolls of Heinrich Handwerck are an attractive collecting specialty. Most of them can be had for half or third the price of French bisque dolls of the same era. Be forewarned, however, that some expensive specimens DO exist.

☐ **Bebe Elite,** *bisque head, blonde vinyl wig, sleep eyes, blue and white floral print, c. 1860, 10½"*	25.00 30.00	27.50
☐ **Bebe Elite,** *bisque head, body, mohair wig, sleep eyes, white christening gown, c. 1894, 18"*	460.00 500.00	475.00
☐ **Bisque,** *ball-jointed body, brown sleep eyes, open mouth with separate tongue, pantaloons and a petticoats, hand embroidered cross-stitched linen dress, original open-work socks and leather shoes, incised 'Handwerck 109/11½ Germany 2½', 21"*	415.00 455.00	425.00

… / HEINRICH HANDWERCK

	Current Price Range		P/Y AVG
☐ **Bisque**, ball jointed body, deep brown threaded sleep eyes, molded brush-stroke brows, red nostril accents, open mouth, four teeth, antique white linen dress with pleated shoulders, jabot, belt and button down cuffs embroidered in lace, feather stitched hemline, incised 109-15½, 31"	900.00	1000.00	925.00
☐ **Bisque**, blonde wig, blue sleep eyes, pierced ears, antique clothes, #69 12 X., 23"	325.00	365.00	330.00
☐ **Bisque**, brown eyes, long brown curls, open mouth, pierced ears, pink low waisted dress, with red print and lace trim, 27"	450.00	550.00	495.00
☐ **Bisque**, head with bisque shoulder plate, fixed eyes, large and very dark, very short painted lashes, open mouth showing three teeth, medium-dark lips, round jaw, dark arched eyebrows, representing a boy of about 4 or 5 years of age, might occasionally be found dressed as a girl, marked HcH and with the mold number 12/0, date of manufacture unknown, probably c. 1900, 14"	175.00	220.00	165.00
☐ **Bisque**, head with bisque shoulder plate, kidskin body, fixed eyes, large, dark, almond shaped, short painted lashes above and below, upturned pug nose, open mouth with a row of upper teeth showing, dimpled chin, dark arched eyebrows, roundish jaw, marked HcH and bearing the mold number 2, date of manufacture unknown, but it would probably be safe to place this doll at c. 1890, 22½"	285.00	340.00	265.00
☐ **Bisque**, head with bisque shoulder plate, fixed eyes, large, dark, not of especially good quality, partially open mouth, flattish nose, thick dark eyebrows, puffy cheeks, very prominent ears turning outward from the head, representing a boy of perhaps 5 or 6 years of age, marked with a four-petaled flower and the letters HcH, also marked Germany, date of manufacture			

	Current Price Range		P/Y AVG

unknown, but the presence of the word "Germany" in the marking places this doll no earlier than 1892, it was probably made about 10 years thereafter, 19½" **240.00 280.00   220.00**

☐ **Bisque,** head with bisque shoulder plate, fixed eyes, large, very short, pale painted lashes, partially open mouth, medium dark lips, thick dark eyebrows, puffy cheeks, roundish jaw, protruding ears, representing a child of 2 or 3 years of age, sometimes dressed as a boy, sometimes as a girl, marked with a horseshoe contained the words Made in Germany, also with the company mark HcH and the mold number 2, date of manufacture unknown but the words "Made in Germany" are a positive indication of post-1892 dating, 22½" **215.00 245.00   200.00**

☐ **Bisque,** head with bisque shoulder plate, fixed eyes, medium large, roundish, short painted lashes above and below, open mouth with teeth showing, pastel lips, thick nose, rather prominent double chin with dimple, dark arched eyebrows, inquisitive facial expression, representing a girl of 4 or 5 years of age, marked HcH, Made in Germany, and with the mold number 9, date of manufacture unknown, but definitely after 1892 and almost certainly, on grounds of style, somewhat after 1900, probably c. 1905, 26" **290.00 335.00   275.00**

☐ **Bisque,** head with bisque shoulder plate, fixed eyes, large, almond shaped, short painted lashes on top of eye socket, much longer painted lashes beneath, open mouth showing teeth, wide nose, thick prominent eyebrows, roundish jaw, prominent ears, marked with the letters HcH and the mold number 5/0, additionally marked with a device which resembles an airplane propeller or a flower with two petals, date of manufacture unknown, but the

	Current Price Range		P/Y AVG
absence of the word "Germany" from the marking would suggest a dating of pre-1892, 17"	230.00	280.00	210.00

MAX HANDWERCK

German firm, whose name translated to English would be "Max's Handcrafts." It was located in Thuringia, a major center for doll manufacture. Max Handwerck went into business around the turn of the century, when the German doll trade was booming (thanks mainly to the enormous sales made to U.S. importers). Most of the dolls of this firm to be found on the antiques market date to the early 1900's.

| ☐ **Bisque,** *jointed composition body, blue eyes, blonde wig, white dress with red trim, 24"* | 400.00 | 450.00 | 440.00 |
| ☐ **Bisque,** *jointed composition body, blue stationary eyes, brown wig, pink dress, lacy hat, 24"* | 350.00 | 400.00 | 360.00 |

LARRY HARMON

| ☐ **Oliver Hardy,** *(finger puppet), vinyl, molded and painted features, marked 1972 Larry Harmon Pictures Corp., 3"* | 1.00 | 1.50 | 1.00 |
| ☐ **Stan Laurel,** *(finger puppet), vinyl, molded and painted features, marked 1972 Larry Harmon Pictures Corp., 3"* | 1.00 | 1.50 | 1.00 |

AILEEN HARRIS

| ☐ **Little Women,** *bisque head, molded and painted hair, dressed to represent a character from the novel by Louisa May Alcott, made in 1963, 9"* | 110.00 | 135.00 | 100.00 |

HAZELLE'S

	Current Price Range		P/Y AVG
☐ **Dagwood**, marionette, plastic head, hands and shoes, cloth over wood body, height 14"	20.00	25.00	22.50

GENE HAZELTON

☐ **Gas Genie**, vinyl mask face, stuffed plush body, molded and painted features, outstretched hands, marked Gas Genie, Gene Hazelton, made in 1969, 21"	4.00	6.00	4.00

HEDAYA

☐ **Love Bug**, vinyl, molded and painted features, painted eyes, oversize head, marked Hedaya & Co., Inc., 1966, Japan, 8"	4.00	6.00	4.00

HEDWIG

☐ **Composition**, character doll Elin from Marguerite de Angeli's book	125.00	175.00	145.00

HUGH M. HEFNER PUBLISHING CO.

☐ **Playboy Bunny**, felt face, stuffed plush body, marked HMH Pub. Co., Inc., made in 1963, 17"	9.00	12.00	8.00

Note: A hand puppet modeled after the famous symbol of Playboy magazine.

HEICO

	Current Price Range		P/Y AVG
☐ **Heico**, vinyl, jointed neck, platinum blonde rooted hair, representing a topless go-go dancer, marked Heico H, made in Western Germany, made in 1963, 7".... **Note: Definitely not one for the kiddies.**	6.00	8.00	6.00

HEUBACH-KÖPPLESDORF

☐ **Baby**, bisque head, five piece composition body, straight redheaded wig, set blue eyes, open mouth, layette gown, toddler shoes and bonnet, 25½"	450.00	500.00	400.00
☐ **Baby**, character, bisque head, composition bent limb baby body, blue sleep eyes, original blonde wig, old christening gown, #342, 23"	550.00	750.00	650.00
☐ **Baby Doll**, unidentified, intaglio eyes, original clothes	440.00	460.00	420.00
☐ **Bisque**, bisque hands, kid body, blue eyes, red mohair wig, open mouth, mold number 275, 18"	225.00	275.00	245.00
☐ **Bisque head**, five piece composition body, glass eyes, open mouth, blond wig, original peasant costume, 6½" ...	100.00	110.00	100.00
☐ **Bisque head**, five piece composition body, open mouth, nice dress with bonnet, #342, 20"	550.00	650.00	600.00
☐ **Bisque**, head with bisque shoulder plate, fitted to a kidskin body, fixed eyes, extremely large and marble-like, and placed close together, long painted lashes on the upper and lower lids, thick arched brows, partially open mouth with teeth visible, medium thick nose, puffy cheeks, round jaw, almost spherical head, representing a girl of 3 or 4 years of age, marked with the number 3095, date of manufacture unknown, on basis of style one would have to imagine that this was among the earlier products of Heubach, dating			

HEUBACH KÖPPLESDORF / 151

| | Current Price Range | P/Y AVG |

possibly to 1890, and the absence of "Made in Germany" from the marking lends support to this, 17¾" 240.00 290.00   225.00

☐ **Bisque,** head, kidskin body, kidskin upper arms, bisque forearms, fixed, large, dark, almond-shaped eyes, painted lashes, more prominent on the lower lids than on the uppers, narrow arched brows, small open mouth with teeth visible, medium-thick nose, not upturned, prominent ears, round jaw, puffy cheeks, representing a boy of about 4 or 5 years of age, marked Made In Germany within a horseshoe, along with the date 1900 and the mold number 6/0, 14⅞" 100.00 130.00 90.00

Note: Slashes in mold numbers, such as in this one, usually indicates plans to issue the doll in more than one size. Such plans were seldom put into action unless the doll sold well.

☐ **Bisque,** fixed eyes, head with bisque shoulder plate, large and bulging, almost resembling marbles, very short painted lashes, thin, slightly arched brows, open mouth showing teeth, medium-wide nose, puffy cheeks, almost spherical head, marked Germany, Heubach Koppelsdorf and with the mold identification number 275/18, date of manufacture unknown, but definitely after 1892 and most likely after 1900, 13½" 120.00 145.00 110.00

Note: One of the standard dolls in the Heubach line, which, to judge from its relative abundance on the market, was kept in production for several years. It probably carried a very low original wholesale price.

☐ **Bisque,** head with bisque shoulder plate, set on a kidskin body, fixed, large, dark, almond-shaped eyes, no lashes, arched brows, small open mouth, showing a row of upper teeth, pastel lips, puffy cheeks, almost spherical head, prominent ears, quizzical

152 / HEUBACH KÖPPLESDORF

	Current Price Range	P/Y AVG

facial expression, representing a youth of 3 or 4 years of age, sometimes dressed as a boy, sometimes as a girl, marked with a horseshoe and the date 1901-1, 22" .... 230.00 270.00 | 215.00

Note: Why is the date given as 1901-1? Possibly this was the first mold to be introduced into the Heubach line that year. Identifying it as 1901-1 would have clearly distinguished it from other #1 molds of earlier years.

☐ **Bisque,** head with bisque shoulder plate, fitted on a kidskin body, fixed, bulging, almond-shaped shaped eyes, very short painted lashes, thick arching brows, open mouth, pastel colored lips, slightly upturned, broad nose, round jaw, facial expression of amazement or wonder, representing a girl of 4 or 5 years of age, marked with the date 1900, and the mold number 0½, 21½" .... 180.00 220.00 | 170.00

☐ **Bisque Shoulder Head,** kid body with gussets at knee, cloth lower legs, bisque hands, blue sleep eyes, open mouth with four porcelain teeth, authentic Sisters of Mercy nun's habit, c. 1890, marks: Made in Germany, incised horseshoe, Hch 5/10, 17" .... 175.00 225.00 | 165.00

☐ **Bisque Shoulder Plate,** cloth and horsehair body, composition lower arms, brown sleep eyes, brown human hair wig, 18" .... 200.00 250.00 | 200.00

☐ **Bisque,** socket head, fixed, medium size, dark, almond-shaped eyes, very wispy short painted lashes, arched brows of conventional style, partially open mouth, teeth visible, pastel lips, round jaw, slight double chin, this doll is normally dressed to represent a woman or young adult, but there is really nothing recognizably adult in the face except the absence of puffy cheeks, marked with horseshoe and the date 1900, and with the mold number 3/0, 14⅞" .... 170.00 210.00 | 155.00

HEUBACH KÖPPLESDORF / 153

	Current Price Range		P/Y AVG

☐ **Bisque,** socket head, fixed, large very prominent, roundish eyes, painted lashes on the upper and lower lids, thin brows, short thick nose, open mouth with teeth visible, bright red lips, double chin, dimpled, puffy cheeks, representing a girl of about 2 or 3 years of age but sometimes dressed in the clothing of an older child, marked Heubach Koppelsdorf and with the mold number 300-9/0, date of manufacture unknown, believed to have been made in the late 1890's or opening years of the 20th century, 12" . 170.00 200.00 160.00

☐ **Bisque Socket Head,** fully jointed composition body, blue sleep eyes, brown human hair wig, open mouth with four teeth, pink silk dress, white brocade cuffs, bib front, ribbon rosettes, matching lined bonnet, original ½" mold split in rear of head at crown, marks: Heubach 250.3 Koppelsdorf Germany, 24" 320.00 370.00 325.00

☐ **Bisque,** socket head, very large, roundish sleep eyes, painted lashes, prominent eyelids, thick dark arched brows, partially open mouth showing three upper teeth, very dark red lips, thick lower lip, moderately broad nose, cheeks slightly puffy, ears somewhat prominent, the most recognizable characteristic of this doll is a set of lines leading downward from the lip corners, flirtatious facial expression, found dressed as a child or adult, marked Heubach Koppelsdorf, and with the mold number 250-4/0, date of manufacture unknown, 16" 170.00 210.00 165.00

☐ **Bisque,** socket head, large, dark, fixed eyes, painted lashes, lashes longer on the lower lid than on the upper, heavy arched brows set close together, small open mouth with teeth showing and pastel colored lips, narrow nose slightly upturned, pierced ears, puffy cheeks, double chin, round jaw, usually dressed to

	Current Price Range		P/Y AVG
represent an adult woman, marked Dep-1900.6, 24"	230.00	280.00	225.00

Note: The numeral "6" following the date is a mold number which probably meant that this was the 6th mold introduced by Heubach during 1900.

HIGHBROW

☐ China Doll, black painted hair, blue painted eyes, rose silk violet dress, 13"	200.00	225.00	210.00

HILL

☐ Movie Queen Natalie, vinyl, sleep eyes, jointed at the waist, marked Made in U.S.A., made in 1959, 21¼"	17.00	23.00	16.00

Note: This doll was not intended to represent Natalie Wood or any movie star in particular.

HOLIDAY FAIR

☐ Holly, cloth, stuffed, painted features, blonde yarn hair, pigtails, double-faced doll, each side of head has its own face, unmarked, sold originally with a tag reading Holiday Fair, N.Y.C., 1971, made in Japan, 19"	5.00	7.00	5.00
☐ Luva Girl, plastic/vinyl, painted eyes, marked Made in Hong Kong, c. 1973, 6".	7.00	10.00	6.00

Note: Definitely inspired by the "trolls" of Thomas Dam of Denmark.

☐ Terry, plastic/vinyl, rooted hair, marked Holiday Fair, Inc., Made in Hong Kong, c. 1973, 9"	3.50	5.00	3.00

HOLLYWOOD DOLL COMPANY

	Current Price Range		P/Y AVG
☐ **Bonnie Blue Bell**, composition head and body, molded and painted features, blonde hair attached by adhesive, marked Hollywood Doll, made in c. 1947, 9½"	9.00	12.00	8.00
☐ **Composition head**, composition arms, legs and body, swivel head, molded and painted hair, painted eyes, closed mouth, dark red lips, jointed at the shoulders and thighs, definitely an "oldie," probably from the mid 1930's, 7"	11.00	15.00	10.00
☐ **Cowgirl**, composition, wears button and gun, 9"	30.00	40.00	34.00
☐ **Hollywood Baby**, plastic, molded and painted hair, blue sleep eyes, jointed, marked Hollywood Doll, date of manufacture unknown, 4½"	11.00	14.00	10.00
☐ **Little Miss Muffet**, composition head and body, molded and painted features, black hair attached by adhesive, wears sunflower-print dress, marked Hollywood Doll, made in 1945, 9"	9.00	12.00	8.00
☐ **Masquerade**, composition head and body, molded and painted features, blonde hair attached by adhesive, marked Hollywood Doll, date of manufacture unknown, believed to be c. 1946, 9½" ...	9.00	12.00	8.00
☐ **Red Riding Hood**, composition head and body, molded and painted features, blonde hair attached by adhesive, unmarked, made in 1946, 9½"	9.00	12.00	8.00

Note: The basic doll used for Red Riding Hood was one that served for a number of the Hollywood dolls including Masquerade and Bonnie Blue Bell. This company issued a great variety of dolls but the changes were mostly in their clothing and props.

HUMMEL

	Current Price Range		P/Y AVG
☐ **Boy,** *rubber, felt clothes, marked, 12"* ..	120.00	150.00	125.00
☐ **Boy,** *rubber, molded brown hair, felt jacket, pants, white shirt, flowered tie, made in Germany, c.1950's, 11"*	115.00	145.00	120.00
☐ **Hansel,** *12"*	50.00	60.00	55.00
☐ **Radi-Bub,** *12"*	50.00	60.00	55.00

HUNGERFORD

☐ **Baby Wet,** *plastic head ("Lastic Plastic"), plastic legs, vinyl arms, vinyl body, nursing mouth, wears checked gown with ruffled neck, dated 1956, 15"*	4.00	5.00	4.00
☐ **Baby Rosie Posie,** *vinyl, molded and painted hair (blonde), sleep eyes (blue), nursing mouth, pug nose, marked Hungerford, made in 1954, 16"*	29.00	37.00	27.00

IDEAL

☐ **Andy Gibb,** *limited issue, c. 1979, 8"* ...	55.00	65.00	58.00
☐ **Baby,** *jointed vinyl, blonde rooted hair, blue sleep eyes, open mouth nurser, antique white gown with tatted trim, 8½"*	12.00	15.00	12.00
☐ **Baby,** *vinyl head, cloth bodied, rooted blond hair, pull string in back and baby wiggles and clutches blanket in arms, pink pajamas, 14"*	13.00	18.00	14.00
☐ **Baby, Baby,** *vinyl, rooted hair (blonde), fixed eyes (blue), nursing mouth, marked 115 Ideal, made in Hong Kong in 1974, 7"*	7.00	10.00	6.00
☐ **Baby Belly Button,** *black, vinyl, black hair (rooted), painted features, brown eyes, smiling closed mouth, in the likeness of an infant, Baby Belly Button has a knob at its stomach which, when turned, makes the arms, legs and head move, dressed in a diaper and white lace-edged smock, marked Ideal Toy*			

	Current Price Range		P/Y AVG
Corp., E9-2-H-165, made in Hong Kong in 1970, 9"	5.50	7.00	5.00
☐ **Baby Big Eyes,** vinyl, blonde hair (rooted), sleep eyes (blue), closed mouth, marked Ideal Doll, made in 1954, 21"	45.00	56.00	42.00
☐ **Baby Flatsy,** vinyl, rooted hair (blonde), ribbon in hair, wears scallop-edged bib, long pants, marked Ideal, 1969, Pat. Pend.	2.75	3.75	2.50

Note: Ideal's "Flatsy Family" included a number of different dolls, sold originally in 1969 and 1970. Some came with elaborate props, which are worth more than the dolls.

☐ **Baby Gurglee,** plastic head, latex arms and legs, latex body, jointed arms, sleep eyes, molded and painted hair, squeeze-activity voice, 19"	11.00	15.00	10.00

Note: Baby Gurglee (the squeeze-voice was intended to represent a gurgle) was marketed in 1951. The identical doll was placed on the market again in 1953, under the name "Touslehead."

☐ **Baby Jo,** plastic, molded and painted hair, sleep eyes (blue), pug nose, closed mouth, holes in nostrils, marked Ideal Doll, Made in U.S.A., 22, made in 1955, 22"	25.00	31.00	23.00
☐ **Baby June,** vinyl, brunette hair (rooted), sleep eyes (blue), marked Ideal Doll VS-15-2, made in 1956, 15"	67.00	82.00	65.00
☐ **Baby Snooks,** composition head, body, feet, cable arms and legs, molded hair, large smiling mouth, painted features, modeled after Fanny Brice, cotton print dress, large bow in hair, marked "IDEAL," 12"	185.00	215.00	200.00
☐ **Baby Snookie,** vinyl head, latex body, molded, painted hair, painted eyes, closed mouth, fingers spaced wide apart, wears diaper with safety pin (no other clothing), made in 1950, 9"	5.00	7.00	5.00

	Current Price Range		P/Y AVG

Note: Obviously inspired (in name at least) from the Fanny Brice character, Baby Snooks.

☐ **Bam Bam,** vinyl, blonde hair (rooted), molded and painted features, painted eyes, Bam Bam is a character in the comic strip "The Flintstones" by Hanna and Barbera, marked Hanna Barbera Products, Inc., BB-17, made in 1963, 15½" 12.00 16.00 11.00

☐ **Betsey Wetsey,** plastic head, vinyl body, sheep's hair wig, blue sleep eyes, lashes, long pink gown, plastic cradle, 14" 75.00 100.00 79.00

☐ **Betsey Wetsey,** plastic head, vinyl body, deep eyes, bent leg, ruffled sun-suit, 14" ... 15.00 20.00 16.00

☐ **Betsey Wetsey,** soft plastic, moulded hair, 1953, 13" 16.00 21.00 15.00

☐ **Black Velvet,** vinyl head, hard body, jointed shoulders, waist and hips, rooted black hair, smiling mouth, pull string in back that makes her twist and look around, in red and green plaid dress, blue shoes, 1972, 15" 63.00 68.00 63.00

☐ **Bonnie Braids,** plastic/vinyl, reddish hair (rooted), sleep eyes (blue), open mouth with teeth, the name Bonnie Braids is adapted from a line in a ballad by 18th century Scottish poet Robert Burns, marked 1951 Chicago Tribune, 13" 34.00 43.00 32.00

☐ **Bonnie Walker,** walker, plastic, sleep eyes blue, open mouth with teeth, bright red lips, marked Ideal Doll W16, 17" 23.00 28.00 21.00

☐ **Brandi,** (sometimes spelled Brandy in dealers' lists, but incorrectly), vinyl, painted features, rooted hair (blonde), hair has "grow" feature (portion of wig is fitted inside head; when hair is pulled gently, it gives the appearance of "growing" out of the scalp), wearing a silky sleeveless gown with scooped neck, eyelet holes at the front, swivel

	Current Price Range		P/Y AVG
waist, marked Ideal Toy Corp., GHB-18-H-185, made in Hong Kong in 1971	13.00	16.00	12.00
☐ **Busy Lizy**, plastic/vinyl, sleep eyes (blue), rooted hair (platinum blonde), pug nose, closed smiling mouth, wears dress with floral-printed cape, marked Ideal Toy Corp. HK-18, dated 1970 on the head and 1971 on the body, 17"	26.00	32.00	25.00
☐ **Casey Flatsy**, vinyl, painted features, molded and painted hair (red), large eyes, smiling face, dressed as a railroad motorman, marked Ideal, 1969, Pat. Pending, made in Hong Kong	2.75	3.75	2.50
☐ **Carol Brent**, vinyl, marked Ideal Toy Corp., M-15-L, made in 1961 for the Montgomery Ward chain, "Carol Brent" was the name used by Ward's for one of its lines of female apparel, 15"	28.00	35.00	25.00
☐ **Charlotte**, Victorian Lady, c. 1983, 12"	15.00	20.00	16.00
☐ **Cinnamon**, plastic/vinyl, painted eyes (blue), open smiling mouth showing teeth, rooted hair (red), hair has "grow" feature (portion of wig is fitted inside head; when hair is gently pulled, it gives the appearance of "growing" out of the scalp), wears short lacy dress, ribbon at front, marked Ideal Toy Corp., GH-12-H-183, 12¼"	8.00	10.00	7.00
☐ **Composition Head**, cloth body, painted eyes, diamond mark on back, c. 1910, 19"	60.00	65.00	62.50
☐ **Constance**, Victorian Lady, c. 1983, 8"	6.00	14.00	7.00
☐ **Constance**, Victorian Lady, c. 1983, 12"	15.00	20.00	16.00
☐ **Cousin Sue**, vinyl head, cloth body, vinyl arms and legs, sleep eyes (blue), unmarked, made in 1957, 17½"	22.00	27.00	20.00
☐ **Cricket**, plastic/vinyl, sleep eyes (brown), open smiling mouth, red hair (rooted), hair has "grow" feature (portion of wig is fitted inside head; when hair is pulled gently, it gives the ap ance of "growing" out of the scalp), wears checked dress with ruffled collar			

160 / IDEAL

	Current Price Range		P/Y AVG
and armholes, jointed at the waist, marked Ideal Toy Corp., CR-15-H-177, made in Hong Kong in 1970, 15¼"	8.00	10.00	7.00

Composition, c. 1910, 19" $60.00-$65.00

☐ **Creampuff,** vinyl, red hair (rooted), sleep eyes (blue), ribbons in hair, marked Ideal Doll OB-19-2, made in 1961, 18" ...	26.00	34.00	25.00
☐ **Crissy,** talking	20.00	25.00	21.00
☐ **Crissy,** vinyl head, hard body, jointed shoulders, waist and hips, blue satin short dress, panties to match, 18"	30.00	36.00	32.00

	Current Price Range		P/Y AVG
☐ **Crissy,** vinyl head, hard body, jointed shoulders, waist and hips, rooted hair, smiling mouth, green and red plaid long dress, panties, matching shoes	35.00	40.00	35.00
☐ **Crissy,** vinyl head, hard body, jointed shoulders, waist and hips, rooted hair, smiling mouth, orange lace dress, panties, orange shoes, 18"	32.00	42.00	38.00
☐ **Crissy,** vinyl head, hard body, jointed shoulders, waist and hips, rooted hair, smiling mouth, pink fancy nightgown with matching panties, #8135-6, 18"	38.00	46.00	40.00
☐ **Crissy,** vinyl head, hard body, jointed shoulders, waist and hips, rooted hair, smiling lips, yellow pajama outfit, quilted yellow short top and matching yellow long pants with lace trim, 18"	32.00	36.00	32.00
☐ **Cuddly Kissy,** vinyl head, cloth body, vinyl arms and legs, blonde hair, marked Ideal Toy Corp., KB-17E, made in 1964, 16½"	45.00	57.00	42.00
☐ **Deanna Durbin,** all composition jointed at neck, shoulder and hips, green sleep eyes accented with eye shadow, brown human hair wig, smiling mouth with porcelain upper teeth, original blue taffeta ball gown accented with yellow ruffles at hem and neckline, original organdy hoop petticoat, marked Deanna Durbin-Ideal Doll, 24"	425.00	475.00	400.00
☐ **Deanna Durbin,** composition head, jointed composition body, sleep eyes, blue full length dress, c. 1950, 21"	200.00	225.00	215.00
☐ **Deanna Durbin,** jointed at waist, poses, marked Durbin, Ideal, U.S.A., 21"	200.00	250.00	210.00
☐ **Dew Drop,** plastic/vinyl, brunette hair (rooted), sleep eyes (blue), nursing mouth, crier, marked V-S-22, made in 1961, 20"	11.00	14.00	10.00
☐ **Diana Ross,** character, 1969 black doll, all vinyl jointed, black rooted hair, black sleep eyes, open smiling mouth with teeth, long gold evening dress with pink boa trim, hair net, 19"	155.00	175.00	155.00
☐ **Dina,** lacy green dress	40.00	50.00	42.00

162 / IDEAL

	Current Price Range		P/Y AVG

- **Dodi**, *plastic/vinyl, rooted hair (brownish blond), painted eyes, open smiling mouth with teeth, two eyelashes drawn outward at the outer corner of each eye ("Cleopatra" style — popular when this doll was made in 1964), marked DO-9-E, 9"* 9.00 11.00 8.00
- **Dracky, Mini Monster**, *plastic/vinyl, molded and painted features, molded and painted hair, designed as a youthful Dracula, marked 1965 Ideal Toy Corp., made in Japan, 8½"* 14.00 19.00 12.00
- **Dr. Evil**, *plastic, adult male model with various face changes (masks), sold in a box marked Ideal Toy Corp., and dated 1965, 11"* 9.00 12.00 8.00
  Note: The stated value is for the doll plus box and accessories.
- **Emma**, *Victorian Lady, c. 1983, 8"* 6.00 14.00 7.00
- **Emma**, *Victorian Lady, c. 1983, 12"* 15.00 20.00 16.00
- **Eric**, *plastic/vinyl, molded and painted features, molded and painted hair, model of young adult, marked 1976 Ideal, made in Hong Kong, 12"* 13.00 17.00 12.00
- **Evel Knievel**, *vinyl, posable, molded and painted hair, painted features, sold with three outfits and various props, representing the daredevil motorcycle stuntman, marked 1972 Ideal, made in Hong Kong*
  Value with all original accessories 7.00 10.00 6.00
  Doll with one outfit, no props 4.00 6.00 4.00
- **Fannie Brice**, *composition head, stuffed wire-encased body, composition hands and feet, molded and painted features, molded and painted hair, Fannie Brice was a star of Ziegfeld's Follies and radio, made in 1939, 13"* 200.00 265.00 185.00
- **Flatsy Family**, *this series of dolls was placed on the market in 1970. Having run their course in the shops, they are now attracting some collector interest.*

	Current Price Range		P/Y AVG

Each Flatsy doll was of very small size, under 5" (some were under 3"), and came boxed with a whole array of scenery and props. For example, Cookie Flatsy (a cook) came with her own kitchen. In general, prices for the dolls by themselves are currently in the $2.75 to $3.75 range. When found with the original accessories, their values are much higher, up to $8.00 to $10.00

☐ **Franky, Mini Monster,** plastic/vinyl, molded and painted features, molded and painted hair, designed as a youthful Frankenstein's monster, marked 1965 Ideal Toy Corp., made in Japan, 8¾" ..   14.00   19.00   13.00

☐ **Flexy Soldier,** composition over wire (posable) with wooden feet, marked Ideal Doll, believed to have been made c. 1944, 13" 50.00   62.00   48.00

☐ **Giggle Toddler,** plastic/vinyl, blonde hair cut in bangs, painted eyes, giggles when arms are extended, marked Ideal Toy Corp., GG18-H77-1967, 18" 36.00   45.00   35.00

☐ **Ginger,** composition, rooted hair, sleep eyes (brown), open mouth with teeth, bright red lips, marked with an X inside a circle, made from a Shirley Temple mold, made in 1939, 15" 65.00   80.00   60.00

☐ **Goody Two-Shoes,** walker, plastic/vinyl, blonde hair (rooted), sleep eyes (blue), marked 1965 Ideal Toy Corp., WT18, Pat. Pending, 18" 36.00   45.00   35.00

Note: The name "Goody Two-Shoes" was created for a character in a play by Oliver Goldsmith in the 18th century.

☐ **Grown-Up Tammy,** plastic/vinyl, rooted hair (blonde), painted eyes, closed mouth, bright red lips, wears heels, intended as a young-adult version of the popular Tammy doll, marked T-12-E, 11½" 9.00   11.00   8.00

☐ **Harriet Hubbard Ayer,** makeup doll, makeup kit and beauty table, 19" 150.00   200.00   170.00

164 / IDEAL

	Current Price Range		P/Y AVG

- ☐ **Honeyball,** vinyl, rooted hair (brunette), painted eyes, marked 1966 Ideal Toy Corp., M9-H4, 9½" 6.00 8.00 5.00
- ☐ **Honeysuckle,** vinyl, brunette hair (rooted), sleep eyes (blue), pug nose, marked Ideal Doll, made in 1955, 20" .. 28.00 35.00 25.00
- ☐ **Howdy Doody,** plastic, cloth body, molded and painted hair, sleep eyes (blue), puppet with movable mouth, based on the TV character, marked Ideal Doll, made in 1950, 20" 75.00 95.00 70.00
- ☐ **Huggee Girl,** vinyl head, oilcloth body (stuffed), sleep eyes (blue), molded and painted hair, marked Ideal Doll BC16, 1952, 15" 18.00 23.00 17.00
- ☐ **Illya Kuryakin,** plastic/vinyl, molded and painted features, molded and painted hair, Illya Kuryakin was a character on the TV series "The Man from U.N.C.L.E.", the doll is designed to resemble the actor David McCallum, marked K-99, made in 1965, 12" 57.00 73.00 55.00
- ☐ **007 James Bond,** plastic/vinyl, molded and, painted features, molded and painted hair, James Bond is a fictional detective created by Ian Fleming, this doll is made to resemble Sean Connery, who was the first actor to portray James Bond in films, marked Ideal Toy Corp., B-12½-2, made in 1965, 12" 65.00 85.00 62.00
- ☐ **Joan Palooka,** vinyl head, latex body, sleep eyes, molded, painted hair, jointed arms, intended as a female counterpart of Joe Palooka, the heavyweight boxing champion of the comic strips, marked 1952, Ham Fisher, Ideal Doll, Ham Fisher was creator of the Joe Palooka character, 14" 20.00 25.00 18.00
- ☐ **Joey Stivic,** vinyl, blonde hair, sexed .. 15.00 20.00 16.00
- ☐ **Judy Garland,** composition head, composition arms, legs and body, sleep eyes, open mouth, bright red lips, represents Judy Garland in the role of

IDEAL / 165

	Current Price Range		P/Y AVG

Dorothy in "The Wizard of Oz.," marked Ideal doll, mold number 18, dated 1939, 17½"	120.00	150.00	110.00

Note: Has human hair wig attached by adhesive. Not a very successful resemblance to Judy Garland, this is nevertheless a very collectible doll.

☐ Judy Splinters, vinyl head, cloth body, latex limbs, marked Ideal Doll, 1951, 18"	45.00	58.00	42.00
☐ Katie Kachoo, sneezer, vinyl, marked 1968, Ideal Toy Corp., SN-17EH37, Katie sneezes when you raise her arms, 16½"	28.00	34.00	25.00
☐ Kerry, plastic/vinyl, blonde hair (rooted), hair has "grow" feature (portion of wig is fitted inside head; when hair is pulled gently, it gives the appearance of "growing" out of the scalp), sleep eyes (blue), partially open mouth, marked 13 EYE, 1970, Ideal Toy Corp, NGH-18, 18"	8.00	10.00	7.00

Note: Kerry was patented in 1960 but did not get on the market until the following year.

☐ Kissy, 16"	30.00	40.00	32.00
☐ Lemonade Flatsy (boy version), vinyl, painted eyes (brown), molded and painted hair (blonde), dressed as a snack vendor, wearing a chef's hat reading "15¢," and a jacket picturing a frankfurter and reading "Dogs," bendable, 2½"	2.00	3.00	2.00
☐ Liberty Boy, World War I uniform, moveable head, arms and legs, 12"	80.00	90.00	82.00
☐ Lindy, plastic, molded and painted hair, sleep eyes, closed mouth, bright red lips, unmarked, made in 1956, 8"	5.00	7.00	5.00
☐ Little Princess (Shirley Temple), composition head, composition arms, legs and body, blonde hair attached with adhesive, open mouth, bright red lips, marked Shirley Temple 18, 18"	80.00	100.00	75.00
☐ Look Around Velvet, plastic/vinyl, sleep eyes (violet blue), long lashes, blonde rooted hair, hair has "grow" feature (portion of wig is fitted inside head;			

	Current Price Range		P/Y AVG
when hair is pulled gently, it gives the appearance of "growing" out of the scalp), wears a brightly colored print dress, head turns by pulling a string, marked Ideal Toy Corp. GH 15-H-157, made in Hong Kong	8.00	10.00	7.00

Note: This doll, designed in 1969, was the "action" version of Ideal's standard Velvet doll.

	Current Price Range		P/Y AVG
☐ **Lydia,** Victorian Lady, c. 1983, 8"	6.00	14.00	7.00
☐ **Lydia,** Victorian Lady, c. 1983, 12"	15.00	20.00	16.00
☐ **Magic Lips,** vinyl head, vinyl over cloth body, vinyl arms and legs, open mouth (which closes by pressing a button, similar to the action of a ventriloquist dummy), marked Ideal Doll T25, made in 1955, 24"	60.00	78.00	55.00
☐ **Magic Skin Baby,** composition head, otherwise made entirely of latex, sleep eyes, molded, painted hair, fully jointed, nursing mouth, made in 1941, 14½" ...	8.00	10.00	7.00
☐ **Magic Squeezums,** plastic head, latex body, sleep eyes, marked Ideal Doll, Made in U.S.A., 1950, 29"	30.00	38.00	28.00
☐ **Marilyn Knowlden,** composition, red hair, sleep eyes (blue), closed mouth, bright red lips, Marilyn Knowlden was a child actress of the 1930's, at the time when every movie studio was trying to get "another" Shirley Temple, marked USA-13, made in 1936, 13"	140.00	170.00	130.00
☐ **Mary Hartline,** plastic head, plastic arms, legs and body, wig attached with adhesive, sleep eyes, skirt has pattern of musical notes, wears boots with tassles, has mold number P91, dated 1952, 15"	30.00	38.00	28.00
☐ **Mary Jane,** composition head and body, blonde hair (wig), marked Ideal 18, believed to have been made c. 1944, 17½"	70.00	85.00	68.00
☐ **Mia,** plastic/vinyl, sleep eyes (blue), black eyelashes, dark brown rooted hair, hair has "grow" feature (portion of wig is fitted inside head; when hair is			

	Current Price Range		P/Y AVG
pulled gently, it gives the appearance of "growing" out of the scalp), striped dress with frilly collar, open mouth, showing teeth, marked Ideal Toy Corp., NGH-15-H173, made in 1970, 15¼"	8.00	10.00	7.00
☐ **Mia,** vinyl head, hard body, jointed shoulders, waist and hips, brown rooted grow hair, blue sleep eyes, smiling mouth, long white dress, 15"	32.00	36.00	32.00
☐ **Mia,** velvet outfit	20.00	30.00	21.00
☐ **Mini-Flatsy Clock,** two dolls with horse and cart, mint in box, 3"	15.00	20.00	16.00
☐ **Mini Monster,** plastic/vinyl, two-tone molded hair (grey and black), marked 1966, Ideal Toy Corp., a little girl with a ghoulish face, and a ghost printed on her dress, the dress was made in Japan, 9"	9.00	12.00	8.00
☐ **Miss Deb Of 1942,** composition head and body, blonde hair attached with adhesive, sleep eyes (brown), open mouth with teeth, bright red lips, marked 18, probably put on sale for the Christmas season of 1941, 18"	30.00	38.00	28.00
☐ **Miss Revlon,** vinyl, brunette hair (rooted), sleep eyes (blue), wears high heels, representing the symbol of the Revlon Cosmetics Co., marked Ideal Doll VT-18, made in 1956, 17"	29.00	37.00	26.00
☐ **Miss Revlon,** yellow striped cotton dress, c. 1955, 20"	30.00	40.00	32.00
☐ **Mortimer Snerd,** composition, stuffed wire-encased body, composition hands and feet, molded and painted features, molded and painted hair, Mortimer Snerd was a character on the Edgar Bergen radio program, the original was a ventriloquist's dummy but this doll is a play-doll only, made in 1939, 13"	140.00	170.00	130.00
☐ **Munchie Flatsy,** green hair, orange dotted outfit	5.00	10.00	6.00
☐ **Munchie Time Flatsy,** boy and girl with hot dog cart	15.00	20.00	16.00

168 / IDEAL

	Current Price Range		P/Y AVG
☐ **New Tiny Tears,** vinyl, fixed eyes (blue), long lashes, rooted hair (blonde), puckered lips with nursing mouth, comes with nursing bottle, doll is designed in such a manner that it drinks from the nursing bottle when held upright, when lying down, the water from the bottle enters the doll through its right arm and becomes "tears," flowing out at the eyes, dressed in a paper diaper, marked Ideal Toy Corp., TNT-14-B-34, made in 1971	5.50	7.00	5.00
☐ **Patience,** Victorian Lady, c. 1983, 8"	6.00	14.00	7.00
☐ **Patience,** Victorian Lady, c. 1983, 12"	15.00	20.00	16.00
☐ **Patty Playful,** vinyl head and limbs, cloth body, white rooted hair, black pupilless sleep eyes, wide open mouth, two teeth, hand operated unit control in back clothing is body, pink pajamas, 16"	20.00	25.00	20.00
☐ **Patti Playful,**	20.00	30.00	21.00
☐ **Patti Play Pal,** black, c. 1982, 36"	25.00	35.00	26.00
☐ **Pebbles,**	12.00	17.00	15.00
☐ **Penny Playpal,** plastic/vinyl, red hair (rooted), sleep eyes (blue), marked Ideal Doll B-32-B, made in 1959, 32"	65.00	79.00	60.00
☐ **Pepper,** plastic/vinyl, rooted hair (blonde), painted eyes, partially open mouth, freckled cheeks, wears short dress with belt and matching collar, marked P9-3, 9"	6.00	8.00	5.00
☐ **Pinocchio,** composition head and body, wooden arms and legs, molded and painted hair, painted clothing, marked Ideal, originally sold with a tag reading Pinocchio, Des. & Copyright by Walt Disney, made in 1940, 11"	90.00	110.00	85.00
☐ **Pinocchio,** wood and composition, socket head, molded yellow cap, brown tufts of hair, long nose, painted features, white sail cloth collar with bow tie, painted molded clothing, fully jointed swivel waist, stick arms and legs, stenciled on front, Pinocchio, Des,			

	Current Price Range		P/Y AVG
& C. By Walt Disney, Made by Ideal Novelty & Toy Co., stenciled on back of head, Ideal Doll, USA, 7½"	150.00	200.00	140.00
☐ **Plassie**, composition/plastic, blonde wig attached with adhesive, sleep eyes (blue), marked P50, Ideal, Made in U.S.A., made in 1948, 17"	24.00	29.00	22.00

Note: Ideal did more experimenting with doll materials in the 1940's than any other company. Plassie did not get her name by accident: she had a hard molded plastic head, but her arms and legs were made of standard composition. Ideal wanted to test the use of these substances in conjunction with each other. In that same year, 1948, Ideal was also experimenting with "magic skin" vinyl-plastic.

☐ **Posie**, walker, plastic/vinyl, sleep eyes (blue), closed mouth, bright red lips, marked Ideal Doll VP17, made in 1954, 17"	28.00	34.00	25.00
☐ **Posie**, vinyl head, plastic arms, legs and body, rooted hair, small sleep eyes, closed mouth, wears short smock-type gown, marked Ideal Doll VP23, not dated, apparently made in early 1950's, called Posie because the doll was fully bendable, 23"	24.00	29.00	21.00
☐ **Pos'n Pete**, plastic/vinyl, molded hair (short, combed down in front), painted eyes, jointed at shoulders and thighs, marked P-8 and dated 1964, 7½"	9.00	11.00	8.00

Note: A posable doll.

☐ **Raggedy Ann, Andy**, porcelain, c. 1983, pair	450.00	550.00	480.00
☐ **Real Live Lucy**, baby, jointed vinyl body, head moves gently when lightly touched, rooted near white hair, blue sleep eyes, open rosebud mouth, fancy blue dress, lots of white lace trim matching underwear and booties, blue ribbon bow in hair, 21"	55.00	65.00	55.00

170 / IDEAL

	Current Price Range		P/Y AVG
☐ **Real Live Lucy,** baby, jointed vinyl body, head moves gently when lightly touched, rooted near white hair, blue sleep eyes, open mouth with two teeth, red dress trimmed in white lace, buttons, rick-rack and braid, red bow in hair, 21"	55.00	65.00	60.00
☐ **Rock Baby Coos,** vinyl head, cloth body, rooted hair (short brownish blond), sleep eyes, wide open mouth (not nursing), wears flannel gown and terry bonnet, marked YTT-19-L-5, 20½"	7.00	9.00	6.00
☐ **Rub-A-Dub Dollie,** all vinyl jointed baby, blond rooted hair, painted blue eyes, pink and white flannel pajamas, 15"	8.00	11.00	8.00
☐ **Rub-A-Dub,** black	20.00	30.00	21.00
☐ **Sandy McCall,** marked McCall Corp., 1959, 36"	110.00	140.00	100.00
☐ **Saucy Walker,** hard plastic, blonde wig, blue sleep flirty eyes, open mouth, two teeth, floating tongue, blue dress, satin collar, blue lace trimmed blue panties with lace and bow, blue bonnet with lace trim, long white stockings, white leather shoes, marked on head, Ideal Doll WR-16, back, Ideal Doll, W-18, 17"	75.00	95.00	75.00
☐ **Saucy Walker,** hard plastic head, jointed walking body, sleep eyes, green and white gingham dress, c. 1950, 20"	35.00	40.00	37.50
☐ **Saucy Walter,** hard plastic, googly eyes, crier, 22"	30.00	40.00	33.00
☐ **Saucy Walker,** plastic head, plastic arms, legs and body, long blonde hair, sleep eyes, open mouth, bright red lips, ribboned hair, silk ribbons on dress, 22"	20.00	25.00	20.00
☐ **Shirley Temple,** Captain January, c.1982, 8"	20.00	25.00	21.00
☐ **Shirley Temple,** Heidi, c.1982, 8"	20.00	25.00	22.00
☐ **Shirley Temple,** Heidi, c.1982, 12"	30.00	40.00	32.00
☐ **Shirley Temple,** Little Colonel, c.1982, 8"	20.00	25.00	21.00
☐ **Shirley Temple,** Little Colonel, c.1982, 12"	30.00	40.00	32.00
☐ **Shirley Temple,** Little Miss Marker, c.1983, 8"	10.00	15.00	11.00

Saucy Walker, hard plastic, c. 1950, 20" **$35.00-$40.00**

	Current Price Range		P/Y AVG
☐ Shirley Temple, *Little Miss Marker,* c.1983, 12"	15.00	20.00	16.00
☐ Shirley Temple, *Littlest Rebel, c.1982, 8"*	20.00	25.00	21.00
☐ Shirley Temple, *Poor Little Rich Girl,* c.1983, 8"	10.00	15.00	11.00
☐ Shirley Temple, *Poor Little Rich Girl,* c.1983, 12"	15.00	20.00	16.00
☐ Shirley Temple, *Rebecca of Sunnybrook Farm, c.1983, 8"*	10.00	15.00	11.00
☐ Shirley Temple, *Rebecca of Sunnybrook Farm, c.1983, 12"*	15.00	20.00	16.00

172 / IDEAL

	Current Price Range		P/Y AVG
☐ Shirley Temple, *Stand Up and Cheer*, c.1982, 8"	20.00	25.00	21.00
☐ Shirley Temple, *Stowaway*, c.1982, 8"	20.00	25.00	21.00
☐ Shirley Temple, *Stowaway*, c.1982, 12"	30.00	40.00	32.00
☐ Shirley Temple, *Susannah of the Mounties*, c.1983, 8"	10.00	15.00	11.00
☐ Shirley Temple, *Susannah of the Mounties*, c.1983, 12"	15.00	20.00	16.00
☐ Shirley Temple, *Wee Willie Winkle*, c.1983, 8"	10.00	15.00	11.00
☐ Shirley Temple, *Wee Willie Winkle*, c.1983, 12"	15.00	20.00	16.00
☐ Shirley Temple, *all composition, 27"*	295.00	360.00	280.00
☐ Shirley Temple, *all composition, 25"*	170.00	205.00	160.00
☐ Shirley Temple, *all composition, 23"*	150.00	185.00	140.00
☐ Shirley Temple, *all composition, 18"*	120.00	145.00	110.00
☐ Shirley Temple, *all composition, 17"*	115.00	140.00	105.00
☐ Shirley Temple, *all composition, 16"*	112.00	135.00	100.00
☐ Shirley Temple, *all composition, 15"*	110.00	130.00	98.00
☐ Shirley Temple, *all composition, 13"*	65.00	80.00	60.00
☐ Shirley Temple, *all composition, 11"*	160.00	190.00	150.00
☐ Shirley Temple, *all composition, jointed, blonde curly mohair wig, brown sleep eyes, open mouth, six teeth, Heidi style dress and pinafore not original, c. 1938, marked on head and body: 13 SHIRLEY TEMPLE, 22"*	525.00	575.00	530.00
☐ Shirley Temple, *all composition jointed neck, shoulders and hips, green sleep eyes, open smiling mouth, original full blonde mohair wig styled in ringlets, original red and white polka kot dress, marked: Original Shirley Temple dress tag; head and body signed Shirley Temple, 25"*	725.00	775.00	700.00
☐ Shirley Temple, *character, vinyl head, plastic body, jointed shoulders and hips, rooted hair painted eyes, smiling mouth, red-polka dot dress, original, mint, 16"*	70.00	80.00	70.00
☐ Shirley Temple, *composition, curly top, Shirley pin, polka dotted red and white dress, c. 1935, 22"*	550.00	650.00	556.00

	Current Price Range		P/Y AVG
☐ **Shirley Temple,** *composition, jointed body, glazed eyes, blonde wig, open smiling mouth, original clothes, marked on head and body: 13 SHIRLEY TEMPLE, 13"*	450.00	550.00	475.00
☐ **Shirley Temple,** *composition, jointed body, glazed eyes, blonde wig, open smiling mouth, original clothes, marked on head and body: 13 SHIRLEY TEMPLE, 25"*	700.00	800.00	750.00
☐ **Shirley Temple,** *composition, pink organdy dress, snap dress, 15"*	275.00	325.00	290.00
☐ **Shirley Temple,** *original, ruffled lace dress, 22"*	495.00	650.00	495.00
☐ **Shirley Temple,** *vinyl and hard plastic jointed neck, shoulders and hips, rooted blonde hair, green sleep eyes, smiling mouth with four porcelain teeth, dimples, original mint condition, petite 1957 model with complete wardrobe, all clothing tagged Shirley Temple, flannel nightgown with cap, pink ballet dress, two piece plaid dress with cap, Swiss dirndl, sunglasses and Shirley Temple pin and purse, wearing a pale yellow organdy dress, marked: Ideal Doll ST-12, 12"*	215.00	225.00	210.00
☐ **Shirley Temple,** *vinyl head, jointed vinyl body, vinyl wig, sleep eyes, sheer blue gown, c. 1950, 17"*	120.00	140.00	125.00
☐ **Shirley Temple,** *vinyl, print dress, marked: Ideal, 12"*	85.00	95.00	89.00
☐ **Shirley Temple,** *vinyl, red dress, plaid trim, marked: Ideal, 12"*	70.00	80.00	73.00
☐ **Shirley Temple,** *vinyl, red dress, script pin, marked: Ideal, 15"*	100.00	150.00	105.00
☐ **Shirley Temple,** *vinyl, red, white dress, marked: Ideal, 12"*	70.00	80.00	73.00
☐ **Shirley Temple,** *vinyl, wig, red dotted dress, 15"*	60.00	70.00	63.00
☐ **Shirley Temple Baby,** *composition head, cloth body, open mouth with teeth, representing actress Shirley Temple as an infant, dressed in gown, bonnet and booties, holds teddy bear, came with a*			

	Current Price Range		P/Y AVG

pin on the gown, bearing a picture of Shirley Temple and reading, "The World's Darling Shirley Temple Doll," 16" .... 160.00 190.00 | 150.00

Shirley Temple, vinyl, c. 1950, 17" $120.00-$175.00

☐ **Shirley Temple Baby,** *composition head with cloth body, marked Shirley Temple,* 17" .... 180.00 215.00 | 165.00
☐ **Shirley Temple Baby,** *composition head with cloth body, marked Shirley Temple,* 18" .... 195.00 230.00 | 175.00

IDEAL / 175

	Current Price Range		P/Y AVG
☐ **Shirley Temple Baby,** *composition head with cloth body, marked Shirley Temple, 22"*	210.00	240.00	200.00
☐ **Shirley Temple Baby,** *composition head with cloth body, marked Shirley Temple, 25"*	245.00	285.00	230.00
☐ **Shirley Temple Baby,** *composition head with cloth body, marked Shirley Temple, 27"*	270.00	335.00	250.00
☐ **Shirley Temple Toddler,** *composition head, cloth body, marked #1 (some specimens do not have this marking but are marked Shirley Temple — stated value applies to both), 23"*	150.00	180.00	135.00
☐ **Shirley Temple Toddler,** *composition, marked 73 Shirley Temple, 25"*	460.00	575.00	425.00
☐ **Snow White,** *composition head, arms and legs, cloth body, molded and painted hair, molded and painted features, open mouth, eyes turned to side, marked Ideal, made c. 1939, 17½"*	70.00	85.00	65.00
☐ **Sparkle Plenty,** *plastic head, latex body, latex arms and legs, blonde hair attached by adhesive, sleep eyes (blue), Sparkle Plenty was a character in the comic strip "Dick Tracy," created by Chester Gould, marked made in U.S.A. Pat. No. 2252077, made in 1947, 15"*	50.00	65.00	45.00
Note: Competition from collectors of "comic character memorabilia" makes the price of this doll much higher than it would otherwise be.			
☐ **Spinderella Flatsy,** *vinyl, painted features, rooted hair (blonde), bendable, mounted on a platform base, to which one foot is attached, when a string is pulled, the platform turns and Spinderella "spins," made in Hong Kong, dated 1969 on the doll and 1970 on the platform*	5.50	7.00	5.00
☐ **Tabatha,** *vinyl head, cloth body, vinyl arms and legs, blonde hair (rooted), painted side-glancing eyes, Tabatha was a character in the TV series "Bewitched," marked 1966 Ideal Toy Corp., 15"*	70.00	90.00	65.00

176 / IDEAL

	Current Price Range		P/Y AVG
☐ **Talking Tot,** *plastic head, vinyl arms and legs, cloth body, molded, painted hair, sleep eyes, open mouth with two teeth, talker with spring-driven talking mechanism located in chest, two voice variations: laughs when upright, cries when lying down, 22"*	16.00	19.00	15.00
☐ **Tammy,** *plastic/vinyl, rooted blonde hair, painted eyes, partially open mouth, wears two-piece bathing suit, 9"*	7.00	9.00	7.00
☐ **Tammy,** *vinyl, seran wig, painted eyes, original shorts and top, c. 1960, 12"*	12.00	14.00	12.50
☐ **Tammy's Mom,** *plastic/vinyl, rooted blonde hair, painted eyes looking upward, closed mouth, dressed in long gown with flowing train, marked W-18-L, also W-13 on doll body, 11⅝"*	10.00	13.00	9.00
Note: Tammy's Mom dates from the early 1960's. It came with a tag reading "Petite Fashions."			
☐ **Ted,** *plastic/vinyl, molded hair, painted eyes, closed mouth, represents an adult man (intended as Tammy's brother), marked B-12-U-2, 12"*	10.00	14.00	9.00
☐ **Theresa,** *Victorian Lady, c. 1983, 8"*	6.00	14.00	7.00
☐ **Theresa,** *Victorian Lady, c. 1983, 12"*	15.00	20.00	16.00
☐ **Thumbelina,** *molded hair, limited edition, c. 1983, 18"*	70.00	90.00	79.00
☐ **Thumbelina,** *porcelain, limited issue, c. 1983, 18"*	250.00	320.00	256.00
☐ **Thumbelina,** *rooted hair, limited edition, c. 1983, 16"*	55.00	65.00	58.00
☐ **Tickletoes,** *crier, vinyl, molded and painted hair, sleep eyes (blue), marked 16 Ideal Doll Made in U.S.A., made in 1948, 16½"*	25.00	30.00	23.00
☐ **Tiffany Taylor,** *plastic/vinyl, representing a teenage high-fashion model, wears a wig which is half blonde and half brunette, set into a revolving disc in the head; by rotating the disc Tiffany can be made to appear (from the front at least) to have either blonde or brunette hair, marked 1973, CG-19-H230 Hong Kong, 18"*	7.00	10.00	7.00

IDEAL / 177

	Current Price Range		P/Y AVG

- ☐ **Tiny Boy,** *plastic, molded and painted hair, sleep eyes (blue), jointed at shoulders and hips, marked Ideal, made in 1960, 8"* 5.00 7.00 5.00
- ☐ **Tiny Girl,** *plastic, molded and painted hair (sandy blonde), sleep eyes (blue), marked Ideal Doll-9, made in 1950, 9¼"* 6.00 8.00 6.00
  Note: A very good quality plastic head which most people would mistake for composition.
- ☐ **Tiny Kissey,** *plastic/vinyl, blonde hair (rooted), sleep eyes (blue), jointed at the wrists, lips pucker when arms are pressed together, marked Ideal Toy Corp., K-L6-3, made in 1962, 16"* 25.00 31.00 23.00
- ☐ **Tiny Tears,** *porcelain, limited issue, c. 1983, 14"* 150.00 240.00 156.00
- ☐ **Toddler,** *hard plastic, 22"* 100.00 150.00 140.00
- ☐ **Toni,** *blonde hair, red striped dress, 14"* 40.00 50.00 43.00
- ☐ **Toni,** *character bride doll, near white wig, blue sleep eyes, closed mouth, elaborate white bridal gown with long train, five layers in skirt, brocade slip, hand beaded Victorian sleeves, tiny functional beaded buttons on cuff and down back, long veil with headpiece, 16"* 145.00 155.00 145.00
- ☐ **Toni,** *composition head, jointed composition body, sleep eyes, yellow dress, red shoes, c. 1950, 14"* 80.00 90.00 82.50
- ☐ **Toni,** *hard plastic, blonde hair, blue sleeping eyes, lashes, dress with pink bodice and green print skirt, 15"* 100.00 150.00 115.00
- ☐ **Toni,** *walker, plastic, blonde hair attached by adhesive, closed mouth, bright red lips, marked Ideal Doll P93, made in 1952, 21"* 65.00 80.00 60.00
- ☐ **Tonie,** *plastic, black hair attached by adhesive, sleep eyes (blue), marked Ideal Doll, Made in U.S.A., and additionally marked with the mold number P-90, made in 1949, 14"* 28.00 36.00 25.00

Toni,
composition,
sleep eyes, c. 1950
$80.00-$90.00

	Current Price Range		P/Y AVG
☐ **Tressy,** vinyl head, hard body, jointed shoulders, waist, hips, rooted hair (black), blue sleep eyes, blue satin short dress and matching panties, blue original shoes, 18"	70.00	80.00	73.00
☐ **Tressy,** plastic/vinyl, black hair (rooted), sleep eyes (blue), pug nose, closed mouth, hair has "grow" feature (portion of wig is fitted inside head; when hair is pulled gently, it gives the appearance of "growing" out of the scalp), marked 1969, Ideal Toy Corp., GH-18, also marked (on hip) with Patent No. 3162976, made in Hong Kong	8.00	10.00	7.00

	Current Price Range		P/Y AVG
☐ **Twins (girl),** vinyl head, cloth body, vinyl arms and legs, blue sleep eyes, marked Ideal Toy Corp., TW-14-2-U, date of manufacture not known, apparently 1960's, 15"	28.00	35.00	25.00
Note: There was also a boy version of Twins, with the same value.			
☐ **Uneeda Kid,** composition head, arms, legs, cloth body, blue painted eyes, molded hair, hat, boots, original romper suit, yellow rain slicker with hat, carrying box of Uneeda biscuits, promotional doll for Uneeda Biscuit Co., mint, 15½"	700.00	800.00	450.00
☐ **Upsy-Dazy,** vinyl head with foam body, foam legs, painted features, rooted hair (blonde), Upsy-Dazy turns herself right side up, when stood on her head, marked Ideal Toy Corp., UD-H-211, made in Hong Kong in 1971, 14½"	7.00	9.00	6.00
☐ **Velvet,** black, vinyl, painted features, rooted hair, smiling face with closed mouth, wears white dress tied with a ribbon at the waist	8.00	10.00	7.00
☐ **Velvet,** white version, vinyl, painted features, rooted hair (blonde), smiling face with closed mouth, wears black dress tied at the waist with a wide white ribbon	7.50	9.50	7.00
☐ **Velvet,** vinyl head, hard body, jointed shoulders, waist and hips, smiling mouth, rooted hair, navy blue sailing outfit with long pants, 15"	38.00	42.00	40.00
☐ **Velvet,** vinyl head, hard body, jointed shoulders, waist, hips, rooted hair, smiling mouth, pink velvet blazer, plaid shirt, 15"	35.00	38.00	35.00
☐ **Victorian Lady,** c. 1983, 8"	20.00	25.00	21.00
☐ **Victorian Lady,** c. 1983, 12"	30.00	35.00	32.00
☐ **Victorian Lady,** vinyl stuffed head, arms, legs, oilcloth body, molded brown hair, blue sleep eyes open closed mouth, original white dress with red and dark blue stripes, large collar, red trim, cotton panties, original shoes, c. 1940's	60.00	70.00	60.00

IMCO

	Current Price Range		P/Y AVG
☐ **Love Me,** *vinyl head and body, blonde hair (rooted), sleep eyes (blue), marked VS20, made in 1953, 19"*	23.00	29.00	21.00

IMPERIAL

	Current Price Range		P/Y AVG
☐ **Boac Airline Hostess,** *plastic/vinyl, painted features, closed mouth, rooted hair (brunette), wearing an airline hostess cap and carrying a flight bag, unmarked on doll, box marked Imperial Toy Corp., 1971, made in Hong Kong, 5"*	3.00	4.00	3.00
☐ **Heidi,** *vinyl head, plastic body, rooted blonde hair cut into bangs, painted eyes, wears peasant costume of Switzerland (Alpine region), marked Made in Hong Kong, 8"*	4.00	6.00	4.00
Note: *The manufacturer's name (Imperial Toy Corp.) appears only on the box, not on the doll.*			
☐ **Japan Airline (J.A.L.) Hostess,** *plastic, vinyl, painted features, closed mouth, rooted hair (black), wearing a Japanese kimono and carrying a flight bag, unmarked on doll, box marked Imperial Toy Corp., 1971, made in Hong Kong, 5"*	3.00	4.00	3.00
☐ **Linda,** *plastic/vinyl, sleep eyes (blue), closed mouth, marked Imperial, made in 1950, 17"*	25.00	31.00	23.00
☐ **Pan Am Airline Hostess,** *plastic/vinyl, painted features, closed mouth, rooted hair (blonde), wearing an airline hostess cap and carrying a flight bag, unmarked on doll, box marked Imperial Toy Corp., 1971, made in Hong Kong, 5¼"*	3.00	4.00	3.00
☐ **Sunny Surfers,** *vinyl, these small dolls (all 5") were made in various poses and facial expressions in the mid 1970's, probably with a view to capturing the sort of market which had bought Thomas Dam's "trolls" about a decade*			

	Current Price Range		P/Y AVG

earlier, some are marked Hong Kong, others have no marking, all products of the Imperial Toy Co., for any style 2.50 3.50 2.50

IMPERIAL CROWN

☐ **Baby Bubbles,** *composition head, cloth body, molded and painted hair, bright red lips, glossy face, made in 1950, 21"* 16.00 21.00 15.00
☐ **Miss Pepsodent,** *vinyl, sleep eyes (blue), open mouth with "action" teeth, when lying down the doll has yellow teeth, upon rising, the yellow teeth roll back and a row of gleaming white ones appear, the message was (of course) that a child who was lazy about brushing would end up with yellow teeth, this doll was apparently sold in stores but may also have been used by the Pepsodent company (makers of toothpaste) as a promotional item, date of manufacture is not known, probably early 1950's* 80.00 100.00 75.00

IMS

☐ **Uncle Sam,** *bisque head, ball jointed, fixed eyes, marked IMS, date of manufacture unknown, presumably 1970's, 12"* 100.00 130.00 95.00

IRWIN

☐ **Baby,** *early plastic, jointed in old plastic high chair, 5"* 45.00 55.00 45.00
☐ **Bashful Boy,** *plastic, molded and painted features, molded and painted hair, marked Irwin, Made in U.S.A., made in 1950, 6½"* 5.00 7.00 5.00

	Current Price Range		P/Y AVG
☐ **Crib Angel,** *vinyl head, cloth body, molded and painted features, fixed eyes (blue), marked Irwin, made in 1961, 8"*	3.00	5.00	3.00
☐ **Knotts' Berry Farm,** *plastic, molded and painted features, molded and painted hair, wears broad-brimmed hat and banner reading "Knotts' Berry Farm," premium doll, date of manufacture unknown, 6½"*	3.00	4.00	3.00

ITALOCREMONA

☐ **Mirella,** *vinyl, sleep eyes, rooted hair, made in Italy for the U.S. Kresge (K-Mart) chain, 12"*	14.00	18.00	13.00
☐ **Sabrina,** *vinyl, sleep eyes, rooted hair, made in Italy for the U.S. Kresge (K-Mart) chain, 12"*	14.00	18.00	13.00
☐ **Vanessa,** *character, 1965, vinyl, jointed lady doll, brown and silver streaked hair, blue sleep eyes, closed mouth, long white sequined evening gown, matching forearms cuffs, genuine white Ermine fur complete with head and tails, 14"*	50.00	60.00	50.00

CHARLES IVES

☐ **Empress Eugenie,** *automan, French bisque head, composition body, original costume and box, one of the rarest in a series designed by Charles Hotchkiss and made by Charles Ives, 11½"*	3200.00	4000.00	3000.00

JACK FROST SUGAR

	Current Price Range		P/Y AVG
☐ **Jack Frost,** *cloth (printed), given as a premium or promotional item in connection with the purchase of Jack Frost Sugar, probably c. 1970, 20"*	8.00	11.00	8.00

JAPAN

☐ **Celluloid,** *black, painted, movable arms, large eyes, wears smock, marked Made in Japan, 8"*	45.00	60.00	42.00
☐ **Nurse,** *celluloid, movable arms, holds infant in one arm, feeding bottle in other hand, wears broad-brimmed hat, old-style nursing uniform with religious insignia, marked Made in Japan, 7"*	32.00	42.00	30.00
☐ **Shirley Temple,** *composition head and body, molded hair, closed mouth, wearing "drum majorette" uniform (sometimes referred to as "marcher"), fully jointed body, 8"*	75.00	100.00	70.00

JERRI

☐ **Blue Boy,** *c. 1983*	350.00	400.00	355.00
☐ **Melody,** *curls, lacy lilac dress, c. 1983*	300.00	350.00	310.00
☐ **Pinkie,** *c. 1983*	300.00	350.00	310.00
☐ **Virginia Dare,** *pilgrim outfit, c. 1983*	300.00	350.00	315.00

JILMAR

☐ **Praying Patti,** *talker, vinyl head, cloth body, painted eyes, recites prayers when button is pushed, unmarked on doll, sold originally with a tag reading TM Jilmar Co., this doll is sometimes referred to as "Sleepy Angel," 18"*	19.00	23.00	18.00

JOLLY

	Current Price Range		P/Y AVG
☐ **Baby Angel,** plastic/vinyl, marked Jolly Toys, Inc., made in 1961, 16"	3.00	4.00	3.00
☐ **Cutie,** vinyl, blonde hair (rooted), sleep eyes (blue), marked Jolly Toys, 1965, 14"	11.00	14.00	10.00
☐ **Dixie Pixie,** vinyl head and body, sleep eyes, closed mouth, marked FR18, made in 1963, 19¼"	28.00	35.00	25.00
☐ **Judy Playmate,** plastic/vinyl, marked Jolly Toy, 1968, 11½"	4.00	6.00	4.00
☐ **Linda,** black, plastic/vinyl, black hair (rooted), sleep eyes (brown), nursing mouth, marked Jolly Toys, Inc., 1969-16, 20"	15.00	19.00	14.00
☐ **Little Love,** plastic/vinyl, sleep eyes (blue), blonde hair (rooted), closed mouth, bright red lips, braided hair, Alpine-type outfit, marked Jolly Toys Inc., 1962, 13½"	4.00	6.00	4.00
☐ **Lovely Lisa,** vinyl head, vinyl arms and legs, cloth body, sleep eyes (blue), rooted hair (light blonde), open puckered mouth, pug nose, dressed in an infant's gown and bonnet, marked 14/4 Jolly Toys Inc., made in 1962, 14½"	4.00	6.00	4.00
☐ **Miss Grow-Up,** plastic/vinyl, fixed eyes, long lashes, long thin eyebrows, blonde hair (rooted), large ribbon in hair, wearing a corduroy dress with ruffled collar, marked Jolly Toys Inc., 1963, 11½"	5.00	7.00	5.00
☐ **Mommy's Baby,** vinyl head, cloth body, vinyl arms and legs, blonde hair (rooted), sleep eyes (blue), marked 15-6 Signature Doll Corp., Signature Doll Division, New York NY 10011, made in 1969, 19"	6.00	8.00	6.00
Note: Whenever a doll is marked with the manufacturer's zipcode, this is positive evidence that it was made no earlier than the 1960's.			
☐ **Nikki,** plastic/vinyl, blonde hair (rooted), sleep eyes (blue), marked Made in Hong Kong, Jolly Toys, made in 1964, 13"	8.00	11.00	7.00

	Current Price Range		P/Y AVG
☐ **Playpen Doll**, plastic/vinyl, blonde hair (rooted), sleep eyes (blue), marked 26 Jolly Toys, Inc., 1967, 14"	5.00	7.00	5.00
☐ **Pretty Girl**, plastic/vinyl, blonde hair (rooted), painted eyes, marked Jolly Toy Co., made in 1964, 17"	9.00	12.00	8.00
☐ **Suzanna Ballerina**, plastic/vinyl, sleep eyes (blue), marked Jolly Toy 1965, 17¼"	7.00	10.00	7.00
☐ **Timmy**, vinyl head, foam body, foam arms and legs, molded and painted features, painted eyes, marked Jolly Toys, Inc., 1967, 14"	12.00	16.00	11.00
☐ **Trudy**, plastic/vinyl, blonde hair (rooted), sleep eyes (blue), marked Jolly Toys, 1962, 13"	11.00	14.00	10.00
☐ **Twistee**, vinyl head, foam body, foam arms and legs, brunette hair (rooted), sleep eyes (black), marked Jolly Toy Inc., made in 1964, 16"	6.00	8.00	6.00

JOY

☐ **Colonial Lady**, composition head and body, sleep eyes (blue), blonde wig, unmarked, believed to have been made in the 1940's, 15"	26.00	32.00	25.00
☐ **Marlene Dietrich**, composition head and body, sleep eyes (blue), blonde wig, made in 1945, 15"	75.00	95.00	70.00
☐ **Sheila From Irleand**, composition head, composition arms, legs and body, painted features, molded and painted hair, closed mouth, neck swivels, dressed in a native costume of Ireland, unmarked on doll, but sold with a stringed tag reading Joy Doll Corp., NYV New York World's Fair 1939, 7½"	23.00	29.00	22.00

Note: Interest from collectors of World's Fair items contributes to the high price. However, when Sheila is lacking the tag her value is somewhat less.

JOYCE-MILLER

	Current Price Range		P/Y AVG

☐ **Grandpa,** *cloth, unmarked on doll, sold originally with a tag reading Joyce-Miller Original, Copyright Sears Roebuck & Co., believed to date from the late 1960's, 16"* 22.00 28.00 22.00

JULLIEN

☐ **Bisque,** *socket head, fixed eyes (very large), painted lashes on upper and lower lids, almost straight horizontal bushy brows, closed pouting mouth, bright red lips, long narrow nose, thin face, representing a girl of 5 or 6 years of age, often dressed as an older girl or an adult, marked Jullien-2, date of manufacture unknown, c. 1885, 13"* 750.00 925.00 725.00
Note: *The Jullien company was located in Paris, and was active from about the time of the American Civil War into the 20th century.*

JUMEAU

This French manufacturer produced some highly exquisite dolls. The quality, reputation and scarcity make for steep prices on the collector's market: anyone interested in Jumeau dolls needs heavy cash or the willpower to admire them behind the glass cases of museums. Jumeau went into business before 1850 and the company was still operating in the late 1800's, having won just about every award for dollmaking that existed on the face of the earth.

☐ **Bebe,** *bisque head, ball jointed composition body, long brown human hair wig, brown paperweight eyes, chiffon dress with eyelet overskirt, 16½"* 3000.00 3500.00 3250.00
☐ **Bebe,** *bisque head, composition body, blonde human hair wig, blue paperweight eyes, pierced ears, long waisted pink eyelet dress with stockings and velvet boots, 23"* 2500.00 2750.00 2600.00

	Current Price Range		P/Y AVG
☐ **Bebe,** *bisque head, composition body, brown paperweight eyes, white crochet dress, ruffled bonnet with long tie, 20½"*	2000.00	2500.00	2250.00
☐ **Bebe,** *bisque head, jointed composition body, blue paperweight eyes, blonde mohair wig, pierced ears and closed mouth, mark: Blue Jumeau Medaille d'or Paris, 12"*	2000.00	2300.00	1800.00
☐ **Bebe,** *bisque head, jointed composition body, blue paperweight eyes, brown wig, closed mouth, pierced ears, lovely antique clothes and shoes, mark: Tete Jumeau 11*	2500.00	3000.00	2200.00
☐ **Bebe,** *bisque head, jointed composition body, brown paperweight eyes, blonde mohair wig, pierced applied ears, closed mouth, rose silk antique ensemble with shoes, mark: Tete Jumeau 14, 30"*	2800.00	3500.00	2800.00
☐ **Bebe,** *bisque head, jointed wood and composition body, blue paperweight eyes, blonde wig, pierced ears, open mouth, mark: Tete Jumeau 12, Bebe Jumeau, 26"*	3200.00	4000.00	3000.00
☐ **Bebe,** *bisque head, kid body with bisque hands, brown loop curl wig, blue sleep eyes, green print dress with lace trim, straw hat, 26"*	3000.00	3500.00	3250.00
☐ **Bebe,** *bisque head, wood and composition jointed body, blue paperweight eyes, blonde mohair wig, closed mouth, pierced ears, rose silk dress and hat, 16"*	2400.00	2600.00	2400.00
☐ **Bebe,** *bisque head, wood and French composition jointed body, blue paperweight eyes, blonde mohair wig, open/closed mouth, pierced applied ears, antique green silk ensemble with shoes, mark: Depose Jumeau 8, 18"*	3800.00	4500.00	3500.00
☐ **Bebe,** *jointed composition body, closed mouth, brown eyes, brown wig, lavender satin dress trimmed with roses, French-style bonnet*	2200.00	2800.00	2450.00

188 / JOYCE-MILLER

	Current Price Range		P/Y AVG
☐ **Bebe Louve,** jointed composition body, corn-flower blue paperweight eyes, blonde mohair wig, pink dress, straw hat, made specially for the Louve Shop in Paris in 1876, 22"	3200.00	4200.00	3600.00
☐ **Bebe Parle,** talker, bisque, sleep eyes (roundish), painted lashes on upper and lower lids, long arching brows, partially open mouth, narrow nose, joined at the elbows, talking mechanism operated by pullcord, says two words ("mama" — "papa"), date of manufacture unknown, probably c. 1895, 32"	900.00	1100.00	850.00

Note: The value indicated is for a specimen in working condition. This is a really impressive doll, both for its size and the fact that it was one of the early foreign talkers. It would be even more expensive but apparently Jumeau turned it out in rather large quantities.

☐ **Bisque,** ball jointed body, blue paperweight eyes, blonde curly wig, open mouth, pierced ears, pink dress with buttons on front, lace, pleated skirt, matching hat, 22"	1800.00	2800.00	2250.00
☐ **Bisque,** blue paperweight eyes, blonde wig, peach taffeta dress, marked: Jumeau, 16"	2800.00	3600.00	3100.00
☐ **Bisque,** blue paperweight eyes, French curls, closed mouth, head and body signed, 15"	2000.00	2600.00	2250.00
☐ **Bisque,** brown paperweight eyes, brown human hair wig, open mouth, pierced ears, lovely costume with hat, 19"	2000.00	2200.00	2000.00
☐ **Bisque,** composition body, bisque hands and feet, paperweight eyes, working mechanism, original costume, 21"	3500.00	4500.00	3500.00
☐ *Bisque,* French, ball-jointed body, human hair wig, blue paperweight eyes, pierced ears, open mouth, pink and green costume, c. 1907	1900.00	2100.00	1850.00
☐ **Bisque,** jointed composition body, blue paperweight eyes, blonde wig, closed mouth, 25"	2200.00	2800.00	2500.00

Description	Current Price Range		P/Y AVG
☐ **Bisque,** *large topaz paperweight eyes, French curls, V hairline, 17"*	1200.00	2000.00	1600.00
☐ **Bisque,** *painted body, blue paperweight eyes, blonde French curls, blue organdy with embroidery, 20"*	5200.00	5800.00	5400.00
☐ **Bisque,** *socket head, walker, fixed eyes, open mouth showing teeth, head turns as doll walks, representing a young girl, marked with an X inside a circle, topped by a checkmark, date of manufacture unknown, presumed to have been made in the 1880's, 22½"*	600.00	750.00	575.00
☐ **Bisque Head,** *brown paperweight eyes, brown human hair wig, open mouth, pierced ears, lovely costume with hat, 19"*	2000.00	2200.00	2000.00
☐ **Bisque Head,** *composition body, bisque hands and feet, paperweight eyes, working mechanism, original costume, 21"*	3500.00	4500.00	3500.00
☐ **Bisque Head,** *French ball-jointed body, human hair wig, paperweight eyes, pierced ears, pink and green dress with hat, marked 1907, 25"*	2000.00	2100.00	2050.00
☐ **Bisque Head,** *French ball-jointed body, human hair wig, paperweight eyes, open mouth, pierced ears, gold satin costume, brown trim, hat to match, 24"*	2300.00	2550.00	2350.00
☐ **Bisque Head,** *French ball-jointed body, human hair wig, blue paperweight eyes, navy blue print dress with hat, marked: No. 9, 1907, 20"*	2000.00	2250.00	2015.00
☐ **Bisque Head,** *French ball-jointed body, human hair wig, brown paperweight eyes, pierced ears, gold satin costume with brown hat, 24"*	2500.00	3000.00	2550.00
☐ **Bisque Head,** *jointed body, dark brown human hair wig, black paperweight eyes, open mouth, pierced ears, French blue brocade two piece dress, 1910, 26"*	1600.00	1800.00	1650.00
☐ **Bisque Head,** *jointed body, medium brown human hair wig, blue paperweight eyes, open mouth, blue silk dress and hat, shoes have "bee mark," marked: #1907, 1905, 22"*	2000.00	3000.00	2250.00

	Current Price Range		P/Y AVG
☐ **Bisque Head,** *jointed French composition body, stationary glass eyes, open mouth, pierced ears, 16"*	2500.00	2600.00	2500.00
☐ **Bisque Socket Head,** *ball-jointed wood and composition body, brown human hair wig in long curls, blue blown glass eyes with lashes, pierced ears, Austrian crystal earrings and necklace, pink fancy dress with large shoulder to waist collar, lace trimmed, matching underclothes, large matching bonnet, head marked in red mark Jumeau, body marked in red mark Jumeau, 23"*	2500.00	3000.00	2700.00
☐ **Black Doll,** *brown paperweight eyes, black wig, closed mouth, plaid taffetta dress, carries own toy, incised Jumeau, 18"*	3200.00	3800.00	3400.00
☐ **Bride,** *fashion, bisque head, lower arms and legs, kid body, blue paperweight eyes, blonde wig, pierced ears, closed mouth, lovely white lace antique bridal gown with veil, 20"*	1500.00	2000.00	1500.00
☐ **Character Doll,** *French-style body, blue eyes, mahogany wig, blue-green satin dress, matching bonnet, incised R.R., 21"*	3000.00	3600.00	3200.00
☐ **Child,** *bisque head, composition jointed body, brown glass paperweight eyes, brown wig, closed mouth, pierced ears, 21"*	3000.00	4000.00	3500.00
☐ **Child,** *bisque head, jointed French composition and wooden body, blue paperweight eyes, closed mouth, dimpled chin, applied, pierced ears, 30"*	4500.00	5500.00	5000.00
☐ **Child,** *bisque socket head, French composition and wooden jointed body, almond shaped brown glass paperweight eyes, brush stroked brows, closed mouth, pierced, applied ears, brown human hair wig, marked 10 jon head and Jumeau Medaille d' Or on body, 24"*	4000.00	5000.00	4000.00
☐ **Closed Mouth,** *ball-jointed composition body, brown eyes, brown hair, marked: VIII, Jumeau stamp, 17"*	1500.00	1800.00	1650.00

	Current Price Range		P/Y AVG

- ☐ **Closed Mouth**, *blue paperweight eyes, blonde curls, pink taffeta dress and hat, 17"* 2200.00 2800.00 2500.00
- ☐ **Closed Mouth**, *blue paperweight eyes, marked, 13½"* 1800.00 2600.00 2200.00
- ☐ **Closed Mouth**, *painted body, large blue eyes, black curls, applied ears, blue outfit, 33"* 6200.00 6800.00 6450.00
- ☐ **Cody**, *bisque, fixed eyes (medium size, dark), lightly painted lashes on upper and lower lids, naturalistic brows (slightly arched), closed mouth, thin pale lips, narrow nose with well-defined nostrils, long thin face, found dressed as a child or adult, marked 13, date of manufacture unknown, c. 1887, one of the most famous and sought-after of the Jumeau dolls, 26"* 3200.00 3900.00 3175.00

  Note: The Jumeau "Cody" doll got its name when Buffalo Bill Cody, the American showman, visited Paris in 1887 and bought a specimen of this doll. Buffalo Bill apparently had taste when it came to dolls: this long-face model represented a sharp departure from the usual mump-cheeked dolls of that era, and its facial features are very well presented.

- ☐ **DEP**, *girl, bisque head, ball-jointed body with stiff wrists and wooden thighs, set brown eyes, six tiny teeth, red silk dropwaisted dress with lace borders and matching hat, 1894 A.M. DEP, 14"* 170.00 205.00 180.00
- ☐ **DEP**, *bisque head, French composition jointed body, brown sleep eyes, auburn French human hair wig, antique white dress with lace, DEP 7, 18½"* 750.00 900.00 725.00
- ☐ **DEP**, *bisque head, French composition ball-jointed body, human hair wig, (blonde) beautiful coloration, heirloom clothing, DEP 9, 22"* 750.00 840.00 765.00
- ☐ **DEP**, *bisque head, French wood jointed body, antique wig, brown sleep eyes, brush stroke brows, small, open mouth with two carved teeth, nostril accents,*

	Current Price Range		P/Y AVG
pierced ears, four piece ensemble of antique pantaloons, slip, petticoat and dress, all with intricate tatting trim and inserts, 2, 12"	475.00	495.00	480.00
☐ E.J. Bebe, bisque head, French composition body, brown paperweight eyes, brown human hair wig, applied, pierced ears, original clothes, marked: DEPOSE E. 7 J., 18"	4800.00	5800.00	4800.00
☐ E.J. Bebe, bisque socket head, composition body with separate ball-joints, unjointed wrists, wig, paperweight eyes, applied ears, pierced ears, antique clothes, marks: head-incised "Depose" mark and check marks, body-"Jumeau Medaille D'or," 20"	4750.00	5500.00	4650.00
☐ E.J. Bebe, bisque socket head, jointed composition body with straight wrists, blonde wig, blue paperweight eyes, closed mouth, pierced ears, unusual clothes, 19"	6000.00	7000.00	6000.00
☐ E.J. Bebe, bisque socket head, jointed composition body with straight wrists, blonde wig, brown paperweight eyes, pierced ears, closed mouth, all original clothes, mint, 20"	7000.00	8000.00	7000.00
☐ Fashion, bisque head, arms, legs, kid body, blue paperweight eyes, blonde mohair wig, pierced ears, closed mouth, original dark green silk dress with matching hat, mark: E. Jumeau, 20"	2800.00	3200.00	2700.00
☐ Fashion Doll, bisque head, kid body, swivel head, upswept wig with tendrils, blue sleep eyes, ivory silk bride suit, 15"	1500.00	2000.00	1750.00
☐ Fashion Lady, bisque, paperweight blue eyes, wig, applied pierced ears, original detailed costume, very elaborate, with her own trunk	3500.00	4000.00	3300.00
☐ French Fashion, bisque head, ball-jointed composition body, human hair wig, brown paperweight eyes, pierced ears, gold gown, 1907, 16"	1500.00	1700.00	1550.00

	Current Price Range	P/Y AVG

- ☐ **French Fashion,** *bisque head, kid body, fancy blonde coiffure, brown glass eyes, watered silk dress, bow trim and bonnet, 14"* .... 1400.00 1500.00 | 1450.00
- ☐ **Girl,** *bisque head, jointed French composition body, brown paperweight stationary eyes, brown wig, closed mouth, pierced ears, antique clothes, marked: J U M E A U / MEDAILLE D'OR/PARIS* .... 2500.00 2600.00 | 2500.00
- ☐ **Girl,** *composition ball-jointed body, brown paperweight eyes, brown human hair wig, closed mouth, marked, 22"* .... 2600.00 3000.00 | 2700.00
- ☐ **Girl,** *French body, blonde, human hair wig, brown paperweight eyes, closed mouth, pierced ears, silk dress, leather shoes, marked: 71EJ, 18"* .... 2000.00 2400.00 | 2100.00
- ☐ **Poupee Parisienne (Paris doll),** *bisque head, wooden body, wooden arms and legs, fixed eyes (oval), painted lashes on upper and lower lids, thin brows, small closed mouth with lightly colored lips, narrow nose, squarish jaw, usually dressed to represent an adult woman, marked E, date of manufacture unknown, but probably 1890's, these are found in a variety of costumes and wearing a variety of wigs, 16"* .... 1375.00 1625.00 | 1325.00

  Note: There is no doubt that the Poupee Parisienne was one of the standard Jumeau dolls for a number of years, however relatively few reached America as the firm was not (at least not at that time) export-oriented.

- ☐ **Papier Mache,** *wooden body, set blue glass eyes, long brown curly wig, open mouth, blue dress with striped collar, picture hat, marked: Paris 301-12, 24"* .. 550.00 650.00 | 586.00
- ☐ **Phonograph Doll,** *bisque head, jointed composition body, wig, brown, blue paperweight eyes, closed mouth, voice box not working, antique clothes* ..... 2500.00 2700.00 | 2500.00
- ☐ **Tete,** *bisque head, jointed composition body, brown paperweight eyes, brown wig, closed mouth, pierced ears,*

	Current Price Range		P/Y AVG

original white taffeta dress with white lace trim, shoes, mark: Tete Jumeau 5, 14½" 2500.00 3000.00 2500.00

☐ **Poured Wax Shoulderhead,** *waxed papier mache arms, legs, cloth body, inset blue eyes, brown wig, open mouth, brown velvet lace trimmed dress, shoes, marked: E. Jumeau Med. Or 1978, Paris, 20"* 375.00 525.00 350.00

☐ **Princess Elizabeth,** *bisque head, blue sleep eyes, blonde human hair wig, blue and white print dress, blue felt coat, 17"* 1600.00 2100.00 1800.00

☐ **Tete,** *bisque head, jointed composition body, blue paperweight eyes, brown human hair wig, closed mouth, pierced ears, marked: Depose Tete Jumeau Bte S.G.D.G. 6, 25"* 4000.00 4300.00 3900.00

☐ **Tete,** *bisque head, jointed composition body, brown wig, blue paperweight eyes, closed mouth, pierced ears, original clothes, fully signed head and body, red head, stamp: Depose Tete Jumeau Bte S.G. D.G. 6, blue stamp or Bebe Jumeau oval sticker on body, 24"* 3800.00 4200.00 3675.00

☐ **Tete Bebe,** *bisque socket head, blue paperweight eyes, light brown human hair wig, light brown eyebrows, painted upper and lower eyelashes, open mouth with four molded teeth, and red accent lines, pierced ears, jointed composition French body, teal blue velvet dress, lace trimmed, satin bow in back, matching hat with feathers, ribbons, leather high button boots, marks: 1907 9, Body blue stamp: Bebe Jumear Bte, S.G.D.G. Depose, 20"* 3000.00 3500.00 3000.00

☐ **Tete,** *bisque socket head, fully jointed French composition body, original cork pate, blonde human hair wig, ringlets, blue paperweight eyes, painted upper and lower lashes, closed mouth with white space between lips, red accent lines, upturned corners, pierced ears, original marked box with large Maison*

	Current Price Range		P/Y AVG
Jumeau label on inside of lid, original pink silk dress, lace panels with silk squares, ribbon embroidered lace, puffed sleeves, neckline with gathered lace, silk ribbon, marks: Depose, Tete Jumeau, Bte, S.G.D.G. 12, various artist initials and check marks, body, oval paper label on back, Bebe Jumeau, Diplome D'Honneur, 26"	4000.00	4200.00	2500.00
☐ **Tete,** bisque socket head, jointed French composition body, brown paperweight eyes, closed mouth with red accent lines, brown human hair wig styled in long ringlets, pierced ears, original cork pate, gold silk dress with lace and brown ribbon, feathered bonnet with lace and silk bow, original body finish, marks: Red stamp on head, Depose Tete Jumeau, S.G.D.G. 12, various artist check marks, body, oval paper label reads Bebe Jumeau, Diplome, D'Honneur, 26"	3600.00	4000.00	3400.00

JUNEL

☐ **Bonny Baby,** mask face cloth, blonde yarn hair, red polka dot dress and hat, name on tag, 15"	50.00	60.00	52.00
☐ **February's Birthday Gift,** composition, brunette hair, painted eyes, jointed at the shoulders, unmarked, made in 1945, 5½"	10.00	14.00	9.00
☐ **Isabella,** composition, molded and painted features, wears reproduction of 15th century costume with large crucifix at neck, representing Isabella of Spain, who was instrumental in sponsoring Columbus' voyage of 1492, unmarked, made in 1946, 7½"	14.00	19.00	13.00

KENNER

	Current Price Range		P/Y AVG
☐ Artoo Detoo, movable legs and a chrome top that clicks, height 2¼" ...	2.00	3.00	2.00
☐ Almond Tea, with Marza Panda	8.00	11.00	8.00
☐ Angel Cake, with Souffle	8.00	11.00	8.00
☐ Apple Dumplin, with tea time turtle	8.00	11.00	8.00
☐ Apricot, with Hopsalot	8.00	11.00	8.00
☐ Baby Alive, vinyl, battery-operated nurser and eater, painted eyes, marked 3564-P13 Kenner Prod., 1973, 16"	11.00	15.00	11.00
☐ Baby Yawnie, vinyl, eyes close and mouth opens in a yawn when bulb is squeezed, made in the late 1970's, 15".	4.00	6.00	4.00
☐ Blueberry Muffin, with Cheese Cake ...	8.00	11.00	8.00
☐ Blythe, plastic/vinyl, rooted hair (blonde), large sad eyes which shift from side to side and change color when pullcord is pulled, wearing a bright print dress, marked Blythe TM, Kenner Products, 1972, also marked General Mills Fun Group (the Kenner company was a subsidiary of General Mills), 12"	7.00	9.00	6.00
☐ Boba Fett, carries a laser with backpack, based on The Empire Strikes Back, height 13¼"	20.00	30.00	23.00
☐ Boba Fett, with laser and back pack, based on The Empire Strikes Back, height 2¼"	2.00	3.00	2.00
☐ Butter Cookie, with Jelly Bear	8.00	11.00	8.00
☐ Cafe Ole, with Burrito	8.00	11.00	8.00
☐ Cherry Cudler, with Gooseberry	8.00	11.00	8.00
☐ Chewbacca, The Space Wookie, crossbow laser rifle, ammunition cartridge is removable, height 15"	15.00	25.00	18.00
☐ Chewbacca, has ammunition belt and special laser rifle, height 4¼"	2.00	3.00	2.00
☐ Crepe Suzette, with Eclair	8.00	11.00	8.00
☐ Crumpet, plastic/vinyl, sleep eyes (blue), rooted hair (blonde), joined at the wrists and waist, pug nose, open smiling mouth with teeth, holds teapot, works by pullcord and battery, marked 1970, Kenner Products Co., 235-225, also marked with address (Cincinnati, Ohio), 18½"	7.00	10.00	7.00

	Current Price Range		P/Y AVG
☐ **Death Star Droid,** *brilliant silver coloring and movable arms and legs, height 3¾"*	2.00	3.00	2.00
☐ **Darth Vader,** *carries light saber, detailed black armor and removable cape, height 15"*	25.00	35.00	28.00
☐ **Darth Vader,** *has retractable light saber and removable cape, height 4¼"*	2.00	3.00	2.00
☐ **Gabbigale,** *plastic/vinyl, painted eyes (blue), rooted hair (dark blonde), talker operated by pullcord and battery, open smiling mouth with teeth, pug nose, marked 1972 Kenner Products Co., 99, 18"*	8.00	10.00	8.00
☐ **Greedo, The Cantina Creature,** *with laser pistol, movable arms and legs, based on The Return Of The Jedi, height 3¼"*	2.00	3.00	2.00
☐ **Han Solo,** *equipped with special laser pistol, height 3¼"*	2.00	3.00	2.00
☐ **Hammerhead,** *holds a laser and has movable legs and arms, based on The Empire Strikes Back, height 4"*	2.00	3.00	2.00
☐ **Huckelberry Pie,** *with Pup Cake*	8.00	11.00	8.00
☐ **Jenny The Quantas Hostess,** *vinyl, representing a hostess for Quantas (Australian) Airlines, marked 3632-189-GMFGI Kenner Products, 12"*	17.00	23.00	16.00
☐ **Lemon Meringue,** *with Frappe*	8.00	11.00	8.00
☐ **Lime Chiffon,** *with Parfait Parrot*	8.00	11.00	8.00
☐ **Luke Skywalker,** *action figure, in Tattoine desert outfit, has light saber grappling hook, removable costume, height 11¾"*	30.00	40.00	34.00
☐ **Luke Skywalker,** *with light saber ready for action with flick of special lever in his arm, height 3¾"*	2.00	3.00	2.00
☐ **Luke Skywalker, X Wing Pilot,** *battle ready in orange flight suit and laser, height 3¾"*	2.00	3.00	2.00
☐ **Meadow,** *vinyl, painted eyes (brown), rooted hair (brunette), wearing sleeveless sweater, holds watering can in right hand, in addition to the watering*			

198 / KENNER

	Current Price Range		P/Y AVG
can, Meadow was originally sold with packets of real garden seeds, marked Garden Gal by Kenner, Hong Kong, made in 1972, 6⅞"	5.00	7.00	5.00

Note: Don't be misled by the name Garden Gal in the marking. This was the name of a series of dolls. There was no single doll named Garden Gal.

☐ **Mint Tulip**, with Marsh Mallard	8.00	11.00	8.00
☐ **Obi-Wan Kenobi**, carries light saber with removable cape, height 12"	25.00	35.00	28.00
☐ **Obi-Wan Kenobi**, has retractable light saber and removable cape, height 3¼"	2.00	3.00	2.00
☐ **Orange Blossom**, with Marma Lade	8.00	11.00	8.00
☐ **Princess Leia Organa**, hair that is able to be styled, costume is removable, height 11½"	25.00	35.00	28.00
☐ **Princess Leia Organa**, has removable cape and laser pistol, height 3½"	2.00	3.00	2.00
☐ **Purple Pieman**, with Berry Bird	8.00	11.00	8.00
☐ **Raspberry Tart**, with Rhubarb	8.00	11.00	8.00
☐ **R5-D4**, red markings, makes clicking sounds, height 2½"	2.00	3.00	2.00
☐ **See Threeplo**, brillant gold color, with movable arms and lips, height 3¾"	2.00	3.00	2.00
☐ **Sippin' Sue**, plastic/vinyl, open mouth with puckered lips into which soda straw can be inserted, marked 1972 General Mills Fun Group, Inc., 6"	3.00	4.00	3.00
☐ **Sleep Over Dolly**, plastic/vinyl, rooted hair, sleep eyes (blue), marked GMFGI, 1976, 16½"	11.00	14.00	11.00

Note: There was also a black version of this doll, whose value is slightly higher.

☐ **Snaggle Tooth**, comes in space outfit and carries laser rifle, based on The Empire Strikes Back, height 3¾"	2.00	3.00	2.00
☐ **Steve Scout**, plastic/vinyl, molded and painted hair (red), painted eyes (blue), representing a youth dressed in a Boy Scout uniform, right arm moves to give scout salute, marked 1974 GMFGL, Kenner Prod., also marked with address (Cincinnati, Ohio) and zip code number (45202), 9"	9.00	12.00	9.00

	Current Price Range		P/Y AVG
☐ **Strawberry Shortcake,** *with Custard* ...	8.00	11.00	8.00
☐ **Storm Trooper,** *black and white space suit and laser rifle, based on Star Wars, height 3¼"*	2.00	3.00	2.00
☐ **Storm Trooper,** *wears a white and black space suit and carries laser, based on Star Wars, height 12"*	20.00	30.00	23.00
☐ **Walrus Man,** *with rifle and articulated arms and legs, based on Return Of The Jedi, height 5¾"*	2.00	3.00	2.00

KERR GHINZ

☐ **Baby,** *bisque, painted, marked, 5"*	7.00	12.00	8.00
☐ **Bisque Babies,** *movable arms, legs, c. 1930's, marked: K & H*	8.00	10.00	8.00

KESTNER

One of the longest-surviving and most successful of the German doll companies, Kestner spanned the era from craft work to factory production, and into the age of heavy overseas exportation. Johann D. Kestner, founder of the firm, started in a very small way as a maker of papier mache novelties. In the early 1800's — while Napoleon ruled most of Europe — Kestner got the idea of making dolls, but it was many years before the firm enjoyed any real success. During the mid 1800's it was the innovator of many important doll types. By the century's close Kestner had built an export empire, supplying dolls to wholesalers in Europe and America, and is said to have employed more workers than any other doll factory of the time.

The Kestner dolls are basically of good quality and the rarity factor on most of them is not especially high, thereby bringing them within financial reach of more hobbyists than the dolls of more exclusive manufacturers. In bisque their value is usually $200.00-$400.00, in composition somewhat less.

☐ **All Bisque,** *jointed at shoulders and hips, glass eyes, human hair wig, closed mouth, lovely clothes, mold #130.7, 7"*	250.00	350.00	295.00

	Current Price Range		P/Y AVG

- ☐ **Character Boy**, bisque head, ball-jointed body, blue sleep eyes, navy blue wool boy suit, marked: 152, 11" 300.00 350.00 325.00
- ☐ **Character Boy**, bisque head, jointed body, brown human hair wig, blue sleep eyes, red boy outfit, marked: 152 ...... 400.00 450.00 415.00
- ☐ **Character Boy**, 15-piece jointed toddler body, human hair boy wig, blue sleep eyes, navy wool suit 600.00 650.00 615.00
- ☐ **Character Doll**, bisque head, toddler body, human hair wig, blue sleep eyes, orchid and white costume with hat, 20" 1000.00 1100.00 1050.00
- ☐ **Character Toddler**, bisque head, jointed five piece body, brown human hair wig, brown sleep eyes, white school girl dress, marked: 152, 18" 375.00 400.00 385.00
- ☐ **Child**, bisque head, jointed composition body, brown sleep eyes, brown human hair wig, open mouth with teeth, lavender organdy dress with lace insets, 28" 700.00 800.00 725.00
- ☐ **Child**, bisque head with composition ball-jointed body, black wig with bangs, brown sleep eyes, open mouth, 27½" . 250.00 300.00 275.00
- ☐ **Child**, bisque head, wood jointed body, long curly brown wig, brown sleep eyes, lacy tiered dress, wide brimmed bonnet, 22" 350.00 400.00 365.00
- ☐ **Composition**, five-piece body, blue glass set eyes, painted eyebrows, stroked eyelashes, dimpled chin, open mouth, upper teeth, brown bobbed mohair wig, white cotton dress, red wool coat, straw hat, 8½" 225.00 275.00 240.00
- ☐ **Daisy**, bisque, ball-jointed body, human hair wig, blue eyes, open mouth, red plaid taffeta costume, marked: 171, 28" 950.00 1000.00 975.00
- ☐ **Daisy**, character, bisque, composition ball-jointed body, human hair wig, blue sleep eyes, open mouth, red plaid taffeta dress, #171, 28" 1000.00 1275.00 1100.00
- ☐ **Daisy**, jointed composition body, brown eyes, blonde wig, white lawn dress, mold number, 31" 725.00 775.00 740.00

KESTNER / 201

	Current Price Range		P/Y AVG
☐ **Girl,** bisque, antique ball-joint body, French human hair wig, blue sleep eyes, rosebud mouth, two teeth, incised Kestner 143, 14"	400.00	450.00	410.00
☐ **Girl,** bisque, platinum wig, brown sleep eyes, closed mouth, crocheted hat, dress, marked 208/4, 7"	200.00	250.00	220.00
☐ **Girl,** character, bisque head, jointed composition body, original mohair wig, blue sleep eyes, fur brows, white lace antique dress, #215, 26"	650.00	800.00	675.00
☐ **Googly-Eyed Character Doll,** bisque head, jointed composition toddler body, blue sleep side glancing eyes, watermelon mouth, 14"	2600.00	3200.00	2500.00
☐ **Heidi,** bisque head and body, blonde mohair wig, brown sleep eyes, blue crochet dress, 6"	150.00	160.00	155.00
☐ **Hilda Baby,** dome head, blue eyes, white christening dress and hat, holds rattle, 13"	1200.00	1800.00	1300.00
☐ **Hilda,** character baby, bisque head, molded hair, composition bent-limb body, brown sleep eyes, baby clothes, 16"	2300.00	2700.00	2450.00
☐ **Hilda,** character baby, bisque head, bent limb composition limbs, blonde wig, blue sleep eyes, open mouth with two teeth, original clothes	2800.00	3000.00	2800.00
☐ **Hilda,** rare original clothes, marked: Made in Germany (245 JDK Jr 000 1914 Hilda), 16"	2600.00	2900.00	2600.00
☐ **Infant,** bisque head, five piece composition body, blue sleep eyes, open mouth, four upper teeth and tongue, baby dress with coat, bonnet, marked: 152, 17"	2000.00	2200.00	2050.00
☐ **Kewpie,** vinyl, only head turns, side glancing eyes, painted features, wears only large red ribbon with bow around body, marks: head, Cameo, back, Cameo, left bottom of foot, JDK, 10½"	42.00	48.00	42.00
☐ **Lady,** bisque head, composition lady body, Gibson girl blonde wig, blue sleep eyes, open mouth with teeth, all original, mold #162, 18"	1200.00	1300.00	1200.00

	Current Price Range		P/Y AVG
☐ **Little Red Riding Hood,** *bisque socket head, five piece jointed composition body, molded, painted heeled shoes and socks, brown set eyes, open mouth with molded teeth, original blonde mohair wig, flowered dress, red felt cape, matching bonnet, marks: 192, 8".*	100.00	125.00	90.00
☐ **Matron,** *bisque head, ball-jointed composition body, brown human hair wig, brown sleep eyes, painted brows, long navy blue flowered gown, 20"*	300.00	350.00	325.00
☐ **Oriental,** *olive tinted bisque head, black human hair wig with que, almond shaped brown glass sleep eyes, silk costume, original, with headdress, 13"*	3500.00	4000.00	3500.00
☐ **Oriental Baby,** *composition bent limb, brown sleep eyes, black human hair wig, mold number 243, 13"*	2200.00	2700.00	2400.00

LUCILLE KIMSEY

☐ **John F. Kennedy,** *bisque head, cloth body, molded and painted hair, a likeness of President Kennedy wearing a double-breasted suit, made in 1971, 14½"*	60.00	75.00	57.00

KING FEATURES

☐ **Henry,** *vinyl, molded and painted features, molded and painted clothing, representing the character Henry from the comic strip of the same name, created by Carl Anderson, made in 1950, 9"* **Note:** *This doll is listed under King Features because the only marking it carries is KF. King Features was a newspaper syndicate, which owned the rights to Henry. However, the company only licensed the production of dolls, it did not manufacture them itself. The actual maker of this item is not known.*	22.00	28.00	20.00

	Current Price Range		P/Y AVG

- **Popeye,** composition and wood, molded and painted features, molded and painted clothing, jointed at shoulders, hips and neck, arms bent at elbows, has tatoo on left forearm, unmarked, date of manufacture unknown, probably late 1930's, 15" **80.00 100.00 70.00**
- **Popeye,** vinyl head, cloth body, vinyl arms, cloth legs, molded and painted features, representing the comic strip character created by L.C. Segar, marked 411 King Features Sy, made in 1960, 21" **100.00 130.00 75.00**
  Note: The value of this doll — and most other old Popeye dolls — more than doubled in 1980, when the motion picture based on Segar's classic comic was released.
- **Sweet Pea,** vinyl head, cloth body, painted eyes, wears baby bonnet (molded), Sweet Pea is a character in the comic strip "Popeye," created by L.C. Segar, marked King Features Sy. Inc., made in 1959, 10" **45.00 60.00 35.00**
  Note: If this doll was 20 years older, the value would be about three times as much.
- **Uncle Walt And Skeezix,** c. 1930, pair of cheesecloth dolls, famous Gasoline Alley characters, height 12" **70.00 80.00 75.00**
- **Wimpy,** vinyl, squeeze toy, molded and painted features, molded and painted clothing, Wimpy is a character in the comic strip "Popeye," created by L.C. Segar, marked King Features Syndicate, date of manufacture unknown, presumably 1960's, 6" **7.00 10.00 5.00**

KLEY & HAHN

- **Bisque Socket Head,** fully jointed composition body, blue sleep eyes, open mouth with four molded teeth, light brown human hair wig, dotted Swiss

	Current Price Range		P/Y AVG

dress, lace trimmed suspenders, green ribbon rosettes, original body finish, marks: 250 K H Walkure 1½, 20" 350.00 375.00 325.00

☐ **Walkure,** *bisque socket head, fully jointed composition body, blue sleep eyes, open mouth with four porcelain teeth, long blonde wig, painted upper and lower eyelashes, printed white cotton dress, marks: 250 K H Walkure 3¼ Germany, 23"* 350.00 450.00 325.00

☐ **Walkure,** *bisque head, compositon body, ball-jointed, paperweight eyes, human hair wig, open mouth, old clothes, excellent condition, 33"* 850.00 1000.00 975.00

☐ **Walkure,** *bisque head, jointed composition body, blonde wig, brown sleep eyes, (glass) open mouth, #250, 20"* ... 400.00 450.00 415.00

KNOTTER

☐ **Girl,** *red cape, green hat, holds package, made in Japan* 30.00 40.00 30.00
☐ **Girl,** *snow suit, holds Teddy Bear* 35.00 45.00 35.00

KÖNIG AND WERNICKE

☐ **Boy,** *bisque head, ball-jointed composition body, short curly brown human hair wig, brown sleep eyes, blue velvet shirt, tie shoes, 37"* 1000.00 1100.00 1050.00

KATHE KRUSE

☐ **Boy,** *molded fabric head, jointed fabric body, beautifully hand painted face with brown eyes and hair, original clothes, signed on foot, 16"* 1100.00 1200.00 1000.00

	Current Price Range		P/Y AVG
☐ **Child,** *all cloth, molded cloth head, jointed body, painted features and hair, original costume, mark: Kathy Kruse on bottom of foot, 17"*	450.00	650.00	450.00
☐ **Girl,** *celluloid base with cloth overlay, human hair wig, painted eyes, c. 1957*	450.00	500.00	475.00
☐ **Girl,** *molded fabric head, jointed fabric body, painted face, original clothes, 20"*	900.00	950.00	900.00
☐ **Riekchen,** *plastic head, cloth body, painted eyes, made in Germany, 1970, 19"*	35.00	42.00	32.00
Note: Made for the Neiman-Marcus department store of Dallas, Texas.			
☐ **Toddler,** *molded cloth head, cloth body, painted face, wig, original clothes, type Puppe VII, 14"*	800.00	1000.00	1000.00

LAKESIDE

☐ **Gumby,** *foam over wire (posable), marked Gumby, Mfg. by Lakeside Ind., Inc., first sold in 1965, 13"*	6.00	8.00	6.00
Note: Gumby was originally a British creation, by Newfeld Ltd. It was made by Lakeside under license from Newfeld. In a sense Gumby was the English answer to G.I. Joe — a male doll wearing various "action and adventure" outfits. The outfits were sold separately.			
☐ **Lone Ranger,** *vinyl, molded and painted features, molded and painted clothing, bendable, marked 24, 1966, Lakeside Ind., Inc., sold in a box marked Wrather Corp., 6"*	4.00	6.00	4.00

Bisque and Composition,
c. 1905, 18"
$600.00-$700.00

A. LANTERNIER	Current Price Range		P/Y AVG
☐ **Bisque Head,** *jointed body, blonde mohair wig, set eyes, molded brows, antique black and white two piece suit, velvet belt and tam, marked with anchor L.C.C., c. 1905, 18"*	600.00	700.00	625.00
☐ **Bisque Shoulder Head,** *composition and cloth body, brown stationary eyes, brown wig, closed mouth, brown wool dress with bonnet, mark: A L, 13"*	400.00	500.00	400.00

	Current Price Range		P/Y AVG

☐ **Caprice,** *French character toddler, bisque head, jointed French composition body, brown wig, blue glass eyes with black rim molded tear ducts, molded open-closed mouth, molded teeth, nice French clothes, 24½"* 1600.00 1800.00 1500.00

☐ **French Le Conte,** *bisque socket head on jointed composition French body, blue sleep eyes, light brown wig with long ringlets and curly bangs, pierced ears, open mouth with porcelain teeth, dimpled chin, molded eyebrows, painted upper and lower lashes, printed green silk dress, marks: L (Anchor) C.C. 12, 27"* 1500.00 1750.00 1350.00

LASTIC PLASTIC

☐ **Bi Bye,** *vinyl head, vinyl arms and legs, stuffed cloth body, painted eyes, molded and painted hair, represents a one-week-old infant with mouth wide open, crying, originally sold with a tag, dated 1949, made for the Fleischaker Novelty Co. by Lastic Plastic, 16"* 14.00 18.00 13.00

☐ **Plastic,** *stuffed, rooted hair, sleep eyes, partially open mouth, wears checkered dress (short) with puff sleeves, two buttons on dress, arms and legs wide apart, marked Copyright 1951 Lastic Plastic, 16½"* 18.00 23.00 17.00

Note: *This doll (unnamed) was manufactured by Lastic Plastic for the Fleischaker Novelty Co. The hairstyle is somewhat "afro."*

H.D. LEE

☐ **Buddy Lee,** *all celluloid, jointed at the shoulders (legs not jointed), molded blonde hair, painted eyes, 13"* 140.00 185.00 135.00

LENCI

In 1919 the Italian doll firm of Lenci was founded by Signora Elena Konig di Scavini. Her nickname was Lenci, hence her dolls were called "Lenci's" dolls.

Madame di Scavini had been a costume designer for her husband Enrico's doll business prior to his joining the Italian military as an aviator. When he left, she began making dolls as a way of keeping busy. This need soon intensified greatly as a result of the death of their only child.

To escape from her sorrow, Madame di Scavini turned to doll making. Lenci dolls were made primarily of felt with painted faces and felt clothing and produced by local women who worked in their homes. Business flourished and by the late 1930's the Lenci factory was built in Turin, Employing several hundred workers. Many celebrities collected her dolls including Mussolini and most of the crowned heads of Europe.

The Lenci firm continued to prosper until depression and war necessitated diversification in the early 1940's. Classic Lenci dolls are reproduced by the company today using the same molds and processes used in the production of their dolls during the 1920's.

	Current Price Range		P/Y AVG
☐ **Amelia Earhart**, composition body and head, jointed blonde wig, blue set eyes, flight engineer's suit, 14"	400.00	425.00	419.00
☐ **Boy**, felt construction, bent limb body, blonde short wig, brown painted eyes, floppy hat, brown riding outfit, 24½"	500.00	600.00	525.00
☐ **Boy**, Swiss guard, pressed felt head, jointed felt body, blue painted eyes, brown wig, striped Swiss guard felt uniform, 2nd hat, 18"	500.00	600.00	500.00
☐ **Character Girl**, pressed felt head, pinted felt body, swivel neck, painted features, blonde wig, Lenci tag, 19"	700.00	800.00	650.00
☐ **Character Girl**, pressed felt head with painted features jointed felt body, corkscrew curls, startled expression at felt, bee poised on her skirt, large bonnet, party slippers, black cloth label, 10"	260.00	290.00	285.00
☐ **Child**, all felt pressed head, jointed felt body, curly mohair wig, pouty faced, stitched fingers, original dress, 21"	450.00	550.00	425.00
☐ **Child**, bride character, all felt head with painted features, felt jointed body, brown hair, brown side glancing eyes, bridal gown in antique white, matching veil & purse, Lenci tag c. 1920's, 12"	285.00	315.00	290.00

	Current Price Range		P/Y AVG
☐ **Child,** *felt construction, bent limb body, curly redhead, brown painted eyes, red pinafore dress with bloomers and hat, 13"*	350.00	450.00	375.00
☐ **Child,** *molded hollow, tagged, 13"*	260.00	320.00	280.00
☐ **Cloth Doll,** *elaborate peasant costume, excellent condition 10½"*	45.00	55.00	50.00
☐ **Cloth,** *pressed felt head, jointed felt body, painted features, original costume, mint, 17"*	700.00	800.00	675.00
☐ **Cowboy,** *felt construction, stationary body, brown wig, brown painted eyes, chaps, vest and shirt with wide bolero, 18"*	650.00	750.00	675.00
☐ **Girl,** *cloth, elaborate peasant costume, excellent condition 8"*	35.00	45.00	40.00
☐ **Girl,** *felt construction, arm raised, blonde wig, brown painted eyes, red dress with over skirt, 32"*	1100.00	1200.00	1050.00
☐ **Girl,** *felt construction, bent arm body, long braided wig, blue painted eyes looking askance, diamond print dress, straw hat, 18"*	350.00	400.00	375.00
☐ **Girl,** *felt construction bent limb body, blonde mohair wig, brown painted eyes, full black ruffled dress with white lacy pantaloons, 22"*	400.00	450.00	425.00
☐ **Girl,** *felt construction, stationary body, black upswept wig, brown painted eyes, long high waisted dress, tall cylindrical hat with tassle, 18"*	350.00	400.00	375.00
☐ **Girl,** *Mascotte, pressed felt head, jointed felt body, painted blue eyes, blonde wig, original costume, cloth label, 9"*	150.00	250.00	175.00
☐ **Girl,** *red curly hair, black and red felt coat, 12"*	375.00	425.00	390.00
☐ **Golfer,** *felt construction, bent arm body, brown wig, brown painted eyes, knickers and vest, holding golf club, 17"*	650.00	725.00	675.00
☐ **Fascist Youth,** *pressed felt head with painted features, jointed felt body, painted blue eyes, brown wig, wearing the black uniform and hat of Hitler's Youth, paper label, 16"*	575.00	675.00	550.00

210 / LENCI

	Current Price Range		P/Y AVG
☐ **Infant,** felt construction, bent joint body, blonde side parted wig, blue painted eyes, modeled features, sweater over ruffled dress, 20"	500.00	600.00	525.00
☐ **Infant,** felt construction, bent joint body, brown curly mohair wig, brown painted eyes, modeled features, lavender ruffled chiffon dress, lacy bonnet, 20"	500.00	600.00	525.00
☐ **Italian Girl,** Laura Face, pressed felt head, jointed felt body, painted eyes, blonde wig, blue eyes, Italian peasant costume, 18"	550.00	650.00	475.00
☐ **Japanese Geisha,** Lucia Face, pressed felt head, jointed felt body, brown painted oriental eyes, brows, black wig, felt Kimono, hair ornaments, footgear, tag, 14"	350.00	450.00	375.00
☐ **Jockey Character,** pressed felt face with painted brown eyes, thick brown mohair wig, felt body jointed at shoulders and hips, swivel neck, individually stitched fingers, beige riding britches, yellow vest, ascot, black boots, red double breasted riding coat, black felt hat, riding crop, 12"	350.00	450.00	375.00
☐ **Lady,** felt construction, bent arm body, painted blue eyes, blonde fancy wig, elaborate blue ball gown with draped tiers, 17"	350.00	400.00	375.00
☐ **Lady,** felt construction, bent limb body, blonde human hair wig, wide blue painted eyes, long plaid dress, match tam, 19"	450.00	500.00	475.00
☐ **Lady,** felt construction, bent limb body, wide blue flirty glass eyes, black gown, flowered hat, 19½"	1400.00	1600.00	1450.00
☐ **Lady,** felt construction, stationary body, blonde curly human hair wig, blue painted eyes, elaborate ball gown with blue chiffon ruffled trim and roses, 23"	400.00	500.00	425.00
☐ **Lady,** felt construction, stationary body, severe blonde bun, wide surprised painted blue eyes, black watered silk gown with flowered hat, 24½"	500.00	600.00	525.00

	Current Price Range		P/Y AVG
☐ **Lady,** felt construction, swivel neck, blonde mohair wig, blue painted almond shaped eyes, French fashion gown, 19"	350.00	400.00	375.00
☐ **Laura,** child, molded felt head, jointed felt body, painted face, wig, original clothes, mint, mark: cloth and paper tags with Lenci written on them, 19"	600.00	850.00	600.00
☐ **Marlene Dietrich,** portrait, pressed felt face, painted features including light blue/grey eyes glancing to side, painted eyelashes, eyeshadow, original full blonde mohair wig parted in center and pulled into ringlets behind head, rouged cheeks, swivel neck, cloth body, well shaped legs with feet formed for high heels, individually stitched fingers and thumb, elaborate pale blue organdy gown, applied felt rosebuds, puffed sleeves, lace mittens, double ruffled organdy collar, yellow felt wide brimmed hat trimmed with flowers, stockings, original garters with blue felt rosebuds, original wired hoop petticoat, marks: cloth and paper labels on back of dress read Lenci, 25"	1000.00	1200.00	1100.00

LESNEY

	Current Price Range		P/Y AVG
☐ **Alice In Wonderland,** vinyl, blonde hair, marked Lesney 1973, made in Hong Kong, not related to Disney, 5"	6.00	8.00	6.00
☐ **Baby,** vinyl jointed, blonde rooted hair, painted blue eyes, open-close nurser mouth, white picque dress with matching bonnet, blue ribbon trim, 14"	18.00	22.00	18.00
☐ **Party Patti,** vinyl, red hair, marked Lesney 1973, made in Hong Kong	6.00	8.00	6.00
☐ **Sailor Sue,** vinyl, marked Lesney 1973, made in Hong Kong, 5"	6.00	8.00	6.00

L.H.K.

	Current Price Range		P/Y AVG
☐ **Bisque,** French body, human hair wig, brown sleep eyes, peach, crepe dress with hat, 18"	650.00	700.00	665.00
☐ **Bisque,** blonde, goat hair wig, marked Germany, 10"	175.00	225.00	185.00
☐ **Bisque,** French ball-jointed body, human hair wig, blue sleep eyes, solid wrists, light blue dress and hat, 18"	925.00	1000.00	950.00
☐ **Bisque Head,** French jointed body, human hair wig, blue sleep eyes, light blue dress and hat	950.00	1000.00	975.00
☐ **Bisque Head,** French jointed composition body, brown set eyes, French human hair wig, pink velvet dress	250.00	325.00	250.00

LIBBY

☐ **I Dream Of Jeannie (Barbara Eden),** plastic/vinyl, sleep eyes (blue), rooted hair (blonde), closed mouth, dressed in the "Jeannie" costume from the popular TV series of the 1960's (still being shown in syndication), marked 4, 1966, Libby, box marked Sidney Sheldon Productions, (Sidney Sheldon was producer of the TV show), 20"	23.00	29.00	22.00

LIBERTY

☐ **King,** cloth, unmarked on doll, sold originally with a tag reading Liberty, Made in England, representing an English king wearing crown and ermine robes, but apparently no king in particular, 8½"	23.00	29.00	22.00

LIMBACH

	Current Price Range		P/Y AVG
☐ **Bisque Head,** *French ball-jointed body, human hair wig, brown paperweight eyes, pierced ears, open mouth, blue velvet dress with antique lace trim, marked clover leaf, 16"*	600.00	650.00	620.00
☐ **Little Girl,** *bisque socket head composition chubby body, mohair glued on wig, in pigtails, black glass pupiless eyes, open mouth with four small teeth, yellow dress, matching bonnet, white pinafore, long white stockings, black leather shoes, Rauenstein Grenier trefoil mark on head, early 1800's, 9½"*	145.00	160.00	145.00

LIMOGES

☐ **Bisque Head,** *French ball-jointed body, brown wig, blue paperweight eyes, pierced ears, green velvet dress, 17"*	685.00	725.00	700.00
☐ **Bisque Head,** *French wooden and composition body, brown set eyes, brown human hair wig, open mouth, lovely old clothes, 20½"*	1150.00	1275.00	1200.00
☐ **French Girl Doll,** *jointed five piece body, set blue paperweight eyes, pierced ears, frilly dress, 12"*	500.00	550.00	510.00
☐ **Francee,** *reproduction, bisque, lacy red velour dress, 22"*	100.00	150.00	125.00

LOUIS AMBERG AND SONS

☐ **Charlie Chaplin,** *cloth body and head, painted face, wool hair, marked Louis Amberg & Son, Charlie Chaplin, date of manufacture unknown, 17"*	165.00	200.00	160.00

LOUISE R. KAMPES STUDIOS

	Current Price Range		P/Y AVG
☐ **Kamkins,** pressed mask cloth face, stuffed cloth body, wig, painted features, original costume, 20"	500.00	600.00	500.00

LOVEE

☐ **Daisy Luv,** plastic/vinyl, marked Made in Hong Kong No. 2618, late 1960's, 11½"	3.00	4.00	3.00

Note: Before being acquired by Lovee, the mold for this doll had been used by Mattel and the Mattel marking will still be found on the back of the doll's head. This has led some collectors and dealers into the error of classifying it as a Mattel doll.

☐ **Unnamed,** plastic/vinyl, nurser, painted eyes, marked 1974, Lovee Doll, 22¼"	5.00	7.00	5.00

MAJBER

☐ **Lindy,** plastic/vinyl, brunette hair (rooted), sleep eyes (blue), partially open mouth, marked Majber, made in 1966, 17½"	14.00	18.00	13.00

MAJESTIC

☐ **Jack And Jill,** printed oilcloth (stuffed), marked 1950 Majestic Dolls, 12" each, value for pair	2.00	3.00	2.00

MARLON

☐ **Sussy,** vinyl, molded and painted hair, sleep eyes, nursing mouth, unmarked, made in 1968, 8"	6.00	8.00	6.00

ARMAND MARSEILLE

Every browser among antique and semi-antique dolls has encountered specimens by Armand Marseille. The factory survived long and was, during its peak years, highly prolific, turning out dolls in large numbers for various contractors. The Armand Marseille dolls chiefly have bisque heads and run a comprehensive gamut in sizes and styles, representing infants, adults and all ages in between. Mostly they have sleep eyes. The faces are mostly very well-modeled, some with strong classical overtones, some suggesting a swing to more progressive designing. From a technical viewpoint the Armand Marseille dolls are probably as good, collectively, as any of their era. The only thing holding down their values is their lack of real scarcity on the market, owing to the large quantities manufactured. This, however, should be a bonus to the hobbyist, as it enables him to get a fine period doll at a bargain price.

Armand Marseille was a German organization. It was founded in 1865 in the town of Koppelsdorf, Thuringia, Westphalia. In its earlier years it was moderately successful but its chief growth occurred after 1890. From 1900 to the onset of World War I (1914) it undoubtedly outproduced all other European doll factories. Its dolls, bearing various distributors' names, were sold in all parts of the western hemisphere. The war hindered all German doll makers, as the local market virtually collapsed and import/export business became difficult or impossible. Armand Marseille succeeded in struggling through the war. The firm was reorganized following the Armistice of 1918, with a view to reattaining the old production levels and heavily exporting into America. This dream was never realized, for various reasons — one of which was the new influence of Japan on the export doll market. In 1927 Armand Marseille closed its doors.

	Current Price Range		P/Y AVG
☐ **Baby,** bent limb, composition body, brown hair, blue eyes, sailor suit, mold number 990, 17"	350.00	400.00	365.00
☐ **Baby,** blue sleep eyes, cloth body, Germany"	250.00	300.00	275.00
☐ **Baby,** blue sleep eyes, dark blonde wig, open mouth, baby outfit of pink gingham checkered dress with white collar, pants to match, 12"	175.00	225.00	185.00
☐ **Bisque Shoulder Plate,** kid body, bisque lower arms, cloth lower legs, brown set eyes, old dress and matching hat, mold number 370, 15"	125.00	165.00	145.00

216 / ARMAND MARSEILLE

	Current Price Range		P/Y AVG
☐ **Black Baby,** *bisque head, five-piece composition body, brown sleep eyes, molded hair, open mouth, white christening gown, mold number 351, 13"*	425.00	550.00	400.00
☐ **Black Dream Baby A.M.,** *dark brown toned bisque solid dome head with flange neck, cloth body, brown toned composition arms, legs, brown sleep eyes, closed mouth, painted red lips, shaded brown hair, white organdy dress, marks: A.M., 10"*	375.00	500.00	375.00
☐ **Character Baby,** *bisque head, bent limb jointed body, red brown human hair wig, blue sleep eyes, short white two-piece dress with bonnet, marked mold number 990, c. 1920, 17"*	400.00	500.00	425.00
☐ **Character Baby,** *bisque socket head, jointed five-piece bent leg baby body, brown sleep eyes, original light brown mohair wig, open mouth with two porcelain teeth, dimpled chin, claret colored velvet jacket, shorts, matching beret, white satin blouse, lace collar, jabot, marks: Armand Marseille A. 975 M. Germany 12, 22"*	550.00	600.00	550.00
☐ **Character Baby,** *bisque socket head, five-piece bent leg baby body, brown sleep eyes, brown wig, open mouth with two porcelain teeth, double chin, white lace trimmed organdy gown, matching bonnet, made for George Brogfeldt by Armand Marseille, marks: Germany G 327 B, A 3 M., D.R.G.M. 259, 15"*	250.00	300.00	250.00
☐ **Character Boy,** *bent limb composition body, dark brown eyes, dark brown wig, three-piece red and blue knit outfit, mold number 990, 10"*	125.00	175.00	140.00
☐ **Character Boy,** *bisque head and hands, kid body, blue intaglio eyes, fancy suit with collar, marked A 600 M, 12"*	450.00	500.00	475.00
☐ **Character Boy,** *bisque head, ball-jointed body, sleep blue eyes, navy blue suit, marked A 326 M, 12"*	400.00	450.00	425.00

	Current Price Range		P/Y AVG
☐ **Character Boy,** bisque head, fully jointed composition body, brown sleep eyes, open mouth with two teeth, light brown human hair wig, navy striped sailor jacket with knickers, marks: Armand Marseille 971 Germany, A 1 M, 17"	300.00	400.00	300.00
☐ **Hoopla Girl,** bisque, socket head set on composition body (fully jointed), fixed dark eyes, closed mouth, marked 590/A. 5 M./Germany, 20"	415.00	470.00	400.00

Note: Hoopla Girl was made during World War I, a period of extreme recession for the factory because its main source of export trade (the U.S.) was cut off as a customer.

☐ **Infant,** bisque head, cloth body, composition hands and feet, molded hair, blue sleep eyes, voice box action, blue shorts outfit with suspenders, 11"	350.00	400.00	375.00
☐ **Infant,** mold number 342, solid dome head, blue sleeping eyes, open/closed mouth with teeth, composition hands, cloth body, crier, wears chemise, diaper and socks, 8½"	165.00	210.00	175.00
☐ **Lilly,** bisque head, arms and hands, kid body, universal joints, blue sleep eyes, open mouth, two piece bustle dress in brown, trimmed in red, white buttons down front, lace trim, straw hat with feather trim, 22"	425.00	475.00	440.00
☐ **Mama Doll,** bisque head and hands, kid body, talker, blue sleep eyes, blue gingham dress, 18"	325.00	375.00	340.00
☐ **Mammy,** black bisque head, jointed composition and wood body, brown sleep eyes, black mohair wig, open mouth red and white kerchief and dress, black stockings and shoes, mark: 390 A 6/0M, 11"	250.00	375.00	225.00

☐ **Musical Marotte,** bisque shoulder head, bisque hands, blue set eyes, black mohair wig, open mouth, original white blouse, fringed red skirt over round wooden casing which covers the musical mechanism, when doll is held

218 / ARMAND MARSEILLE

	Current Price Range		P/Y AVG
by wooden handle and twirled, it plays a tune, in working order, marks: on shoulder head-3200 AM 9/0 Dep, 13"	200.00	350.00	180.00
☐ **Oriental Baby,** bisque head, bent limb composition body, brown oriental eyes, molded hair, silk kimono, mark: A.M. 353, 13"	750.00	975.00	725.00
☐ **Oriental Baby,** bisque head, bent limb composition body, brown oriental eyes, molded hair, silk kimono, mark: A.M. 353, 20"	950.00	1500.00	950.00
☐ **Queen Louise,** bisque head, ball-jointed body, flapper, set blue eyes, long lashes, long blonde human hair wig, open mouth, fully beaded dress, silver head band, pink feathers, silver shoes, 23"	450.00	550.00	485.00
☐ **Queen Louise,** bisque head, ball-jointed composition body, human hair wig, brown sleep eyes, red dress with white lace trim, 22"	600.00	650.00	625.00
☐ **Queen Louise,** bisque socket head on fully jointed composition body, blue sleep eyes, original brown mohair wig, open mouth, double chin, dark green printed dress with white velvet ribbon, marks: Germany, Queen Louise 10, 26"	200.00	300.00	175.00
☐ **Queen Louise,** bisque socket head, fully jointed composition body, brown sleep eyes, real upper lashes, open mouth with four teeth, brown wig, blue batiste dress covered with antique lace, wide lace collar, and blue embroidered satin sash, matching bonnet, marks: Queen Louise 100 Germany, 24"	300.00	400.00	275.00
☐ **Queen Louise,** bisque head, jointed composition body, original reddish human hair wig, brown set eyes, feathered brows, eleborate red velvet dress and matching hat, 26"	450.00	550.00	450.00
☐ **Queen Lousie,** composition ball-jointed body, blue sleep eyes, blonde hair, 24"	360.00	410.00	380.00
☐ **Queen Louise,** composition, jointed open mouth, four teeth, brown sleep eyes, German, 27"	450.00	500.00	456.00

	Current Price Range		P/Y AVG

MARVEL COMICS GROUP

- **Spiderman,** *plastic/vinyl, molded and painted, based on the comic character from Marvel Comics Group, marked Marvel CG, 1971, 8"* 6.00 8.00 5.00

MASCOTTE

- **Bisque Head,** *jointed French composition and wood body, brown human hair wig, blue paperweight eyes, original clothes* 3200.00 3500.00 3000.00

MATTEL

- **Baby First Step,** *plastic/vinyl, blonde hair (rooted), sleep eyes (blue), toddles (battery operated), marked 1964 Mattel, Inc., Hawthorne, Calif., 18"* 12.00 16.00 12.00
- **Baby Fun,** *vinyl, blonde hair (rooted), painted eyes, can blow up balloons, wears dress with three small flowers on it, marked 1968 Mattel, Inc., Hong Kong, 8"* 6.00 9.00 6.00
- **Baby Secret,** *talker, vinyl head, foam body, vinyl hands, stuffed legs, red hair (rooted), painted eyes, made in Japan in 1965, 17½"* 12.00 16.00 12.00
- **Baby Teenie Talk,** *vinyl head, cloth body, vinyl arms and legs, platinum blonde hair (rooted), painted eyes (blue), a talker with a novel feature: its mouth moves while it talks, marked Mattel, Baby Teenie Talk, 1965, 17"* 12.00 16.00 12.00
- **Baby Tenderlove,** *foam head and body, platinum blonde hair (rooted), painted eyes, nursing mouth, marked 652C, 1969, 15"* 5.00 7.00 5.00
- **Beany,** *vinyl, molded and painted features, molded hair, marked Mattel Inc. Toymakers, made in Hong Kong in 1969, 18¼"* 36.00 45.00 32.00

MATTEL

	Current Price Range		P/Y AVG
☐ **Big Jack**, black, plastic/vinyl, molded and painted hair, painted eyes, fully jointed, figure of an adult black male, marked 1971 Mattel Inc., US Patent Pending, made in Hong Kong, 9½"	7.00	10.00	7.00
☐ **Bouncy Baby**, vinyl head, plastic body, vinyl arms and legs, blonde hair (rooted), painted eyes, set with springs to make baby bounce, marked 1968 Mattel, 11"	5.00	7.00	5.00
☐ **Boy Baby Brother Tenderlove**, black vinyl, rooted hair, sexed, 15"	12.00	17.00	13.00
☐ **Buffie**, plastic/vinyl, blonde hair (rooted), painted eyes, marked 1967 Mattel Inc., U.S. and For. Pats. Pend., 10"	16.00	21.00	15.00
☐ **Bugs Bunny**, vinyl face, plush body (stuffed), vinyl hands, holds carrot, marked Mattel Bugs Bunny, Warner Bros. Pictures, made in 1969, 19"	9.00	12.00	8.00
☐ **Callisto From Jupiter**, vinyl, posable, a space alien with corrugated arms and legs, marked 1968 Mattel, Inc., made in Hong Kong, 6"	7.00	10.00	6.00

Note: By 1968 the "man from Mars" theme was wearing thin, so toy manufacturers turned attentions to more distant planets.

☐ **Captain Lazer**, plastic/vinyl, molded and painted features, molded and painted hair, wearing spaceman-type suit, carries gun, gun shoots "lazer beam" (operated by battery), marked 1967 Mattel, Inc., 12"	11.00	15.00	10.00

Note: Investigation into the possible uses of lazer light was in its infancy when Mattel brought out "Captain Lazer."

☐ **Character Doll**, rubber head, cloth body	12.00	14.00	10.00
☐ **Charmin' Chatty**, talker, plastic/vinyl, blonde hair (rooted), sleep eyes (blue), marked Charmin' Chatty, 1961, 25"	35.00	46.00	33.00

Character Doll,
rubber and cloth
$12.00-$14.00

	Current Price Range		P/Y AVG
☐ **Chester O'Chimp (a monkey),** vinyl head, plush body (stuffed), bendable fingers, molded and painted features, marked Mattel, Chester O'Chimp, 1964, 14½"	8.00	11.00	7.00
☐ **Dancerina,** ballerina, blonde rooted hair, big blue eyes, open rosebud mouth, painted features, bright pink ballerina outfit and slippers, 24"	25.00	30.00	25.00

222 / MATTEL

	Current Price Range		P/Y AVG
☐ **Dancerina,** *mechanical (dances), plastic/vinyl, platinum blonde hair (rooted), painted eyes, operates by knob on top of head, battery powered, marked 1968 Mattel, 24"*	13.00	16.00	12.00
☐ **Doug Davis, Spaceman,** *vinyl, molded and painted features, molded and painted hair, dressed in space suit with helmet, marked Mattel, Inc., 1967, made in Hong Kong, 6"*	5.00	7.00	5.00
☐ **Dr. Doolittle,** *talker, vinyl head, cloth body, pullcord operated, says a variety of short phrases, marked Dr. Doolittle, MCMLXVII (1967), Twentieth Century Fox Film Corp., Inc. 22½"*	28.00	37.00	26.00

Note: Some added interest as "movie memorabilia."

☐ **Gentle Ben (a bear),** *talker, all plush (stuffed), plastic eyes and nose, marked Mattel, Gentle Ben, 1967, 18"*	10.00	14.00	9.00
☐ **Liney Lou,** *sweet treats, mint in box, enclosed in spoon*	3.00	6.00	4.00
☐ **Lola Liddle,** *vinyl, blonde hair (rooted), molded and painted features, marked Mattel 1965. 3"*	6.00	8.00	6.00
☐ **Major Matt Mason,** *vinyl, posable, molded and painted features, molded and painted hair, wears space suit, marked Mattel, Inc., 1967, made in Hong Kong, 6"*	5.00	7.00	5.00
☐ **Marie Osmond,** *mannequin modeling doll, 1976, 30"*	30.00	45.00	27.00
☐ **Monkees,** *talker, hand puppet representing all four members of this singing group, plastic, molded and painted features, molded and painted hair, made in 1967*	40.00	55.00	32.00

Note: If this one wasn't collectible as "rock music memorabilia," its value would be much lower.

☐ **Mrs Beasley,** *1967 Family Affair, vinyl head blonde rooted hair, blue cloth body, big blue eyes, painted features, yellow polk-a-dots, 22"*	22.00	28.00	22.00

Marie Osmond,
1976, 30"
$45.00-$55.00

	Current Price Range		P/Y AVG
☐ **Pioneer Daughter,** *bicentennial series,* #7940	12.00	17.00	13.00
☐ **Randy Reader,** *talker, plastic/vinyl, platinum blonde hair (rooted), operated by battery, eyes move as he reads, marked 1967 Mattel, Inc., 19"*	38.00	49.00	35.00
☐ **Raspberry Rosie,** *sweet treats, mint in box, enclosed in spoon*	3.00	6.00	4.00
☐ **Saucy,** *plastic/vinyl, rooted hair, changing facial expressions, the left arm serves as a crank, by which the doll's face changes expression, marked 1972 Mattel, Inc., 16"*	16.00	22.00	15.00

Note: One of the more imaginative novelty dolls sold by this firm.

224 / MATTEL

	Current Price Range		P/Y AVG
☐ **Sgt. Storm**, vinyl, posable, molded and painted features, molded and painted hair, wears space suit, with oxygen tank on back, marked Mattel, Inc., 1967, made in Hong Kong, 6"	5.00	7.00	5.00
☐ **Shrinking Violet**, cloth head and body, blonde mop hair, sewn-on eyes, ventriloquist mouth operated by pullcord, marked Mattel Shrinking Violet, The Funny Company, made in 1962, 15"	85.00	100.00	80.00
☐ **Singin' Chatty**, plastic/vinyl, blonde hair (rooted), sleep eyes (blue), singing version of the Chatty Cathy doll, with which Mattel had great success, marked Singin' Chatty, 1964, Mattel, Inc., Hawthorne, Calif., 17"	22.00	28.00	20.00
☐ **Sister Belle**, talker (11 expressions), plastic head, cloth body, cloth arms and legs, molded and painted features, mop hair (blonde), marked Mattel, Hawthorne, Calif., made in 1961, 17"	27.00	35.00	25.00
☐ **Sister Smallwalk**, walker, plastic/vinyl, brunette hair (rooted), painted eyes (blue), open smiling mouth with teeth, operates by battery, marked 1967 Mattel, 11½"	8.00	11.00	7.00
☐ **Slugger**, vinyl head, cloth body, cloth arms and legs, holds cloth baseball bat (stuffed), red hair (rooted), molded and painted features, marked 1975 Mattel, Inc., Taiwan, 5½"	3.00	5.00	3.00
☐ **Small Talk**, plastic/vinyl, blonde hair (rooted), painted eyes, open mouth with teeth, pullring operated, marked 1967 Mattel Inc., Japan, 11"	7.00	10.00	7.00
☐ **Sweet Sixteen**, vinyl/plastic, molded and painted features, blonde hair, marked 1-Mattel, Inc., 1958, Korea, made in 1975 (the date in the marking refers to a mold date), 11½"	8.00	11.00	8.00
☐ **Stephanie**, of the Sunshine Family, print dress, made in 1973	2.00	8.00	5.00

MATTEL / 225

	Current Price Range		P/Y AVG
☐ **Talk-A-Little**, *talker, printed cloth, stuffed, cloth arms and legs, mop hair (red), pullcord operated, says several brief phrases, sold originally with a tag reading 1970 Mattel, Inc., Hawthorne, Calif., 8"*	6.00	8.00	6.00
☐ **Talking Baby First Step**, *talker/walker, plastic/vinyl, blonde hair (rooted), painted eyes, marked 1967 Mattel, Inc., 18"*	15.00	19.00	14.00
☐ **T-Bone (a dog)**, *talker, head, stuffed body, molded and painted features, unmarked on doll, sold originally with a tag reading T-Bone TM 1964 Mattel Inc., 11"*	8.00	11.00	8.00

MATTEL — BARBIE AND BARBIE-RELATED

☐ **Allan**, *fashion doll, straight leg, yachting outfit*	20.00	25.00	21.00
☐ **All Star Ken**	12.00	15.00	13.00
☐ **Angel Face Barbie**, *c. 1983*	12.00	15.00	13.00
☐ **Baby**, *(from "Barbie Babysits"), plastic, molded and painted features, blonde hair, wears an apron, marked 953, sold in 1963, 3"*	7.00	10.00	7.00
☐ **Baby**, *(from "Barbie Babysits"), plastic, molded and painted features, revised version of the doll introduced in 1963, with different hair, marked 0953, sold in 1964, 3"*	6.00	8.00	6.00
Note: *Prices shown are for the doll PLUS all original accessories with which it was sold. The dolls by themselves without accessories, or with partial accessories, do not bring the full listed prices.*			
☐ **Barbie**, *blonde, orange dress*	20.00	30.00	21.00
☐ **Barbie**, *blonde, white net bathing suit, orange trim*	20.00	30.00	21.00
☐ **Barbie**, *bubble cut blonde, angel outfit, c.1963*	40.00	50.00	42.00

226 / MATTEL

	Current Price Range		P/Y AVG
☐ **Barbie,** *fashion queen, red bubble cut wig, blue wool sheath*	30.00	40.00	32.00
☐ **Barbie,** *fashion queen, red flip wig, wedding outfit*	30.00	40.00	32.00
☐ **Barbie,** *live action, turquoise bathing suit*	15.00	25.00	16.00
☐ **Barbie,** *living, lavendar knit dress, elbow slit*	10.00	15.00	11.00
☐ **Barbie,** *plastic, molded and painted features, ponytail with bangs, slotted feet designed to fit in stand, loop earrings, marked 850, made in 1959, 11½"*	725.00	950.00	700.00

Barbie,
sunstreaked hair
$150.00-$200.00

	Current Price Range		P/Y AVG
☐ **Barbie,** *plastic, molded and painted features, ponytail with bangs, feet NOT slotted (change in design from the original version), marked 850, made in 1960, 11½"*	650.00	825.00	600.00
☐ **Barbie's Friend Christie,** *black, plastic, molded and painted features, talker, brown hair (parted), wears knitted green shirt and red shorts, marked 1126, sold in 1968, 11½"*	120.00	150.00	100.00
Note: The first black doll in the Barbie group. The second, introduced a year later, was modeled after a living person (singer/actress Diahann Carroll).			
☐ **Beauty Secret Barbie**	10.00	15.00	11.00
☐ **Ken's Buddy Allen,** *plastic, molded and painted features, painted hair (reddish brown), non-posable legs, wears blue shorts and striped jacket, marked 1000, sold in 1964, 12"*	15.00	19.00	13.00
Note: The first Allen doll.			
☐ **Ken,** *dark flocked hair*	15.00	25.00	16.00
☐ **Ken,** *dark molded hair, business suit*	20.00	25.00	21.00
☐ **Ken,** *flocked hair, hat*	20.00	25.00	21.00
☐ **Ken,** *hard plastic, molded brown hair in crew cut #1, 11½"*	45.00	55.00	45.00
☐ **Ken,** *modern*	40.00	50.00	42.00
☐ **Ken,** *molded blonde hair, tennis outfit, racket, glasses, ball*	20.00	25.00	21.00
☐ **Ken,** *talking*	30.00	40.00	32.00
☐ **Kissing Barbie**	10.00	13.00	11.00
☐ **Midge,** *blonde, hot pink lounge pants*	30.00	40.00	32.00
☐ **Midge,** *blonde, jeans and shirt*	30.00	40.00	32.00
☐ **Midge,** *dark hair, pink dress*	30.00	40.00	32.00
☐ **Midge,** *red hair*	30.00	40.00	32.00
☐ **Miss Barbie,** *plastic, molded and painted features, sleep eyes, posable legs, wears pink suit (one piece), sold with three interchangeable wigs, marked 1060, sold in 1964, 11½"*	250.00	300.00	225.00
☐ **Mod Hair Ken,** *plastic, molded and painted features, rooted hair, wears brown jacket, marked 4224, sold in 1973, 12"*	7.00	10.00	6.00
☐ **My First Barbie**	7.00	13.00	8.00

228 / MATTEL

	Current Price Range		P/Y AVG
☐ **Newport Barbie**, *plastic, molded and painted features, wears yachting outfit, Malibu skintone, marked 7807, sold in 1974, 11½"*	14.00	20.00	12.00
☐ **Night Night Tutti**, *plastic, molded and painted features, marked 3553, sold in 1966, 6¼"*	5.00	7.00	4.00
☐ **Pink And Pretty Barbie**	12.00	15.00	13.00
☐ **P.J.**, *suntan, blonde hair, purple eyes*	6.00	10.00	7.00
☐ **P.J.**, *talking, necklace, ponytail advertising doll*	40.00	50.00	42.00
☐ **Pretty Change Barbie**	8.00	12.00	9.00
☐ **Quick Curl Barbie**, *plastic, molded and painted features, wears pink dress, marked 4220, sold in 1973, 11½"*	14.00	20.00	12.00
☐ **Quick Curl Francie**, *plastic, molded and painted features, wears yellow dress, marked 4222, sold in 1973, 11"*	8.00	10.00	7.00
☐ **Quick Curl Skipper**, *plastic, molded and painted features, wears blue dress, marked 4223, sold in 1973, 9¼"*	7.00	10.00	6.00
☐ **Skating Barbie**	10.00	13.00	11.00
☐ **Skating Ken**	8.00	12.00	9.00
☐ **Skipper, Barbie's Little Sister**, *plastic, molded and painted features, wears single-piece white and red suit, marked 0950, sold in 1964, 9¼"* **Note: The first Skipper doll.**	13.00	16.00	12.00
☐ *Skipper, dress and boots*	30.00	40.00	32.00
☐ **Skipper's Friend Ricky**, *plastic, molded and painted features, painted hair (reddish brown), non-posable legs, wears jacket and blue shorts, marked 1090, sold in 1965, 9¼"*	8.00	10.00	7.00
☐ **Skipper**, *Malibu, orange two-piece swimsuit*	10.00	20.00	11.00
☐ **Skooter, Skipper's Playmate**, *plastic, molded and painted features, freckled face, non-posable legs, wears two-piece red suit, marked 1040, sold in 1965, 9½"*	9.00	12.00	8.00
☐ **Spanish Talking Barbie**, *plastic, molded and painted features, wears ponytail, talker, dressed in shorts and knitted shirt, marked 8348, sold in 1968, the same as the standard talking Barbie,*			

	Current Price Range		P/Y AVG
introduced that same year, except that she speaks Spanish, intended for sale in Spanish-speaking areas of New York, California and Texas, 11½"	130.00	160.00	120.00
☐ **Spanish Talking Ken**, *plastic, molded and painted features, talker with bendable legs, dressed in red, Spanish-speaking version of the standard Talking Ken doll, intended for sale in Spanish-speaking communities of New York, California and Texas, marked 1111, sold in 1970, 12"*	70.00	90.00	65.00
☐ **Sport And Share Ken**	9.00	13.00	10.00
☐ **Stacey, Barbie's English Friend,** *plastic, molded and painted features, talker, wears to-piece striped outfit, marked 1125, sold in 1968, 11½"* .... **Note:** *The first Stacey doll.*	16.00	20.00	15.00
☐ **Stacy,** *red flip wig, swimsuit*	30.00	40.00	32.00

McDONALD

☐ **Ronald McDonald,** *printed cloth, representing the symbol of the McDonald restaurant chain, used as a promotional item, made in 1967, 17"*	4.00	6.00	4.00

METTI

☐ **Bindi,** *black, vinyl, sleep eyes, open mouth with teeth, representing a child of the Australian aboriginals ("bushmen"), marked Metti, Australia, date of manufacture unknown*	70.00	90.00	65.00
☐ **Mon Cherie,** *vinyl, sleep eyes (blue), puffy cheeks, pug nose, unmarked, sold originally with a paper tag reading My Name is Mon Cheri, Made in Australia, made in 1975, 12½"*	22.00	28.00	20.00

	Current Price Range		P/Y AVG
☐ **Vanessa,** *vinyl, sleep eyes (blue), pug nose, open mouth, unmarked, sold originally with a paper tag reading My Name is Vanessa, The House of Metti, made in 1975, 24½"*	45.00	56.00	42.00

MIDWESTERN

☐ **Darleen,** *plastic/vinyl, sleep eyes (blue), marked 25-6AE, made in 1961 for the Speigel mail-order house of Chicago, 24"*	7.00	10.00	6.00
☐ **Nun Nurse,** *plastic, sleep eyes (blue), dressed as nun with hood, cape and gown, unmarked, made in 1958, 12"* ...	8.00	11.00	7.00
☐ **Tiny Little,** *vinyl head and body, rooted hair, nursing mouth, bright red lips, marked PTN-18, made in 1964, 15"*	4.00	6.00	4.00

MIGLIORATI

☐ **Vinyl Head,** *soft body, painted features, pink yarn hair tied with bows, pink dress and hat, known as "Nuvolette," made in Italy, 14"*	35.00	45.00	38.00
☐ **Vinyl Head,** *soft body, painted features, red yarn hair tied with bows, blue dress and hat, known as "Nuvolette," made in Italy, 14"*	35.00	45.00	38.00
☐ **Vinyl Head,** *hands, and feet, soft body, painted features, brown wig, lavender floor length gown, matching hat silver shoes, stand, made in Italy, 26"*	50.00	100.00	70.00

MINERVA

	Current Price Range		P/Y AVG

☐ **Metal**, *shoulder head, set on cloth body with bisque forearms and cowhide feet, fixed eyes, open mouth showing two teeth, marked Minerva, 20"* 90.00 115.00 85.00
Note: Figure of a young girl.

☐ **Metal**, *shoulder head, set on cloth body, bisque forearms, molded reddish hair, painted head, fixed eyes, open mouth showing three teeth and traces of others, marked Minerva, 18¾"* 100.00 130.00 95.00
Note: This is a model of a boy about 3 or 4 years of age.

EDWARD MOBERLY

☐ **Candy**, *vinyl, molded and painted features, molded and painted hair, marked The Edward Moberly Co., 1958, 8"* 4.00 6.00 4.00
Note: Actually made by Arrow Plastics.

MOLLENECHT

☐ **Gucki**, *felt with rubber head, representing an alpine peasant in traditional costuming, made in Bavaria, 12"* 11.00 14.00 10.00

MOLLYE

☐ **Angel Face**, *crier, composition head with cloth body, made in 1948, 24"* 46.00 57.00 45.00

☐ **Belgium Girl**, *cloth, marked Mollye's Doll, T.M. Reg., representing a young girl in a Belgian national costume, date of manufacture unknown, probably 1930's, 15"* .. 70.00 85.00 65.00

☐ **Debbie Deb**, *music box, composition, sleep eyes, blonde wig, 17½"* 350.00 425.00 330.00
Note: In working order.

232 / MONICA STUDIOS

	Current Price Range		P/Y AVG
☐ **Dutch Girl**, *cloth, elaborately costumed, made in 1941, 18"*	95.00	115.00	90.00
☐ **Hi Buzzy**, *cloth, a child in cowboy outfit, made in 1949, 22"*	115.00	135.00	110.00
☐ **Irene Dunn**, *music box, composition, human hair wig, made c. 1950, 20"*	160.00	190.00	150.00
☐ **Peggy Rose The Royal Bride**, *hard plastic, sleep eyes (blue), made in 1950, 16"*	80.00	95.00	75.00
☐ **Sabu**, *composition, representing the motion picture actor Sabu dressed for his role in "The Thief of Bagdad," made c. 1948, 15"*	190.00	225.00	175.00

MONICA STUDIOS

☐ **Monica**, *composition, blue painted eyes, brown wig, red and white organdy gown with red ribbon and rickrack trim, 14½"*	225.00	275.00	240.00
☐ **Monica**, *composition, rooted hair, painted eyes, dressed as bride, unmarked, date of manufacture unknown, believed to have been made in the 1950's, 16"*	70.00	90.00	65.00

MORIMURA BROTHERS

☐ **Baby Darling**, *bisque, jointed, painted, marked Nippon*	65.00	75.00	70.00
☐ **Bisque Head**, *kid body, long red hair, blue stationary glass eyes, open mouth, teeth, green velvet dress with fur trim, feather butterfly in hair, 22"*	250.00	300.00	270.00
☐ **Bisque**, *German doll, set brown eyes, long brown hair, open mouth, white dress, baby bonnet, 30"*	550.00	650.00	588.00
☐ **Bisque Shoulder Head**, *kid body, pin jointed arms, legs, knees, bisque hands, nail detail, blue sleep eyes with real upper lashes, open mouth with four molded teeth, dimpled chin, light brown*			

	Current Price Range		P/Y AVG
wig, white two piece suit, embroidered red lace trim, Made by Morimura Bros. marks: 5 MB within incized circle, Japan 4, 21"	120.00	135.00	120.00
☐ **Toddler**, nine-piece jointed body, painted eye, navy blue wool suit, 13"	300.00	350.00	325.00

NANCY ANN STORYBOOK DOLL COMPANY

The Nancy Ann Storybook Doll Company began in San Francisco, California in 1941. It was founded by Nancy Ann Abbott and A.L. Rowland. In the beginning, they imported the bodies from various Japanese and European sources but due to the poor quality of these imports they soon began producing their own dolls.

As demand for the charming 5½" elaborately wigged and costumed dolls grew, a factory was built and dolls were produced at a rate of over 8,000 per day. The storybook dolls were originally made of bisque with painted faces, lovely wigs, one-piece head, body, legs, and jointed arms. Miss Abbott designed all the beautiful costumes herself, basing the themes on nursery rhymes, fairy tales, and her own creativity.

In the 1950's the dolls were made of hard plastic and vinyl and were fully jointed. These lovely dolls continued in production until 1960. The Nancy Ann Storybook Doll was produced again in the 1970's by Giant Consolidated Industries of Salt Lake City, Utah.

☐ **A Flower Girl For May,** bisque, molded and painted features, blonde hair attached by adhesive, wears flowered broad-brimmed hat, long lace-trimmed dress, unmarked, sold originally in a box which gave the mold number as 191, made in 1943, 6½"	15.00	21.00	15.00
☐ **April,** bisque, one-piece body with jointed arms, painted eyes, wig, original costume, #190 box, 5½"	35.00	45.00	40.00
☐ **Boy,** bisque, jointed, blonde hair, ring bearer, one-piece pants set, bow, 4"	45.00	55.00	50.00
☐ **Big Sister,** hard plastic, straight leg walker, brown mohair wig, sleep blue eyes, long pink taffeta dress, white lace trim, pink matching slippers, 10"	60.00	70.00	60.00

234 / NANCY ANN STORYBOOK DOLL COMPANY

	Current Price Range		P/Y AVG
☐ **Big Sister And Little Sister,** hard plastic, one-piece body with jointed arms, painted eyes, wig, original costume, 5½"	55.00	65.00	60.00
☐ **Bisque,** blonde hair, dotted white, yellow dress, 6"	15.00	25.00	20.00
☐ **Bisque,** blonde hair, white satin, flowered, pink hat	25.00	35.00	30.00
☐ **Bisque,** dark hair, pink satin dress, pink felt, 6"	25.00	35.00	30.00
☐ **Bisque,** dark hair, purple satin dress, white apron	20.00	30.00	25.00
☐ **Bisque,** reddish brown mohair wig, gold satin dress, black lace trim, lavender bow	20.00	25.00	20.00
☐ **Bisque,** straight leg, red hair, lacy white dress, pink felt hat, purple ribbons, 6"	25.00	35.00	25.00
☐ **Bride,** hard plastic, one-piece body with jointed arms, painted eyes, wig original brides gown with taffetta skirt and lace flock, 5½"	25.00	35.00	30.00
☐ **Bride,** jointed, swivel neck, hand painted, wedding outfit, veil, flowers, 6"	20.00	30.00	25.00
☐ **Bride,** plastic, sleep eyes, marked Nancy Ann Storybook Doll, 6"	16.00	21.00	15.00
☐ **Bridesmaid,** bisque, one piece body with jointed arms, painted eyes, wig, original costume blue gown, #87 box, 5½"	45.00	55.00	50.00
☐ **Bridesmaid,** bisque, one piece body with jointed arms, painted eyes, wig, original pink gown, #87 box, 5½"	45.00	55.00	40.00
☐ **Christening Baby,** plastic, molded and painted hair, sleep eyes, (blue), marked Storybook Dolls, U.S.A., made in 1952, 3½"	13.00	17.00	12.00
☐ **Cinderella,** hard plastic, one piece body with jointed arms, painted eyes, wig, original costume, stand, 5½"	45.00	55.00	50.00
☐ **Commencement,** plastic, blonde hair attached by adhesive, sleep eyes, (black), marked Storybook Dolls, U.S.A., made in 1952, 6"	9.00	12.00	9.00

	Current Price Range		P/Y AVG
☐ **Composition,** jointed, blonde mohair wig, pink satin dress, white lace trim, flowers	20.00	25.00	20.00
☐ **Composition,** jointed brown mohair wig, red full dress, yellow and green trim, large grey hat with feather	18.00	22.00	18.00
☐ **Daffidown Dilly,** plastic, blonde hair attached by adhesive, painted features, unmarked, sold originally in a box which gave the mold number as 171, made in 1952, 5½"	9.00	12.00	9.00
☐ **Daisy,** hard plastic, one piece body with jointed arms, painted eyes, wig, original costume long pink gown, 5½"	25.00	35.00	30.00
☐ **"December,"** bisque, one piece body with jointed arms, painted eyes, wig, original costume, 5½", #198 box	35.00	45.00	40.00
☐ **December,** bisque, straight legs, blonde hair, green net gown, #198, 7"	40.00	50.00	40.00
☐ **December,** plastic, lacy red taffeta, matching felt, feathered hat, mint in box, #198, 7"	30.00	40.00	35.00
☐ **Diaphanie,** hand painted, red hair, open close eyes, multicolored floral print dress, pink apron, hat, mint in box, 6" ..	30.00	60.00	35.00
☐ **Diller A Dollar,** plastic, blonde hair attached by adhesive, sleep eyes, (blue), marked Storybook Dolls, U.S.A., made in 1952, 7½"	9.00	12.00	9.00
☐ **Elsie Marley,** bisque, molded and painted features, red hair attached by adhesive, unmarked, sold originally in a box which gave the mold number as 31, and carried the following couplet: "Elsie Marley's grown so fine, She won't get up 'till eight or nine," made in 1942, 5½"	14.00	19.00	13.00
☐ **"Feb,"** bisque, one piece body with jointed arms, painted eyes, wig, original costume, #188 box, 5½"	35.00	45.00	40.00
☐ **Flossie Came,** bisque, one piece body with jointed arms, painted eyes, wig, original costume, #174 box, 5½"	45.00	55.00	50.00

NANCY ANN STORYBOOK DOLL COMPANY

	Current Price Range		P/Y AVG
☐ **Girl**, *bisque, jointed leg, blonde hair, ruffled, pink polka dotted gown, feathered hat, 6"*	15.00	25.00	20.00
☐ **Girl**, *plastic, lacy pink nylon outfit, flowered hat, 6"*	15.00	25.00	20.00
☐ **Give Me A Lass**, *bisque, one piece body with jointed arms, painted eyes, wig, original costume, #178 box, 5½"*	35.00	45.00	40.00
☐ **Goose Girl**, *bisque, one piece body with jointed arms, painted eyes, wig, original costume, #169, box, 5½"*	35.00	45.00	40.00
☐ **Goose Girl**, *red hair, dotted red, white dress, green skirt, dotted red, white apron, mint in box*	30.00	40.00	35.00
☐ **Hard Plastic**, *jointed shoulder and neck, sleep eyes, brown mohair, white dress with pink flowers*	20.00	25.00	20.00
☐ **Hard Plastic**, *one piece, jointed arms, painted eyes, wig, original red bodice, hearts on skirt, red felt hat, 5½"*	25.00	35.00	30.00
☐ **Hard Plastic**, *one piece body with jointed arms, painted eyes, wig, original costume with green felt hat with cherries*	35.00	40.00	35.00
☐ **Hard Plastic**, *one piece body with jointed arms, painted eyes, wig, original long green gown, floral bodice and slip, 5½"*	25.00	35.00	30.00
☐ **"May,"** *bisque, one piece body with jointed arms, painted eyes, wig, original costume, #191, box, 5½"*	35.00	45.00	40.00
☐ **Miss Muffet**, *plastic, blonde hair attached by adhesive, sleep eyes, (blue), unmarked, originally sold with a tag reading Styled by Nancy Ann, Nancy Ann Storybook Dolls, San Francisco, made in 1956, 6½"*	9.00	12.00	9.00
☐ **Muffie**, *plastic, brunette hair attached by adhesive, sleep eyes, blue, marked Storybook Dolls, California, made in 1952, 7"*	9.00	12.00	9.00
☐ **Muffie**, *vinyl, a female version of Daniel Boone, made in 1956, 8"*	22.00	27.00	20.00
☐ **Muffie**, *walker, dark pigtails, blue eyes, molded lashes*	60.00	70.00	60.00

NANCY ANN STORYBOOK DOLL COMPANY / 237

	Current Price Range		P/Y AVG
☐ **Muffie Around The World,** *hard plastic. This was a series released in the 1970's, showing the basic Muffie doll in various national costumes. Each came in a colorfully printed display package. All are 8" tall and the values are $11.00-$14.00.*			
☐ **Nellie Bird,** *swivel neck, jointed, open close eyes, red hair, purple, blue floral print dress, blue apron, lacy white hat, mint in box, 6"*	30.00	40.00	35.00
☐ **Nun,** *hard plastic, one piece body with jointed arms, painted eyes, wig, original costume, 5½"*	45.00	55.00	50.00
☐ **October,** *hard plastic, one piece body with jointed arms, painted eyes, wig, original costume, 5½"*	30.00	40.00	35.00

October,
hard plastic, 5½"
$30.00-$40.00

NANCY ANN STORYBOOK DOLL COMPANY

	Current Price Range		P/Y AVG
☐ **One Two Button My Shoe,** hard plastic, one piece body with jointed arms, painted eyes, wig, original costume, 5½"	30.00	40.00	35.00
☐ **On Two, Button My Shoe,** bisque, brunette hair attached by adhesive, painted eyes, (blue), closed mouth, marked Storybook Doll, U.S.A., made in 1941, 5"	19.00	24.00	18.00
☐ **Operetta-Bittersweet,** bisque, one piece body with jointed arms, painted eyes, wig, original costume, #311 box, 5½"	35.00	45.00	40.00
☐ **Polly Put The Kettle On,** bisque, brunette hair attached by adhesive, painted eyes, (blue), holds ceramic kettle, marked Storybook Doll, U.S.A., made in 1941, 5"	18.00	24.00	17.00
☐ **Queen Of Hearts,** bisque, molded and painted features, brunette hair attached by adhesive, unmarked, sold originally with a tag reading 117, Queen of Hearts, made in 1942, 5"	14.00	19.00	14.00
☐ **Rain Rain,** bisque, one piece body with jointed arms, painted eyes, wig, original costume, #170 box, 5½"	45.00	55.00	50.00
☐ **Ring Around The Roses,** bisque, one piece body with jointed arms, painted eyes, wig, original costume, #159 box, 5½"	35.00	45.00	40.00
☐ **Ring Bearer And Flower Girl,** hard plastic, one piece bodies with jointed arms, painted eyes, wigs, original costumes, 5½" tallest figure	90.00	110.00	100.00
☐ **"September,"** bisque, one piece body with jointed arms, painted eyes, wig, original costume, #195 box, 5½"	35.00	45.00	40.00
☐ **Spring,** bisque, painted, green, net gown, flower motif, seasons series, #90, 6"	30.00	40.00	35.00
☐ **Star Light-Star Bright,** hard plastic, one piece body with jointed arms, painted eyes, wig, original costume, stand, 5½"	45.00	55.00	50.00
☐ **Sugar And Spice,** hard plastic, one piece body with jointed arms, painted eyes, wig, original costume, 5½"	35.00	45.00	40.00

	Current Price Range		P/Y AVG
☐ **Valentine,** bisque, painted, lacy gown with red heart, lacy bonnet, 5½"	17.00	22.00	16.00
☐ **Winter,** plastic, brunette hair attached by adhesive, molded and painted features, marked Storybook Dolls USA., made in 1952, 5¾"	9.00	12.00	9.00

Note: From a series of "seasons" dolls, all of which have the same retail value. Each is dressed appropriately for the season she represents.

NASCO

☐ **Andy,** vinyl/plastic, yarn hair, marked Nasco Dolls Inc., The Bobbs-Merrill Co., Inc., Bobbs-Merrill was the publishing company that owned the rights to Raggedy Ann and Andy, made in 1973, 24".	11.00	14.00	11.00
☐ **Debbie Lou,** composition head and body, sleep eyes, (blue), closed mouth, blonde hair, fully jointed, made in 1944, 14"	31.00	37.00	30.00
☐ **Raggedy Ann,** vinyl/plastic, yarn hair, marked Nasco Dolls Inc., The Bobbs-Merrill Co., Inc., Bobbs-Merrill was the publishing company that owned the rights to Raggedy Ann, made in 1973, 24"	11.00	14.00	11.00
☐ **Stumbles,** walker, vinyl head, cloth body, vinyl hands, representing a toddler just learning to walk, who takes many "stumbles," marked Nasco Doll Co., Inc., Taiwan, date of manufacture unknown, probably c. 1973, 13"	10.00	14.00	10.00

NEMS ENTERPRISES

☐ **George,** vinyl, hair attached by adhesive, molded and painted features, representing George Harrison of the Beatles, marked NEMS ENT. Ltd. 1964, 5"	210.00	250.00	200.00

240 / NESTLE'S CHOCOLATE

	Current Price Range		P/Y AVG
☐ **John,** hard plastic, hair attached by adhesive, molded and painted features, representing John Lennon of the Beatles, marked NEMS ENT. Ltd. 1964, 5"	290.00	345.00	275.00
☐ **Paul,** vinyl, hair attached by adhesive, molded and painted features, representing Paul McCartney of the Beatles, marked NEMS ENT. Ltd. 1964, 5"	240.00	280.00	230.00
☐ **Ringo,** hard plastic, hair attached by adhesive, molded and painted features, representing Ringo Starr of the Beatles, marked NEMS ENT. Ltd. 1964, 5"	1100.00	1350.00	915.00

NESTLE'S CHOCOLATE

☐ **Chocolate Man,** cloth (printed), given as a premium in connection with the purchase of Nestle's Chocolate, date of manufacture unknown, c. 1970	7.00	9.00	7.00

RUTH E. NEWTON

☐ **Babee Bee,** vinyl, molded and painted hair (blonde), sleep eyes (blue), nursing mouth, marked Sunbabe, Babee Bee, Ruth E. Newton, New York, NY, made in 1954, 12"	11.00	14.00	11.00
☐ **So-Wee,** plastic, baby doll, comes with bottle, booties, jacket, towel and soap	30.00	40.00	35.00

ADELHEID NOGLER

☐ **Friedel,** celluloid, molded and painted features, brown hair attached by adhesive, representing a youth in Alpine costume, made in Innsbruck, Austria, in 1937, 9"	35.00	45.00	33.00

	Current Price Range		P/Y AVG

Note: Scarce, without any doubt. Foreign dolls in national costumes of their land of manufacture were almost always intended for local sale — as souvenirs for tourists — rather than for wholesale export. Considering that not too many Americans were visting Austria in the troubled late '30's, only a relatively few specimens could have been brought to this country.

ROSE O'NEILL

☐ **Kewpie**, bisque head, jointed arms and neck, stationary legs, marked on foot, 4½"	150.00	200.00	175.00
☐ **Kewpie**, composition, all one molded piece torso and legs on rounded base, jointed arms, starfish hands, molded blonde top forelock, two side curls, blue wings, mischievous, painted, brown eyes glancing to side, marks: round paper label on bottom reads Rose O'Neill c. 1913, 12"	100.00	175.00	75.00
☐ **Kewpie**, composition doll with moveable arms, tiny blue tipped wing buds on back, decal intact, height 11"	80.00	90.00	85.00
☐ **Kewpie**, composition head and jointed arm body, molded hair, painted googly eyes, closed mouth, open fingers, 11"	150.00	200.00	175.00
☐ **Kewpie**, composition, head turns, jointed shoulder, hips, side glaring eyes, molded blonde hair peaked on top, painted features, smiling face, pink sunsuit trimmed in lace, 13"	120.00	130.00	120.00
☐ **Kewpie**, composition, jointed at head, shoulders, hips, side glancing eyes, exceptional facial coloring, blue dress with white polka dots, 13"	145.00	155.00	145.00
☐ **Kewpie**, female, composition head, molded composition body, painted eyes, red and white dress, c. 1920, 12"	120.00	130.00	120.00

242 / P & M

Kewpie Girl, composition, painted features, c. 1920, 12"
$120.00-$130.00

P & M	Current Price Range		P/Y AVG
☐ **Belinda,** *black, plastic/vinyl, black hair, (rooted), sleep eyes, (brown), marked P & M Sales, Inc., 1966, marked additionally with a mold number BD19, 23"*	14.00	19.00	13.00
☐ **Royal Princess,** *plastic/vinyl, brunette hair, (rooted), sleep eyes, (blue), nursing mouth with teeth, marked 17EYE, 1967, P&M Doll Co., 17"*	8.00	11.00	7.00

Note: *The idea for a Royal Princess doll might have been inspired by Caroline of Monaco, who in 1967 was about the age of the girl represented by this doll.*

PARKSMITH

	Current Price Range		P/Y AVG
☐ **Googly**, *vinyl, eyes spin when squeezed, a boy wearing horn-rimmed eyeglasses, holding an ice cream cone, marked U.S. Pat. No.3451160, made in Japan in 1969,* 6"	4.00	6.00	4.00

ADELAINE PATTI

☐ **Lady**, *china head, porcelain arms and legs, desirable hairdo, centerpart, swept back at temples, 12 vertical curls at sides, raised pompador over forehead, red eye lines, circular nostrils, full molded lips with painted separation lines, stylish black lace trimmed walking suit,* 21" 375.00 415.00 385.00

GUTTA PERCHA

☐ **Bisque**, *shoulder head, cloth body, painted black eyes and hair, original dress,* 21" 425.00 550.00 425.00

PEREGO

☐ **Topo Gigio**, *(a mouse), vinyl head, cloth body, vinyl hands, rooted hair, marked 1963 Maria Perego,* 12⅞" 11.00 14.00 10.00
Note: Topo Gigio, a puppet-mouse, was featured many times on the Ed Sullivan TV program.

PERFECTA

	Current Price Range		P/Y AVG

☐ **Sad Song,** *vinyl, brunette hair, (rooted), molded and painted features, teardrop emerging from left eye, holds hands clasped, marked Perfecta, Made in Hong Kong, made in 1965, 6½"* 5.00 7.00 5.00

PERFEKTA

☐ **Pregnant Doll,** *plastic/vinyl, sleep eyes, (blue), rooted hair, marked Perfekta, Made in Hong Kong, 14"* 10.00 14.00 10.00
Note: *We have been unable to locate any information on the Perfekta Doll Co., which almost certainly was not located in Hong Kong even though this doll was made there. To judge from the progressive nature of the doll it was possibly a West German product.*

PETER PUPPET PLAYTHINGS

☐ **Princess Summerfall Winterspring,** *(marionette puppet), composition head, wood body, composition hands and feet, wears Indian-style clothing, Princess Summerfall Winterspring was a character on the "Howdy Doody" TV program, unmarked, made in 1950, 13½"* 50.00 65.00 45.00

PETITE PORTRAITS

☐ **Campbell Kid,** *composition, 12"* 325.00 375.00 340.00
☐ **Liz Taylor,** *bisque head, cloth body, bisque arms and legs, painted features, black wig, marked Petite Portraits and L.W., for the sculptor, Lita Wilson, date of manufacture unknown, c. 1970, 15½"* 500.00 650.00 475.00

	Current Price Range		P/Y AVG

☐ **Prince Ranier Of Monaco,** *bisque head, cloth body, bisque arms and legs, molded and painted hair, marked Petite Portraits and L.W., for the sculptor, Lita Wilson, made in 1971, 16"* 325.00 400.00 300.00

PIACENXA

☐ **Athena,** *plastic, sleep eyes, (blue), bright red lips, marked Athena, Piacenxa, 40P, date of manufacture unknown, 18"* 90.00 115.00 90.00
Note: The manufacturer's name is pronounced Piacen-ZA.

PILLSBURY

☐ **Doughboy,** *printed cloth, (stuffed), wearing a chef's hat with the Pillsbury logo, used as a premium, made in the 1960's, 13"* 7.00 10.00 7.00
☐ **Poppin' Fresh,** *vinyl, molded features, all one piece, representing the symbol of the Pillsbury Flour Co., marked 1971, The Pillsbury Co., Minneapolis, Minn., undoubtedly a premium or promotional item, 7"* 5.00 7.00 5.00

PIEROTTI

☐ **Shoulder Head,** *poured wax head, arms, legs, cloth body, blonde mohair inset hair, blue glass inset eyes, original navy blue taffeta dress, 19"* 900.00 1250.00 925.00
☐ **Wax Head,** *ball jointed body, blue sleep eyes, floral yoked dress with straw hat, marked 1875* 500.00 600.00 530.00

PRINCESS CHRISTINA

	Current Price Range		P/Y AVG
☐ **Chiffon,** *vinyl head, cloth body, vinyl hands, long blonde hair tied with ribbons, floral print dress, white stockings, black shoes, unmarked on doll, made in France in 1974, 12"*	22.00	28.00	20.00
☐ **Corina,** *black vinyl, jointed, mint in box, West Germany, 12"*	40.00	50.00	40.00
☐ **Sweet Sue,** *vinyl, jointed, mint in box, 16"*	40.00	50.00	40.00

PRODUCT PEOPLE

☐ **Charlie The Tuna,** *vinyl, molded and painted, representing the symbol of the StarKist Tuna Co., a tuna wearing cap and eyeglasses, made in 1973, 7"*	4.00	6.00	4.00

GRACE STOREY PUTNAM

☐ **Bye-Lo Baby,** *all bisque, human hair, brown eyes, painted shoes and socks, rare, 6"*	750.00	825.00	750.00
☐ **Bye-Lo Baby,** *all bisque infant, comes with cradle and toy, 5½*	260.00	300.00	270.00
☐ **Bye-Lo Baby,** *all bisque, jointed limbs, painted features, incised mark on back, 3½*	250.00	300.00	265.00
☐ **Bye-Lo Baby,** *bisque head, celluloid body, blue sleep eyes, white dress with bonnet, 12½"*	550.00	600.00	575.00
☐ **Bye-Lo Baby,** *bisque head, celluloid body, painted skin head, brown sleep eyes, closed mouth, long christening gown, 13½"*	400.00	500.00	425.00
☐ **Bye-Lo Baby,** *bisque head, celluloid hands, cloth body, 11½"*	425.00	475.00	440.00
☐ **Bye-Lo Baby,** *bisque head, cloth body, celluloid hands, sleep blue eyes, long white baby dress with lace trim, 12"*	625.00	675.00	640.00

	Current Price Range		P/Y AVG
☐ **Bye-Lo Baby,** *bisque head, composition bent limb, jointed body, molded painted hair, 14"*	650.00	750.00	650.00
☐ **Bye-Lo Baby,** *bisque head, original body, blue sleep eyes, beautiful antique dress, large size 14" head circumference*	675.00	775.00	650.00
☐ **Bye-Lo Baby,** *black, bisque, long white baby gown, 23"*	250.00	300.00	270.00
☐ **Bye-Lo Baby,** *blue sleep eyes, christening gown, rare extra large size, original marked head and body, 16" head circumference*	850.00	1250.00	1000.00
☐ **Bye-Lo Baby,** *brown sleep eyes, straight legs*	375.00	450.00	350.00
☐ **Bye-Lo Baby,** *celluloid head and hands, cloth body, brown set eyes, ruffling hat and clothes, 11"*	600.00	650.00	625.00

QUESTER

☐ **Cinderella,** *all cloth, printed face, open mouth, (smiling), sold with mop, pail and extra skirt, 9½"* **Note: Not a Disney product.**	8.00	10.00	7.00

RATTI

☐ **Girl,** *brown mohair wig, goo goo, sleep, blue eyes, lashes, green corduroy dress, 18"*	150.00	200.00	160.00
☐ **Happy Andrina,** *vinyl head, vinyl arms, legs and body, rooted hair, sleep eyes, open mouth with broad smile, freckled cheeks, wears short-sleeved dress with floral appliques, marked Ratti, made in Italy, date 1964, 11"* **Note: The mark of the Ratti Co., which its dolls carry, is a pair of seated rats.**	14.00	18.00	14.00

BERNARD RAVCA

	Current Price Range		P/Y AVG
☐ **Elderly Dutch Couple**, *cloth stockinette faces sculptured with needle stitching, hand painted features, white hair, individually stitched fingers, stuffed bodies, working clothes, wearing painted Dutch type shoes, marks, both have paper labels reading "Original Ravca-Paris," cloth label attached to clothing - Made in France, 13"*	75.00	150.00	100.00
☐ **Old Fisherman**, *all cloth doll has hand painted stockinet needle stitched face, white mohair wig, beard, black felt beret, wine colored trousers, shirt, carries a "fishing net," marks, paper label reads -Original Ravca, Fabrication Francaise, cloth label on clothing reads - Made in France, 9½"*	65.00	85.00	55.00

RDF

☐ **Tiny Tim**, *vinyl, grotesque caricature, marked RDF 67, 3½"*	13.00	17.00	12.00

RECKNAGEL

☐ **Bisque**, *ball jointed body, blue eyes, long red curls, blue satin dress, 14"*	150.00	175.00	160.00
☐ **Bisque**, *ball-jointed body, dark brown eyes, dark brown wig with wavy hair, blue satin dress, 12"*	100.00	140.00	118.00
☐ **Bisque**, *brown eyes, brown wig, white and blue dress, 21"*	300.00	350.00	340.00
☐ **Bisque**, *jointed composition body, blue eyes, black curls, pink dress and hat, 21"*	350.00	400.00	370.00
☐ **Bisque Socket Head**, *jointed five piece jointed papier mache composition body, molded socks and shoes, blue sleep eyes, open mouth with four teeth, red lace trimmed dress, original brown wig, marks, 1907 R/A DEP, 6½"*	50.00	75.00	50.00

	Current Price Range		P/Y AVG
☐ **Bisque,** stick figure, set blue glass eyes, blonde wig, open mouth, pink patterned taffeta dress with black stripes and lace, 15"	150.00	200.00	170.00
☐ **Composition,** five-piece composition body, brown eyes, brown hair, molded hair	100.00	150.00	120.00
☐ **Googlie,** boy, bisque head, five piece composition body, molded blonde hair, blue intaglio eyes, closed watermelon mouth, marked R49A, 8"	600.00	700.00	625.00
☐ **Googlie,** five piece body, blue sleep eyes, 11"	625.00	675.00	640.00

REGAL

☐ **Eskimo,** vinyl head, plush body stuffed with excelsior, black hair, (rooted), fixed eyes, marked Regal, Made in Canada, 1965, 16"	23.00	29.00	21.00
☐ **Louise,** vinyl head, plastic body, sleep eyes, rooted hair, puffy cheeks, partially open mouth, wide-eyed facial expression, wears white dress with small floral print, marked Regal Toy, Made in Canada, 1962, 13"	6.00	8.00	6.00

OTTO REINECKE

☐ **Baby Name Doll Grete,** bisque, long blonde curls, grey sleep eyes, two upper teeth, commercial organdy dress with lace tatting on sleeves, "GRETE," 12"	310.00	340.00	320.00
☐ **Character Baby,** bisque head, five piece bent-limb composition body, original wig, blue sleep eyes, brush-stroke brows, two upper teeth, molded tongue, old pink cotton striped play dress with matching full romper, knit socks, incised "P.M. 914, Germany 9," 16"	365.00	400.00	375.00

	Current Price Range		P/Y AVG
☐ **Character Baby,** *bisque socket head, jointed bent leg body, brown wig, brown sleep eyes, open smiling mouth with two porcelain teeth, illusion of tongue, dimples, lace trimmed white gown, hand made crochet yellow sweater, matching bonnet, made by Otto Reinecke, marks P.M. 914 12, 28"*	375.00	450.00	375.00

RELIABLE

☐ **Mary Baby,** *plastic head, plastic arms, legs and body, rooted hair in elaborate high-fashion coiffure, sleep eyes with thick long eyelashes, 13½"*	4.00	6.00	4.00

RELIABLE OF CANADA

☐ **Barbara Ann Scott,** *composition, sleep eyes, (blue), open mouth, marked Reliable of Canada, 14"*	90.00	115.00	85.00

ROYAL DOULTON

HEIRLOOM DOLLS

☐ **Firstborn,** *this baby doll is a beautiful blue-eyed infant in a basket crib trimmed in lace, the infant is dressed in a traditional christening robe of white figured cotton with a lace front panel, bonnet is of white satin and lace*	175.00	225.00	195.00
☐ **Little Bridesmaid,** *dress in cream satin, trimmed with cream lace which matches the lace on the bride (Wedding Day), flowers are yellow, orange and white, hair is light auburn, and headdress is a ringlet of similar flowers*	150.00	200.00	170.00

	Current Price Range		P/Y AVG

☐ **Royal Baby Doll**, *to commemorate the birth of His Royal Highness Prince William of Wales, born June 21, 1982, baby wears a dress and bonnet of cream lace and net over taffeta, underneath are cream cotton bloomers, bonnet is cream trimmed in matching lace and ribbons, the canopied crib is draped with a white and cream figured cotton, trimmed with baby blue, the face, hands and feet are a delicate baby tone, limited edition of 2,500* 275.00 325.00 295.00

☐ **Wedding Day**, *bride wears a wedding dress of ivory silk which is almost entirely covered with ivory lace, the veil is matching lace and pink and cream flowers accentuate her brunette reall hair, she carries a miniature bouquet of yellow, orange and white flowers, height 14"* 200.00 250.00 220.00

KATE GREENAWAY SERIES

☐ **Big Sister**, *white dress with lacey underskirt, royal blue ribbon at the waist, hat is white trimmed in same color blue, slippers white, carrying dark brown basket with white and red flowers, limited edition of 5,000, height 12"* 150.00 200.00 170.00

☐ **Little Model**, *gown is light beige with blue ribbon at waist, hat is blue matching ribbon on dress with deep maroon ties, cape is maroon, limited edition of 5,000, height, 12"* 150.00 200.00 170.00

☐ **The Muff**, *dressed in tailored full length coat with a fur cape collar and carrying a fur muff, the coat has a pink lining, dress is maroon satin, hat is plum colored and trimmed with chocolate and pink feathers, hair is auburn, limited edition of 5,000, height 12"* 175.00 225.00 195.00

☐ **Pink Ribbon**, *dress is white taffeta line with pink underskit, hat white pink satin ribbon and white feathers, carrying a miniature bouquet of silk rosebuds, limited edition of 5,000, height 12"* 175.00 225.00 195.00

252 / ROYAL DOULTON

	Current Price Range		P/Y AVG
☐ **Pink Sash,** *dressed in white taffeta over a pink underskirt, wearing white hat decorated with feathers and pink ribbon, over blonde hair, carrying a miniature bouquet of silk rosebuds, limited edition of 5,000, height 10"*	125.00	175.00	140.00
☐ **Small Sister,** *small child has all white dress with white shoes tied with pink ribbons, bonnet is white with pink bows over dark blonde hair, limited edition of 5,000, height 8"*	100.00	150.00	120.00
☐ **Swansdown,** *dressed in a white figured satin fur trimmed coat over a white satin dress, she carries a white fur muff and wears a lace trimmed hat over her blonde curly hair, decorated with Swansdown and yellow ribbons, limited edition of 5,000, height 12"*	175.00	225.00	195.00
☐ **Vera,** *deep beige dress with matching color overdress, hat matches dress, light auburn hair, carrying basket of pink flowers, limited edition of 5,000, height 12"*	150.00	200.00	170.00
☐ **Waiting,** *simple white gown of silk with frilled neckline and cuff, wide sash of orange satin ribbon at waistline, matching the lining of her dark brown lace and feather hat, under the hat is a white linen cap trimmed in lace, limited edition of 5,000, height 12"*	175.00	225.00	195.00
☐ **Winter,** *costume is scarlet red trimmed with black fur, carrying fur muff, beautiful black hat showing underneath is her red hair, black shoes, limited edition of 5,000, height 12"*	150.00	200.00	170.00

VICTORIAN BIRTHDAY DOLLS

The well remembered nursey rhyme inspired this charming new collection. While each Day's child is represented by a boy and girl doll, each girl has a hairpiece while the boys hair is sculptured in the ceramic. Their costumes follow the 19th century tradition. This is a non-limited edition.

☐ **Monday's Child,** *is fair of face*	120.00	160.00	140.00
☐ **Tuesday's Child,** *is full of grace*	120.00	160.00	140.00

Monday's Child,
Heirloom series
$120.00-$160.00

	Current Price Range		P/Y AVG
☐ **Wednesday's Child,** *is full of woe*	120.00	160.00	140.00
☐ **Thursday's Child,** *has far to go*	120.00	160.00	140.00
☐ **Friday's Child,** *is loving and giving*	120.00	160.00	140.00
☐ **Saturday's Child,** *works hard for a living*	120.00	160.00	140.00
☐ **Sunday's Child,** *a child that is born on the Sabbath Day is bonny and blithe and good and gay*	120.00	160.00	140.00

SCHMID

☐ **Clown,** *musical, cloth, brown yarn hair, red and white clown outfit with polka dots, plays "Send In The Clowns," marked 286-009, 10"*	30.00	40.00	30.00

254 / BRUNO SCHMIDT

	Current Price Range		P/Y AVG
☐ **Duck**, *musical, cloth, yellow fur, pink checkered bonnet, plays "Raindrops," marked 286-005, 8½"*	30.00	40.00	30.00
☐ **Nurse**, *musical, cloth, yellow yarn hair, white dress and nurse's cap, plays "Spoonful Of Sugar," marked 286-008, 8½"*	30.00	40.00	30.00
☐ **Tennis Player**, *musical, cloth, brown yarn hair, holds small cloth tennis racquet, plays "It's A Small World," marked 286-001, 8½"*	30.00	40.00	30.00

BRUNO SCHMIDT

☐ **Baby**, *bisque head, five piece composition body, short black wig, blue flirty eyes, long layette gown, lacy bonnet, 26"*	400.00	500.00	450.00
☐ **Character Doll**, *bisque head, ball-jointed body, human hair wig, brown sleep eyes, pierced ears, corduroy print dress, 20"*	500.00	550.00	515.00

SCHOENHUT

When Albert Schoenhut arrived in America from Wurttenberg Germany at the age of 17, he was already an accomplished wood carver. The Schoenhut family in Germany had been wood carvers for generations. Albert continued this family tradition, teaching the trade to his six sons and, in the 1870's, the Schoenhut family opened a toy factory in Philadelphia, Pennsylvania. However, it was not until 1911 that he began to market his unique all wood dolls. These first Schoenhut dolls had swivel necks, spring jointed bodies with a hole in the bottom of each foot which permitted the use of a stand for display purposes.

When Albert Schoenhut died in 1912, his sons carried on the Schoenhut doll and toy business. In 1913, Albert's oldest son designed a bent-limb baby and or toddler doll, and in the 1920's a less expensive elastic jointed doll was introduced into production. Before it ceased operation in the 1930's, Schoenhut also marketed a fully jointed, all composition doll.

SCHOENHUT / 255

	Current Price Range		P/Y AVG
☐ **Acrobat,** wooden toy man, hinged at hips, tall molded red fez and tassel, goatee and moustache, two-piece brown patterned cotton suit, 7"	60.00	70.00	63.00
☐ **Baby,** all wood, molded wooden head, doweled bent limb wooden body, painted blue eyes, open/closed moth, 12"	350.00	450.00	350.00
☐ **Baby,** bent limb, blonde skin wig, closed mouth, 11"	350.00	400.00	365.00
☐ **Baby Character,** wooden head, jointed wooden body, brown intaglio eyes, original wig, pouty mouth, original clothes and shoes, 21"	1200.00	1300.00	1200.00
☐ **Baby,** wooden construction carved features, ball-joint body, painted eyes, open mouth, layette suit with bonnet, c. 1911, 12"	300.00	400.00	325.00
☐ **Boy,** carved wooden head and spring jointed wood body, painted brown eyes, with blonde wig, two-piece black velvet suit and white shirt, paint peeling across face, marks: Schoenhut Doll Pat. Jan. 17″11, USA, 14"	95.00	100.00	200.00
☐ **Boy,** sombre face, blonde wig, sailor suit, 16"	350.00	400.00	365.00
☐ **Boy,** spring jointed, bald, painted blue eyes, partially open mouth	400.00	450.00	410.00
☐ **Boy,** wooden, blue painted eyes, closed pouty mouth, striped woolen suit, marked head and marked incised body	550.00	650.00	550.00
☐ **Circus Clown,** wooden, striped cotton suit in green, pink, and white, large red feet, 8"	90.00	100.00	92.00
☐ **Dolly Face,** brown mohair wig, 22"	275.00	325.00	295.00
☐ **Dolly Face,** red pigtail mohair wig, sticker, 17"	225.00	275.00	240.00
☐ **Dolly Face,** 15½"	400.00	450.00	420.00
☐ **Girl,** all-wood, jointed wooden body, blue intaglio eyes, brown wig, dressed in sailor suit, 16"	625.00	725.00	600.00
☐ **Girl,** character, wooden head, jointed wooden body, pouty, brown wig, painted features, original clothes, 16"	900.00	1000.00	950.00

	Current Price Range		P/Y AVG
☐ **Girl**, molded brown pulled over ears and tied in back with molded blue ribbon, fully jointed wooden body, painted blue eyes, pink gingham dress, 16"	975.00	1175.00	900.00
☐ **Girl**, sombre face, blonde wig, 15"	350.00	400.00	360.00
☐ **Lady Bareback Rider**, bisque head, painted blue eyes, brown hair, pink and green outfit, 7½"	425.00	475.00	440.00
☐ **Pouty**, wooden head on spring jointed wooden body, painted blue intaglio eyes, new blonde human hair wig, wearing pink checked pinafore over white lace trimmed blouse, nose rub, discreet retouching of face, marks: oval label reads "Schoenhut Doll, Pat. Jan. 17th, 1911 U.S.A., 14"	275.00	300.00	270.00
☐ **Rolly Dollys**, clown, 9"	100.00	150.00	120.00
☐ **Rolly Dollys**, policeman, 7"	90.00	110.00	98.00
☐ **Toddler**, brown, mohair wig, painted eyes, partially open mouth, 11"	350.00	450.00	365.00
☐ **Walker**, wooden head, jointed wooden five piece body, painted blue eyes, blonde mohair wig, open/closed mouth, sailor suit, paper label	400.00	575.00	425.00
☐ **Walker**, wooden, original mohair wig, blue painted eyes, closed pouty mouth, walker body, cute sailor suite, marked head and body, 16½"	695.00	850.00	650.00
☐ **Walker**, wood, spring jointed, carved head, blue ribbon headband with bow in back, brown intaglio eyes, Schoenhut stick in back, original sailor suit, underwear and shoes, 14"	1500.00	1700.00	1450.00

SCHULTE

	Current Price Range		P/Y AVG
☐ **Turtle Girl**, celluloid head, bisque hands, cloth body, brown sleep eyes, blue stripe print dress with hat, 23"	275.00	325.00	300.00

SIMPLICITY

	Current Price Range		P/Y AVG
☐ **Holly Hobbie,** sew-it-yourself cloth doll, simplicity pattern #6248, 17"	4.00	6.00	4.00

SKIPPY

☐ **Baby Ellen,** vinyl head, cloth body, vinyl arms and legs, blonde hair (rooted), sleep eyes (blue), open mouth with two teeth, marked S1968 Skippy Doll, 21"	9.00	12.00	8.00
☐ **Julia,** plastic/vinyl, sleep eyes (blue), marked A Skippy Doll, 1967, 17"	9.00	12.00	8.00

ELLA SMITH

☐ **Alabama Indestructible Doll,** all cloth, molded oil painted head, painted features and shoes, cotton dress, 25"	600.00	750.00	600.00

SONSCO

☐ **Bonnie Dee,** talker, plastic/vinyl, blonde hair, sleep eyes (blue), battery operated, unmarked, made in 1973, 14"	11.00	14.00	10.00
☐ **Lady Baseball Player,** stockinette, posable, representing an adult woman holding a baseball bat, unmarked on doll, sold originally with a tag reading Sonsco Toys, Japan, believed to date from about 1967, 12¼"	22.00	27.00	21.00

MAJORIE SPANGLER

☐ **Cynthia,** vinyl, jointed, blonde pigtails, blue sleep eyes, pink dotted swiss party dress, white leotards, black patent leather shoes, 13"	45.00	50.00	45.00

	Current Price Range		P/Y AVG

☐ **Emerald Isle Doll,** *long blue dress, bonnet, commemorative collection, c. 1980, 15"* 45.00 55.00 50.00

STAHLWOOD

☐ **Buck,** *vinyl, squeeze toy, molded and painted features, made of scented vinyl, marked Buck, Soft Standing, Scented, made in 1955, 8"* 4.00 6.00 4.00

KARL STANDFUSS

☐ **Juno,** *metal head, kid body, cloth arms and legs, painted features, pink and green floral print dress, straw bonnet with flowers, made in Germany, 18"* ... 50.00 100.00 70.00

STREET CORNER PRODUCTIONS

☐ **Flip Wilson/Geraldine,** *(two-sided doll), black, talker, printed cloth, one side pictures comic Flip Wilson as himself, the other as "Geraldine," marked 1970, Street Corner Productions, 16"* 42.00 53.00 36.00

STEIFF

☐ **Fireman,** *plastic face, helmet, felt clothes, c. 1960's, 12"* 137.00 168.00 135.00
☐ **Man,** *farmer, character, cloth, wig, glass eyes, large hands and feet, original costume, 20th century, 14"* 650.00 800.00 700.00
☐ **Shepherd Doll,** *velvet outfit, 8"* 25.00 35.00 30.00

STUART

	Current Price Range		P/Y AVG
☐ **Baby's Doll,** vinyl head, cloth body, cloth arms and legs, molded and painted hair, fixed eyes (blue), partially open mouth, marked Styled by Stuart, St. Paul, Minn., made in 1961, 8"	6.00	8.00	5.00
☐ **Muff Doll,** cloth mask-type face, painted, yarn hair, stuffed body, unmarked, made in 1939, 10"	16.00	21.00	15.00

SWEDLIN

☐ **Mimi The Martian,** vinyl head, vinyl arms, legs and body, rooted hair, painted eyes, marked J. Swedlin, Inc., 1967, Made in Japan, 4⅞"	4.00	6.00	4.00

TECNOGIOCATTOLI

☐ **Bettina,** vinyl head, plastic body, rooted hair, sleep eyes, strung doll made to represent an adolescent girl, made in Italy, marked Sebino, 16¼"	14.00	18.00	13.00

TEEN

☐ **Calamity Jane,** posable legs, marked Azark-Hamway, 12"	4.00	6.00	4.00
☐ **Emma Peel,** plastic/vinyl, painted eyes, representing a character from the TV program "The Avengers," marked Made in Hong Kong, presumably c. 1965, 11½"	26.00	33.00	25.00

TERRI LEE

	Current Price Range		P/Y AVG
☐ **Benji,** black, walker, vinyl, brown sleep eyes unmarked, date of manufacture unknown, believed to have been made in the late 1950's or early 1960's, 10"	90.00	115.00	85.00
☐ **Connie Lynn,** plastic, red hair, blue sleep eyes, partially open mouth, unmarked, made in 1955, 18½"	65.00	80.00	60.00
☐ **Gene Autry,** plastic, molded and painted, wears Gene Autry button, marked Terri Lee, Pats. Pending, date of manufacture unknown, presumably c. 1950, 16"	225.00	275.00	220.00
☐ **Terri Lee,** composition body, blonde wig, tin eyes, closed mouth, original clothes, 12"	215.00	235.00	220.00
☐ **Terri Lee,** plastic, dark hair, hairnet, two piece pink play suit, 16"	100.00	165.00	105.00

VANITY

☐ **Big Girl,** black, plastic head, cloth body, latex arms and legs, black hair, sleep eyes (brown), wears a baby bonnet, unmarked, made in 1949, 23"	58.00	70.00	55.00

VERLINGUE

☐ **Girl,** five piece body, brown eyes, closed mouth, dark hair, molded shoes and socks, 8"	100.00	150.00	120.00

VIDEO CRAFT

☐ **Pinocchio,** vinyl head, cloth body, cloth arms and legs, molded and painted features, molded and painted hair, painted eyes, marked Video Craft Ltd., 1962, made in Japan, 13"	8.00	11.00	7.00

Note: No connection with the Disney version of Pinocchio.

VIRGA

	Current Price Range	P/Y AVG
☐ **Lucy,** *plastic, walker, comes in plaid suitcase, 8"*	40.00 50.00	45.00

VOGUE

Vogue was founded by doll costume designer Jennie Graves in 1937 but it wasn't until the advent of the Ginny doll in 1948 that Vogue really got off the ground. From that point on, however, Vogue was firmly established in the doll world. The 1948 Ginny was a 7" jointed composition doll with mohair wig, painted facial features and various charming costumes. She was later made of hard plastic, and then vinyl, and acquired a complete wardrobe, jewelry and accessories as well as a family.

The Vogue company has introduced many dolls over the years such as Ginny's little sister, Baby Ginnette, Teenage Jill, Baby Dear, Star Brite, Posie Pixie, Lil Imp, Too Dear, Bunny Hug, Jama Baby and Love Me Linda to name but a few.

Vogue absorbed Arranbee in 1959 and was itself acquired by Ilonka Corporation in 1973. Lesnoy bought Vogue from Tonka and is in current production.

☐ **Baby Dear One,** *vinyl head and limbs, cloth body, blonde rooted hair, blue sleep eyes, closed mouth, mama cryer, blue dress with white pinafore, blue booties, 21"*	55.00	65.00	55.00
☐ **Ballerina,** *brown eyes, brown mohair hair, pink tutu with green and gold trim, flowers in hair*	125.00	175.00	140.00
☐ **Becky,** *strung, brown eyes, red hair, velvet top, organdy skirt, straw hat*	120.00	160.00	138.00
☐ **Boy,** *strung, blue eyes, red hair, aqua corderoy overalls, knitted hat*	110.00	160.00	128.00
☐ **Brickette,** *plastic/vinyl, reddish hair (rooted), sleep eyes (green), closed smiling mouth, white shoes, unmarked, made in 1960, 22"*	38.00	48.00	35.00
☐ **Bride,** *strung, brown eyes, blonde*	200.00	250.00	220.00
☐ **Bridegroom,** *strung, blue sleep eyes, dark blonde hair*	200.00	250.00	220.00
☐ **Bridesmaid,** *strung, blue eyes, red hair*	200.00	250.00	220.00
☐ **Cheryl,** *redhead, mold number 44*	190.00	230.00	205.00
☐ **Cinderella,** *strung, hazel eyes, blonde wig*	200.00	250.00	240.00

	Current Price Range		P/Y AVG
☐ **Dutch Boy,** strung, brown eyes, blonde hair	125.00	175.00	140.00
☐ **Fairy Godmother,** strung, light brown eyes, blonde wig	200.00	250.00	240.00
☐ **Ginny,** ballerina, blue eyes, molded lashes, blonde wig, pink and white tutu, flowers in hair, braid leather shoes	150.00	200.00	170.00
☐ **Ginny,** ballerina, blue eyes, molded lashes, brown hair, pink taffeta top, white net, pearl crown	110.00	160.00	128.00
☐ **Ginny,** walker, painted lashes, red hair, pink sweater and skirt, beenie	140.00	180.00	155.00
☐ **Ginny,** walker, blue eyes, red braids, painted lashes, graysilk dress with white ruffled organdy hat	110.00	160.00	125.00
☐ **Ginny,** walker, straight leg, majorette outfit, marked Ginny Vogue Dolls, 8"	70.00	80.00	75.00
☐ **Ginny of Foreign Lands,** hard plastic, Polish outfit, 8", c. 1972	22.00	28.00	23.00
☐ **Jan,** auburn hair, blue sleep eyes, lashes, skating outfit, skates, cap #3364, c. 1958	40.00	50.00	45.00
☐ **Jill,** blonde hair, wedding outfit, earrings, necklace, flowers	45.00	55.00	47.00
☐ **Jill,** composition body, black curly wig, painted eyes, 10"	125.00	140.00	135.00
☐ **Jill,** golden blonde hair in angel hairstyle, black exercise outfit, pearl earrings and necklace	60.00	70.00	62.00
☐ **Jill,** plastic, brunette hair attached by adhesive, blue sleep eyes, jointed at the knees, dressed in bridal gown, marked Jill-Vogue Doll-Made in U.S.A., 1957, 10"	10.00	14.00	10.00
☐ **Jill,** strawberry blonde ponytail, knit top, pleated skirt, navy blazer, gold earrings, straw purse	40.00	50.00	45.00
☐ **Jill,** strawberry blonde wig, beige taffeta dress with lace trim, stand, head band, pocketbook	160.00	210.00	175.00
☐ **Jill,** underwear, earrings with box, #3013	30.00	40.00	30.00
☐ **Prince Charming,** strung, brown eyes, blonde wig	200.00	250.00	240.00
☐ **Red Riding Hood,** strung, brown eyes, golden blonde hair, carries basket	125.00	175.00	140.00

Jill,
walker, c. 1960
$8.00-$12.00

	Current Price Range		P/Y AVG
☐ **Skier,** *walker, blue eyes, painted lashes, red and white sweater, blue pants, skis and poles* .... *composition*	170.00	220.00	190.00
☐ **Toodles Sailor Boy,** *composition, molded and painted features, molded and painted hair, wears sailor suit, marked Vogue, date of manufacture unknown, 7½"*	38.00	46.00	35.00
☐ **Wanda,** *brown eyes, brown hair, white cotton dress with yellow flowers, matching shoes and straw hat*	160.00	210.00	178.00

IZANNAH WALKER

	Current Price Range		P/Y AVG
☐ **Lady,** *fabric, pressed head, oil painted face and hair, applied ears, original outfit*	3000.00	4000.00	2800.00
☐ **Rag Doll,** *all cloth, stockinet molded oil painted head, cloth body, painted hair, eyes, arms, legs, stitched toes, original cotton dress, 17"*	1700.00	2300.00	1500.00
☐ **Rag Doll,** *stockinet molded oil painted head, cloth body, painted hair, eyes, shoes, original cotton dress, early, 19"*	2000.00	2500.00	2000.00

SHEILA WALLACE

☐ **Jenny Jerome Churchild,** *wax, 21", c. 1979*	500.00	550.00	515.00

WALT DISNEY PRODUCTIONS

☐ **Bashful (one of the Seven Dwarfs),** *composition, molded and painted features, beard attached by adhesive, unmarked, made in 1939, 8½"*	58.00	72.00	55.00
☐ **Christopher Robin,** *polyfoam-covered wire, molded and painted features, molded and painted hair, posable, marked Made in England, Walt Disney Productions, 1966, 10"*	15.00	19.00	14.00

Note: Christopher Robin was a character from A.A. Milne's "Winnie the Pooh."

☐ **Donald Duck,** *hard plastic, musical roly-poly, closed mouth, molded clothing, coat has two buttons, carries no markings, believed to date from the late 1960's or early 1970's and probably made in Hong Kong, 11"*	8.00	10.00	8.00
☐ **Donald Duck,** *vinyl head, plastic body, arms spread wide apart, wears felt jacket with four buttons, made in Hong Kong, 8"*	4.00	6.00	4.00

	Current Price Range		P/Y AVG

Note: Don't let this one fool you. It looks much older than it is. It was made in the mid 1970's but was designed to show Donald as he appeared about 40 years earlier, very different than the modern version.

☐ **Donald Duck**, vinyl head, vinyl body, molded clothing, wide open mouth, hands held together (as if about to dive from diving board), no movable parts, marked Dell, Walt Disney, 6" 5.00 7.00 5.00

☐ **Dopey (of the Seven Dwarfs)**, vinyl head, plush body (stuffed), two buttons at front, arms wide apart, wide open eyes looking upward, 8½" 8.00 10.00 7.00

Note: Dopey was a character in "Snow White and the Seven Dwarfs," a Disney animated film.

☐ **Ferdinand The Bull**, composition head and body, fully jointed, marked Walt Disney Enterprises, Ideal Novelty & Toy Co., 9" 65.00 80.00 62.00

Note: Ferdinand was the docile bull who refused to charge matadors or do other bullish things.

☐ **Grumpy**, rubber, molded and painted features, marked Gund, W.D.P., 1938 ... 40.00 55.00 37.00

Note: Representing a character from Disney's animated film, "Snow White and the Seven Dwarfs,"

☐ **Jiminy Cricket**, plastic, molded and painted features, clothing attached by adhesive, marked Marx Toys, Made in Hong Kong, made in 1963, 5½" 9.00 12.00 8.00

Note: Jiminy Cricket was an animated character from the film, "Pinnochio."

☐ **Mickey Mouse**, wood, painted, stump hands without fingers, large bulbous nose, marked Mickey Mouse, Copyright By Walt Disney, 3" 80.00 110.00 75.00

Note: Mickey's primitive appearance in this doll places it in the early 1930's. A companionpiece, MINNIE MOUSE, was also issued, and is worth about the same price.

266 / WALT DISNEY PRODUCTIONS

	Current Price Range		P/Y AVG
☐ **Mickey Mouse Hobo,** vinyl head, all vinyl body, molded clothing (including a shirt with two buttons, the letter M and a crown atop it), squeaks when squeezed, 10"	5.00	7.00	5.00
☐ **Minnie Mouse,** vinyl swivel head, plastic body, molded clothing, a wheeler doll (wheel in each foot, but no walking mechanism — doll had to be pushed manually), marked Walt Disney Productions, 11"	10.00	14.00	10.00

Mickey and Minnie, cloth, c. 1920 .... $45.00-$85.00

☐ **Minnie Mouse,** vinyl head, plastic body, bow-tied ribbon on top of head, wears fabric clothing, including polka-dotted skirt, oversized shoes, in addition to Disney mark, also carries mark of Dakin and Co., almost certainly made in Hong Kong but not marked to that effect, 6"	4.00	5.00	4.00
☐ **Peter Pan,** seated vinyl figurine with cloth jacket, c. 1950	22.00	35.00	27.50

	Current Price Range		P/Y AVG

☐ **Pinocchio**, *composition head and body, wooden arms and legs, molded and painted hair, painted clothing, marked Ideal, originally sold with a tag reading Pinocchio, Des. & Copyright By Walt Disney, made in 1940, 11"* 90.00 110.00 85.00
Note: The Disney film, "Pinocchio," was released in 1937, three years before this doll came out.

☐ **Pinocchio**, *composition head, composition arms, legs and body, painted eyes, wears Tyrolean-style (or mountain climber) cap, marked Pinocchio, Walt Disney Pr., Knickerbocker Toy Co., 12"* . 80.00 100.00 75.00

☐ **Pluto Pulltoy**, *all wood construction overlaid with printed paper, set with wheels, equipped with a leash with which Pluto could be "walked," as the toy was pulled along, the wheels activated its front and hind legs and set them in walking motion, length, 15"* ... 120.00 150.00 110.00
Note: First placed on the market around 1946, still being sold at retail in 1950 and possibly later — but these have nevertheless become scarce, when complete and in good operating condition.

BEVERLY WALTER

☐ **Bisque Father Christmas**, *dressed as Daniel Boone, bisque shoulder head, hands, black boots, cloth body, 1980 UFDC Souvenir doll from the Washington, D.C. Convention made by Beverly Walter, molded white hair, beard, moustache, eyebrows, blue intaglio eyes, detailed facial modeling, sombre expression, Daniel Boone tan fringed velveteen hunting suit, mink hat, marks: Father Christmas, Beverly Walter, 1980, 16½"* 225.00 250.00 230.00

BERGMAN WALTERSHAUSEN

	Current Price Range		P/Y AVG
☐ **Bisque,** *spring-jointed body, original wig, blue-grey sleep eyes, two tone lips, four porcelain teeth, incised CM Bergman Walters Hausen 1916 6½"*	295.00	330.00	300.00
☐ **Girl,** *bisque head, spring, jointed body, original long brown wig, fine antique cotton dress with elaborate panelling and embroidered white on white flowers, original slip, shoes, incised Bergman Waltershausen, 1916, 6, 22".*	360.00	395.00	365.00

WARNER BROTHERS

☐ **Elmer Fudd,** *vinyl, molded and painted features, painted eyes, jointed at the shoulders and hips, wears one-button jacket, derby hat, Elmer Fudd is a character in the comic strip "Bugs Bunny," created by R. Schlesinger, marked Warner Brothers, 1968, made in Hong Kong, 7"*	15.00	20.00	14.00

NORAH WELLINGS

☐ **American Indian Character,** *English doll, 19"*	220.00	240.00	200.00
☐ **Fellow,** *comic, very expressive, perfect clothes, 8"*	35.00	40.00	35.00
☐ **Native Boy,** *brown red wig, brown glass eyes, 15"*	100.00	120.00	110.00
☐ **Norah Sue,** *mask face, stuffed body, painted facial features, human hair wig, wears bowtie, unmarked on doll, sold originally with a tag reading Made in England by Norah Wellings, date of manufacture unknown, 15½"*	50.00	65.00	47.00
☐ **Queens Guard Character,** *all cloth, molded painted features, authentic queens guard uniform, cloth tag on foot, made in England by Norah Wellings, 9"*	60.00	65.00	60.00

PAPERDOLLS

	Current Price Range		P/Y AVG
☐ **Air Hostess,** *1947 Saalfield*	12.00	18.00	14.00
☐ **Airline Stewardess,** *1957 Samuel Lowe*	2.00	8.00	5.00
☐ **Alice Faye,** *1941 Merrill #4800, three dolls, forty-three pieces of clothing*	70.00	80.00	74.00
☐ **A Little French Doll Cut-Out,** *with dresses like those Queen Marie Antonnette wore, 1931, newspaper doll, sorted clothes, uncut*	8.00	12.00	9.00
☐ **All Aboard For Shut-Eye-Town,** *Dionne Quints, 1937, uncut*	30.00	40.00	34.00
☐ **Annie Oakley With Tagg And Lofty,** *1956 Whitman book #1960, statuette dolls, eight pages of Western outfits, uncut*	45.00	55.00	48.00
☐ **Bild-A-Set,** *by Pachter, Chicago, 1943, eight dolls with front and back uniforms, cut*	40.00	50.00	43.00
☐ **Billy Boy,** *Samuel Lowe, uncut*	2.00	6.00	4.00
☐ **B Is For Betsy,** *1954 Merrill*	2.00	6.00	4.00
☐ **Blondie,** *1944 Whitman book #981, four dolls — Blondie, Dagwood, Cookie, and Alexander, assorted outfits, cut*	30.00	40.00	34.00
☐ **Blondie,** *1945 King Features book #987, Blondie, Dagwood, Alexander, Cookie, and Daisy, assorted outfits, cut* .	30.00	40.00	32.00
☐ **Blondie,** *from the T.V. show, Saalfield book #1334, Comic characters also, uncut*	20.00	30.00	23.00
☐ **Blondie Doll,** *by Betty Campbell, numerous front and back outfits, cut*	8.00	12.00	9.00
☐ **Buffy,** *from the T.V. show (Family Affair), 1968 Whitman book #1995, carries Mrs. Beasley, assorted outfits*	20.00	30.00	22.00
☐ **Charlie McCarthy,** *by Queen Holden, 1938 Whitman book #995, one doll, another head, assorted outfits, cut*	12.00	18.00	14.00
☐ **Charming,** *Saalfield book #1323, three ladies, assorted clothes, uncut*	8.00	12.00	9.00
☐ **Chatty Cathy,** *1964 Whitman book #1961, Mattel doll, blonde hair, uncut* .	16.00	24.00	19.00
☐ **Children Around The World,** *1955 Merrill, wrap-around clothing*	5.00	10.00	7.00
☐ **Double Dolls,** *five dolls — two girls and three boys, dressed in different styles, no outfits*	18.00	22.00	19.00

	Current Price Range		P/Y AVG
☐ Double Wedding, *1939 Merrill, uncut* ..	25.00	35.00	28.00
☐ Down On The Farm, *Samuel Lowe, uncut*	10.00	18.00	13.00
☐ Elaine Stewart, *1955 Whitman book #2048, two dolls, eight pages of clothes, uncut*	70.00	80.00	71.00
☐ Elaine Stewart, *1955 Whitman book #2048, two dolls, assorted outfits, cut* .	30.00	40.00	34.00
☐ Elizabeth, *1963 Samuel Lowe, uncut* ..	2.00	6.00	4.00
☐ Elizabeth Taylor, *1949 Whitman book #968, assorted outfits, cut*	40.00	50.00	44.00
☐ Elizabeth Taylor, *1955 Whitman book #1951, two large dolls, cut*	30.00	40.00	34.00
☐ Elly May, *1963 Watkins/Strathmore book #1819A, small book, two dolls, eight pages of clothes, uncut*	40.00	50.00	43.00
☐ Emilie, *Merrill*	45.00	55.00	48.00
☐ Emily And Mimi, *by Queen Holden, 1971 James and Jonathan book #2711, assorted dresses, uncut*	8.00	12.00	9.00
☐ Esther Williams, *1950 Merrill book #1563, three dolls, numerous outfits, uncut*	55.00	65.00	58.00
☐ Esther Williams, *1950 Merrill book #1563, two dolls, several outfits, cut* ...	35.00	45.00	38.00
☐ Erte' Fashion Paper Dolls Of The Twenties, *by Erte', six paper dolls, forty-three costumes including gowns, coats, hats, and accessories with elaborate details, book production supervised by Erte', thirty-two pages, 9¼" x 12¼"*	2.00	6.00	4.00
☐ Eve Arden, *1953 Saalfield, uncut*	25.00	35.00	28.00
☐ Evelyn Rudie, *1958 Saalfield book #1745, four front and back dolls, four pages of clothes, thin cover, uncut*	20.00	30.00	23.00
☐ Evelyn Rudie, *1958 Saalfield book #1745, signed by Aralo, four dolls, four pages of outfits, soft cover, cut*	10.00	20.00	14.00
☐ Gloria Jean, *1941 Saalfield #2231, uncut*	10.00	18.00	14.00
☐ Gone With The Wind, *1940 Merrill, eighteen dolls, assorted clothes, cut* ...	125.00	175.00	140.00
☐ Gone With The Wind, *1940 Merrill #3404, uncut*	85.00	95.00	88.00

PAPER DOLLS / 271

	Current Price Range		P/Y AVG
☐ **Gone With The Wind,** by Charlotte Whatley, two dolls — Rhett 13" and Scarlette 11", sixteen authentic movie costumes, black and white, limited edition of 500	8.00	12.00	10.00
☐ **Gone With The Wind,** characters from the movie: Scarlette, Rhett, Melanine, Carreen, Ellen Suellen, Aunt Pittypat, Mammy, Gerald, assorted outfits	35.00	45.00	38.00
☐ **Kim Novak Paperdolls And Colorbook,** 1957 Saalfield book #4459, two dolls, four pages of dresses, coloring book, uncut	55.00	65.00	58.00
☐ **Kim Novak,** 1958 Saalfield, uncut	25.00	35.00	28.00
☐ **Lana Turner,** 1945 Whitman #975, two dolls, twenty-seven outfits, nineteen accessories, cut	20.00	30.00	24.00
☐ **Large Babies,** c.early 1950's, three dolls, thirty-one pieces of clothing	2.00	8.00	5.00
☐ **Large-Sized Doll,** Raphael Tuck, white top, lavender petticoat, three dresses, two coats — one brown and one red	45.00	55.00	50.00
☐ **Mod Fashions — Jane Fonda,** 1966 Saalfield book #1369, assorted clothes, uncut	18.00	24.00	20.00
☐ **Mods,** 1967 Milton Bradley #4727, large headed dolls — one boy and one girl, mod clothes from the 1960's, cut	2.00	8.00	4.00
☐ **Molly Bee,** 1962 Whitman book #2091, one doll, assorted clothes, tall thin book, uncut	20.00	30.00	22.00
☐ **Molly Bee,** 1962 Whitman book #2091, one doll, assorted outfits, cut	10.00	18.00	13.00
☐ **Mother Goose Rhyme Punch Out,** 1965, four scenes to punch out and put together	2.00	6.00	4.00
☐ **Munsing Family,** 1909, set of eight dolls, with accessories, cut	40.00	50.00	42.00
☐ **Playmates,** 1958 Whitman, four dolls, cut	3.00	9.00	6.00
☐ **Playtime Pages,** Circus Sam, by Stella Delcosta, July 1952, Jack and Jill set, uncut	2.00	6.00	3.00

SPECIAL LIMITED OFFER

40% Discount on

...an indispensible book for every collector, hobbyist, dealer and investor!

THE MOST VALUABLE BOOK YOU'LL EVER OWN...

Successful collectors know —
What they have... What they paid... and
What it's worth... at a moments notice!

- *The ultimate collection organizer.*
- *Your complete inventory at a glance.*
- *An indisputable insurance & tax record.*
- *Track price trends.*

(256 pp., paperback, 5¼" x 7⅞")

PLUS...

- A directory for Clubs, Dealers, and Fellow Collectors.
- List of recommended Museums and Publications.
- Special advice on — Appraisals — Insurance — Taxes — Buying & Selling — Care & Storage — Restoration and Detecting Fakes & Reproductions.

A Regular $4.95 Value...
Now Only $2.50 (plus 50¢ postage)

ORDERING INSTRUCTIONS

To be eligible for this special limited offer *you must fill out completely,* the reader survey questionnaire on the back of this order form.

SEND ORDERS TO: *THE HOUSE OF COLLECTIBLES,* DEPARTMENT RS
1900 PREMIER ROW, ORLANDO, FLORIDA 32809

☐ Please send one copy of "The Official Collector's Journal" at my special discount price of $2.50 + $.50 postage = $3.00
☐ Check or money order enclosed $_____ (include postage)
☐ Please charge $_____ to my: ☐ MASTERCARD ☐ VISA

Account No. (All Digits)_____ Expiration Date _____

Signature _____

NAME (please print)_____ PHONE _____
ADDRESS_____ APT. # _____
CITY_____ STATE _____ ZIP _____

Note: This offer is limited to one copy per customer. Additional copies may be ordered at the regular price. See order blank at back of book.

READER SURVEY

The House of Collectibles continually seeks to improve, expand and update the material in *The Official Price Guide Series*. The assistance and cooperation of numerous collectors and dealers have added immeasurably to the success of the books in this series. Please take a few seconds and give us your help so we can provide you with information needed to become a successful collector.

Name _____ Phone (___) _____
Address _____
City _____ State _____ Zip _____
Age Group: ☐ under 18 ☐ 18-24 ☐ 25-34 ☐ 35-44 ☐ 45-54 ☐ 55 & over
Title of book purchased _____
Date of purchase _____
Name & address of bookshop _____
_____

Reason for purchase:
☐ I had the previous edition.
☐ I saw it in a public library.
☐ I was looking for a book about this subject.
☐ I saw it advertised.
☐ It was recommended to me.

Do you plan to buy the new revised
edition of this book when it's published? ☐ Definitely ☐ Probably ☐ No

Did you have difficulty locating a bookshop
that carries The House of Collectibles titles? ☐ Yes ☐ No

Is this the first House of
Collectibles book that you've purchased? ☐ Yes ☐ No

Is there any way you feel this book could be improved? _____
_____

How do you feel this book compares with other books about the same subject?
_____
_____

Check the publisher's catalogue at the back of this book, then tell us:
are there any titles you'd like to see added to our series? _____
_____

Would you consider yourself primarily a:
☐ Collector ☐ Dealer ☐ Investor ☐ Home Decorator ☐ General Reader

Do you have any information not included
in the book but which you think should be? ☐ Yes ☐ No

If you do, would you be interested
in becoming a contributor to a future edition? ☐ Yes ☐ No
(If your answer is yes, we'll be contacting you with full details on how you can become an "Official Member" of the world's largest hobby publishing team!)

There is only one...
THE OFFICIAL®
PRICE GUIDE

THE MULTIPURPOSE REFERENCE GUIDE!!

THE OFFICIAL PRICE GUIDE SERIES has gained the reputation as the standard barometer of values on collectors' items. When you need to check the market price of a collectible, turn first to the OFFICIAL PRICE GUIDES ... for impartial, unbiased, current information that is presented in an easy-to-follow format.

- **CURRENT VALUES FOR BUYING AND SELLING.** ACTUAL SALES that have occurred in all parts of the country are CAREFULLY EVALUATED and COMPUTERIZED to arrive at the most ACCURATE PRICES AVAILABLE.

- **CONCISE REFERENCES.** Each OFFICIAL PRICE GUIDE is designed primarily as a *guide to current market values.* They also include a useful summary of the information most readers are seeking: a history of the item; how it's manufactured; how to begin and maintain a collection; how and where to sell; addresses of periodicals and clubs.

- **INDEXED FORMAT.** The novice as well as the seasoned collector will appreciate the unique alphabetically *indexed format* that provides *fast retrieval* of information and prices.

- **FULLY ILLUSTRATED.** All the OFFICIAL PRICE GUIDES are richly illustrated. Many feature COLOR SECTIONS as well as black and white photos.

Over 21 years of experience has made
THE HOUSE OF COLLECTIBLES
the most respected price guide authority!

TRADE PRICE GUIDE SERIES

■ **American Silver & Silver Plate** — Due to recent **skyrocketing** demand, **American Silverware** has become the most profitable collectible field in the nation. • Over **16,000 current market values** *for all types of American antique and modern silverware and holloware.* • *A handy pattern reference guide.* • *Valuable advice on starting and building a collection.* • *Silversmiths' marks.* • *Care and storage tips.* • *ILLUSTRATED.*
3rd Edition, 608 pgs., 5⅜" x 8", Paperback, ISBN: 402-X, $9.95.

■ **Anheuser Busch Collectibles** — **The official guide endorsed by Anheuser Busch** • *Thousands of values are given for every known product of this prestigious brewery.* • *Includes steins, glasses, umbrellas, T-shirts, pool cues, aprons, trays, beer cans, key rings, insulators, playing cards, tie tacks, belt buckles, hats, caps, coolers, dart games, light fixtures, towels, and more.* • *ILLUSTRATED.*
1st Edition, 576 pgs., 5⅜" x 8", Paperback, ISBN: 417-8, $9.95.

■ **Antique Clocks** — Acclaimed by clock enthusiasts as the most **comprehensive** guide to antique American clocks in print today! • Over **10,000 current market values.** • *Over 1,000 line drawings from actual manufacturers' catalogs dating back to the 19th century.* • *Advice on displaying, cleaning, and storing your collection.* • *Complete list of clock suppliers, museums, libraries, periodicals, and books.* • *ILLUSTRATED.*
2nd Edition, 576 pgs., 5⅜" x 8", Paperback, ISBN: 420-8, $9.95.

■ **Antique & Modern Dolls** — Historically a **favorite hobby**, antique and modern dolls are a **hot investment.** • More than **6,000 current retail selling prices** *for dolls in all price ranges.* • *Antique dolls in wax, carved wood, china, and bisque.* • *Modern and semi-modern dolls in celluloid, chalk, plastic, composition, and cloth.* • *Shirley Temples, Barbie, G.I. Joe, Peanuts, Kewpies and more.* • *ILLUSTRATED.*
1st Edition, 576 pgs., 5⅜" x 8", Paperback, ISBN: 381-3, $9.95.

■ **Antique & Modern Firearms** — Serious gun enthusiasts have long **recognized** this work to be the **official definitive source for pricing collector firearms.** • Over **20,500 current market values** *for pistols, rifles, and shotguns made by more than 1,300 manufacturers!* • *Colonial muzzle-loaders, semi and automatic handguns, sub-machine guns, revolvers, shotguns, and bolt and lever action rifles.* • *ILLUSTRATED.*
4th Edition, 576 pgs., 5⅜" x 8", Paperback, ISBN: 421-6, $9.95.

■ **Antiques and Other Collectibles** — • Over **100,000 current market values** and **detailed listings** *for more than 200 categories of antiques and collectibles.* • *A special price column indicates which items have increased in value offering the best investment potential.* • *Learn expert tactics for successful collecting from how to build a collection to understanding market trends.* • *Fully Indexed.* • *ILLUSTRATED.*
4th Edition, 832 pgs., 5⅜" x 8", Paperback, ISBN: 374-0, $9.95.

■ **Antique Jewelry** — Acclaimed by critics, jewelers, appraisers, and collectors, this is the **most respected** and **extensive** guide to antique and collectible jewelry **ever published.** • Over **8,300 current prices,** *organized for easy reference by category, all cross-referenced in a complete index.* • *A history lesson in Georgian, Victorian, Art Nouveau, and Art Deco jewelry designs.* • *ILLUSTRATED.*
3rd Edition, 672 pgs., 5⅜" x 8", Paperback, ISBN: 401-1, $9.95.

■ **Bottles Old & New** — Long recognized by the experts as the most **comprehensive and reliable value guide** in the antique and collectible bottle field! • Over **22,000 current collector values** *for antique, figural, and current production collectible bottles. Ale, Bitters, Flasks, Medicine, Poison, Soda, Avon, Jim Beam, and more.* • *Complete glossary.* • *ILLUSTRATED.*
7th Edition, 672 pgs., 5⅜" x 8", Paperback, ISBN: 399-6, $9.95.

For your convenience use the handy order form.

TRADE PRICE GUIDE SERIES

■ **Collectible Cameras** — Today **astonishing prices** are being paid for many **fine antique, classic,** and even **secondhand cameras.** • More than **5,000 selling prices** *for all types of popular collector cameras.* • *Information on manufacturer, model name, model number, specifications, and date.* • *Advice on buying and building a collection.* • *A step-by-step guide through the hobby.* • *ILLUSTRATED.*
1st Edition, 320 pgs., 5⅜" x 8", Paperback, ISBN: 383-X, $9.95.

■ **Collectibles of the Third Reich** — **Phenomenal** is the only word to describe the **rising interest** in Nazi militaria. *Perhaps our desire never to forget the horror of Hitler is the root cause of this astonishing collectible field.* • *Included in this extensive guide are firearms, badges, insignia, flags, standards, banners, uniforms, bayonets, daggers, swords, and much more.* • *ILLUSTRATED.*
1st Edition, 320 pgs., 5⅜" x 8", Paperback, ISBN: 422-4, $9.95.

■ **Military Collectibles** — The **definitive guide** to war memorabilia containing military objects from all over the world, 15th century to date: armor, weapons, uniforms, bayonets, rare, and unusual objects. • *Over* **12,000 totally revised prices** *assembled from actual nationwide sales results!* • *Advice on buying and selling from auction houses, mail order, and retail dealers.* • *Museums.* • *Glossary.* • *ILLUSTRATED.*
3rd Edition, 608 pgs., 5⅜" x 8", Paperback, ISBN: 398-8, $9.95.

■ **Music Collectibles** — This revised and expanded edition is the **best selling reference guide** in the music memorabilia field. • **Over 11,000 current market values.** • *Detailed descriptions, historical backgrounds, and values for all types of American and foreign made music machines from the 15th century to the present.* • *Expert advice on grading condition, restoration, and buying and selling.* • *ILLUSTRATED.*
3rd Edition, 576 pgs., 5⅜" x 8", Paperback, ISBN: 406-2, $9.95.

■ **Old Books & Autographs** — Fully revised and updated, this is the **most comprehensive** guide to vintage books and autographs **in print today.** • *Over* **11,000 current market values** *for children's books, the old West, novels, detective fiction, book sets, Bibles, and collectible autographs.* • *Glossary of collector terminology.* • *Biographies of the great printers and bibliophiles.* • *Care and repair of old books.* • *ILLUSTRATED.*
5th Edition, 576 pgs., 5⅜" x 8", Paperback, ISBN: 410-0, $9.95.

■ **Oriental Collectibles** — **Unravel the mystique** of the Orient with this fascinating guide **documented in detail.** • *Over* **10,000 current market values** *compiled from actual sales records from auctions and private sales throughout the U.S.* • *Detailed listings for Chinese, Japanese, and Asian collectors' items including pottery, Japanese weapons, jade carvings, ivories, netsuke, rugs and more.* • *ILLUSTRATED.*
1st Edition, 512 pgs., 5⅜" x 8", Paperback, ISBN: 375-9, $9.95.

■ **Paper Collectibles** — Tour the **fabulous** world of paper collectibles. • **Over 27,000 prices** *for paper items of every description dating from medieval times to the present including books, posters, checks, documents, photographs, newspapers, celebrity autographs, and much more!* • *Sections on buying, selling, and caring for paper collectibles.* • *Find the bargains and enjoy the hobby like never before!* • *ILLUSTRATED.*
3rd Edition, 608 pgs., 5⅜" x 8", Paperback, ISBN: 394-5, $9.95.

■ **Pottery & Porcelain** — This comprehensive guide has **over 12,000 current market values** for American pottery and porcelain **of all types** and **all periods** from the 18th to the 20th century! • *Art pottery, tableware, functional pieces, and novelties.* • *Backgrounds for all the major manufacturers including Rookwood, Roseville, Weller, Hull, and more.* • *Trademark reference guide.* • *Tips on building a collection.* • *ILLUSTRATED.*
3rd Edition, 576 pgs., 5⅜" x 8", Paperback, ISBN: 403-8, $9.95.

For your convenience use the handy order form.

TRADE PRICE GUIDE SERIES

■ **Radio, TV, and Movie Memorabilia** — For the first time ever, *a comprehensive value guide is devoted **exclusively** to these collectibles.* • *Includes thousands of actual selling prices gathered from across the country on animated cels, autographs and autographed articles, books. buttons, pins, rings, costumes, design sketches, fanzines, figurines, games, magazines, posters, press kits, and much more.* • *ILLUSTRATED.*
1st Edition, 576 pgs., 5⅜" x 8", Paperback, ISBN: 416-X, $9.95.

■ **Records** — Find out if your **'golden oldies"** are worth a small fortune. • *More than 32,000 current collector prices for all categories of old, rare, and modern records from 1953 to date!* • *Exclusive photos and biographies of nearly 200 recording stars.* • *Collecting advice on condition, care, and storage.* • *Complete discographies for Motown and Philles records* • *Inventory checklist.* • *ILLUSTRATED.*
5th Edition, 576 pgs., 5⅜" x 8", Paperback, ISBN: 409-7, $9.95.

■ **Royal Doulton** — Acclaimed by critics as the **definitive value guide** to the delightful world of **Royal Doulton figurines.** • *Over 5,500 current collector market values.* • *Features market trends, areas of collector interest, and the investment potential.* • *A handy "quick" reference numerical index for all HN and M model numbers.* • *Includes the Kate Greenaway series, Gilbert and Sullivan, and more.* • *ILLUSTRATED.*
3rd Edition, 576 pgs., 5⅜" x 8", Paperback, ISBN: 407-0, $9.95.

■ **Science Fiction and Fantasy Collectibles** — The interest has never been greater for a guide devoted exclusively to this fascinating field. • *Thousands of values given for "sci-fi" autographs, original art, posters, paperbacks, novels, Big Little books, games, fanzines, lobby cards, comics, toys, and much more.* • *Advice on buying and selling, care, display, and condition.* • *ILLUSTRATED.*
1st Edition, 576 pgs., 5⅜" x 8", Paperback, ISBN: 418-6, $9.95.

■ **Wicker** — The most detailed guide to the fabulous world of vintage wicker on the market today! • *All types of American made wicker furniture and accessories from the Victorian, Turn of the Century, and Art Deco eras.* • *Over 600 photos* • *Detailed descriptions for positive identification.* • *Current collector values.* • *A guide to restoring wicker with professional repair methods.* • *ILLUSTRATED.*
2nd Edition, 480 pgs., 5⅜" x 8", Paperback, ISBN: 380-5, $9.95.

■ **Collectible Toys** — This is the **book** no toy collector can afford to be **without!** • *Over 25,000 current values for trains, windups, autos, soldiers, boats, banks, guns, musical toys, Disneyana, comic characters, Star Trek; Star Wars, and more.* • *Major manufacturers from the Civil War to the present.* • *Valuable collecting tips.* • *Toy manufacturing in America.* • *The Evolution of toy collecting.* • *ILLUSTRATED.*
1st Edition, 576 pgs., 5⅜" x 8", Paperback, ISBN: 384-8, $9.95.

■ **Collector Cars** — The worldwide love affair with the automobile has **resulted in unprecedented profits.** • *Over 37,000 actual current prices for 4,100 models of U.S. and Foreign antique and classic automobiles.* • *United States production figures — 1897 to date.* • *A list of reference publications, museums, and collector clubs.* • *Advice on how to buy and sell successfully at auctions, to dealers, and individuals.* • *ILLUSTRATED.*
5th Edition, 576 pgs., 5⅜" x 8", Paperback, ISBN: 408-9, $9.95.

■ **Collector Handguns** — No other book on the subject **comes close** to supplying the **concise** and **comprehensive information** found here. • *More than 5,000 current retail prices for handguns of all styles and all calibers.* • *Every gun identified by manufacturer, model name, action, caliber, length, date, type of stock, weight, serial number, and markings.* • *Extensive ammo section.* • *Advice on buying and selling.* • *ILLUSTRATED.*
1st Edition, 544 pgs., 5⅜" x 8", Paperback, ISBN: 367-8, $9.95.

— For your convenience use the handy order form. —

TRADE PRICE GUIDE SERIES

■ **Collector Knives** — **Endorsed by the American Blade Collectors.** • Over 14,000 current collector values. • *1,250 worldwide knife manufacturers.* • *Special section for Case, Ka-Bar, and limited edition knives.* • Valuable collector information. • *Exclusive identification guide for pocket knife shields, knife nomenclature, and blade and knife patterns.* • Up-to-date list of knife organizations and trade publications. • *ILLUSTRATED.*
6th Edition, 736 pgs., 5⅜" x 8", Paperback, ISBN: 389-9, $9.95.

■ **Collector Plates** — **The plate collector's bible!** Contains the **most complete listing of all U.S. and foreign plate manufacturers and distributors in print!** • Over 18,000 current collectors values. • *Includes thousands of collector plates from 1895 to date.* • Tips on cleaning, shipping, storing, and displaying. • *A glossary and complete list of plate publications and clubs.* • How to buy and an investment review. • *ILLUSTRATED.*
2nd Edition, 672 pgs., 5⅜" x 8", Paperback, ISBN: 393-7, $9.95.

■ **Collector Prints** — The **most accurate** and **authoritative** work on limited edition prints in publication today. • **Over 14,750 listings of collector prints for more than 400 of the world's leading artists.** • *A list of galleries, agents and publishers.* • Information on buying, selling, storing, and caring for prints. • *A glossary of printmaking and print collecting terminology.* • Artists' biographies. • *ILLUSTRATED.*
5th Edition, 672 pgs., 5⅜" x 8", Paperback, ISBN: 395-3, $9.95.

■ **Comic Books and Collectibles** — **America's indispensable guide** to comic books and related collectibles. • Over 50,000 current values compiled from marketplace transactions. • *Exclusive sections on Big Little Books, Comic Character Memorabilia, Original Art, and Newspaper Comic Art.* • Advice on buying, selling, investing, and swapping. • *An in-depth glossary.* • *ILLUSTRATED.*
7th Edition, 672 pgs., 5⅜" x 8", Paperback, ISBN: 411-9, $9.95.

■ **Depression Glass** — **The largest price guide devoted exclusively to depression glass in print today!** Thousands of items listed, every known pattern and manufacturer included. • *Clear and concise line drawings illustrate each pattern.* • Valuable collector tips on buying and selling, care and display, fakes, reproductions, and much more. • *Complete list of collector publications, museums, and clubs.* • *ILLUSTRATED.*
1st Edition, 576 pgs., 5⅜" x 8", Paperback, ISBN: 433-X, $9.95.

■ **Glassware** — For the first time in print, the **most comprehensive** price guide to collectible glassware **ever produced!** • Over 60,000 current market values for all of the major types of collectible glass including Art, Carnival, Cut, Depression, and Pattern. • *Collecting advice and informative background histories.* • Includes museums, clubs, and manufacturers' marks. • *ILLUSTRATED.*
1st Edition, 576 pgs., 5⅜" x 8", Paperback, ISBN: 125-X, $9.95.

■ **Hummel Figurines & Plates** — Hummel collectors are **unanimous** in their **praise** of this **comprehensive** guide! • Over 18,000 current market values for every known Hummel. • *Complete guide to trademarks and variations.* • A detailed history of Berta Hummel and the Goebel factory. • *Tips on collecting, care, and repair.* • Information on clubs, exhibits, publications, and contests. • *ILLUSTRATED.*
4th Edition, 480 pgs., 5⅜" x 8", Paperback, ISBN: 390-2, $9.95.

■ **Kitchen Collectibles** — This is the only value guide in print today devoted **exclusively** to collectible kitchenware. • More than 28,000 current selling prices. • *China, glassware, silver, copper, iron, and wood.* • Historical backgrounds. • *Comprehensive descriptions of every item, including use, manufacturer, material, style, date, and size.* • Hints on buying, selling, care, and storage. • *ILLUSTRATED.*
1st Edition, 544 pgs., 5⅜" x 8", Paperback, ISBN: 371-6, $9.95.

For your convenience use the handy order form.

MINI PRICE GUIDE SERIES

■ **Antiques & Flea Markets** — Do your antique browsing with the experts . . . take along this **super compact guide** to more than **15,000 old, rare, and unusual collectors' items!** • Spot the bargains . . . avoid the fakes . . . make the best deals when you buy or sell at antique shops, auctions, flea markets, and garage sales. • Current market values for thousands of collectors' items in all categories. • Learn the professional approach to grading, storage, and restoration. • ILLUSTRATED.
2nd Edition, 320 pgs., 4" x 5½", Paperback, ISBN: 392-9, $3.95.

■ **Antique Jewelry** — The indispensable guide to **valuable, but affordable jewelry** — for collecting, wearing, and investing. • Over **2,500 current values** for jewelry from 1750 to 1930. • **Complete descriptions** of styles, patterns, and identifying features. • Date of manufacture. • **Important collector's advice** — buying, selling, cleaning, storing, and displaying. • **Grading information** for diamonds, gold, and silver. • **Historical background** of jewelry. • ILLUSTRATED.
2nd Edition, 288 pgs., 4" x 5½", Paperback, ISBN: 442-9, $3.95.

■ **Baseball Cards** — For thousands of fans, young and old, baseball card collecting is **a year round hobby**. This newly revised edition is the collector's standard reference. • Over **100,000 current market values**. • **Valuable collecting information** — The history of card manufacturing in the U.S., tips on buying and selling, and how to grade condition to determine the value of your collection. • A special price column indicates which items have increased in value. • **Exclusive checklist "grading" system**. • ILLUSTRATED.
4th Edition, 352 pgs., 4" x 5½", Paperback, ISBN: 438-0, $3.95.

■ **Beer Cans** — Collectors agree this handy carry along guide contains everything you will ever need to know about one of America's fastest growing hobbies! • Over **6,000 actual selling prices** for old, modern, rare, and common beer cans. • **All brands** and all types of cans. Includes all label design variations, with information for identifying every variation. • **History of brewing through 6,000 years!** • Tips on how to find valuable cans and how to buy, sell, and trade • ILLUSTRATED.
2nd Edition, 288 pgs., 4" x 5½", Paperback, ISBN: 440-2, $3.95.

■ **Bottles** — Never before in pocket size! Here is the **most convenient** guide to collectible **bottles** in print! Thousands of values given for all types of old and new bottles. • Includes ale & gin, beer, bitters, cure, flasks, fruit jars, Hutchinson, ink, medicine, mineral, poison, Pontil, soda, spirits, Avon, Jim Beam, Brooks, Old Fitzgerald, and many more. • Also valuable collecting tips on buying and selling, grading condition, conducting a dig, background histories, bottle clubs, basic bottle shapes, trademarks, and investment advice. • ILLUSTRATED.
1st Edition, 288 pgs., 4" x 5½", Paperback, ISBN: 431-3, $3.95.

■ **Cars and Trucks** — You could have a fortune parked in your own garage! Over **10,000 current auction and dealer prices** for all popular U.S. and foreign made antique, classic, and collector cars. • **Each detailed listing includes:** the model name and year of production, engine specifications, body style, and a price range value from fair to excellent condition. • **Learn how to evaluate** the condition of a collector car the way the professionals do! • ILLUSTRATED.
1st Edition, 240 pgs., 4" x 5½", Paperback, ISBN: 391-0, $2.95.

For your convenience use the handy order form.

MINI PRICE GUIDE SERIES

■ **Collectible Records** — One of the **most enjoyable and profitable hobbies** today. • Over 11,000 current market prices for Rock and Country recordings. A chronological listing of discs from 1953 to date. • Listed by their original label and issue number. • **Collecting tips** — How to begin a collection, buying, selling, and grading the condition of records and jackets. • A handy guide to "Golden Oldie" shops, conventions, flea markets, and garage sales. • ILLUSTRATED.
1st Edition, 240 pgs., 4" x 5½", Paperback, ISBN: 400-3, $2.95.

■ **Collector Guns** — This handy pocket guide contains **over 9,000 dealer prices** compiled from nationwide sales records for handguns, rifles, and shotguns. Covers American and foreign manufacturers. • **Complete data** on model names, barrel lengths, calibers, and sight types. • Information on the history of firearms, biographies of famous gunmakers, and collecting techniques! • ILLUSTRATED.
1st Edition, 240 pgs., 4" x 5½", Paperback, ISBN: 396-1, $2.95.

■ **Comic Books** — Join the **thousands** who have discovered the fascinating world of comic collecting, one of the nation's fastest-growing hobbies. • **Current market values for over 5,000 old and new comics.** • **Learn how** to start a comic collection and watch it grow into a profitable investment. • Tips on buying, selling, and swapping your comics. Start a comic collection with purchases from the newsstand. • ILLUSTRATED.
2nd Edition, 288 pgs., 4" x 5½", Paperback, ISBN: 382-1, $3.95.

■ **Dolls** — Reap pleasure and profit! • **Over 3,000 current market prices** for dolls of all types and all manufacturers. • **Positive identification** by maker, name of doll, markings, hair color, eye color, type of eye, date of manufacture, and size. • Valuable collector information on buying and selling, fakes, repairs, and how to care for your dolls. • Extensive glossary of doll making and collecting terms. • ILLUSTRATED.
2nd Edition, 288 pgs., 4" x 5½", Paperback, ISBN: 434-8, $3.95.

■ **Football Cards** — Call the right signals every time with the most **authoritative** guide to football cards **in print today!** This revised edition features all the latest cards and price changes. • **Over 50,000 current market values** for collectible football cards. • Valuable collector information — tips on trading, buying and selling, and how to grade condition to determine the value of your collection. • **Exclusive checklist system.** • ILLUSTRATED.
3rd Edition, 288 pgs., 4" x 5½", Paperback, ISBN: 388-0, $2.95.

■ **Glassware** — The handiest guide to collectible glassware on the market today! Contains thousands of values for the five major types of collectible glass — art, carnival, cut, depression, and pattern. • Includes history of each period, manufacturer's marks, pattern and motif identification guide, extensive glossary, and much more. • Plus valuable collector advice on buying, selling, care, display, collector publications, clubs, organizations, and museums. • ILLUSTRATED.
1st Edition, 288 pgs., 4" x 5½", Paperback, ISBN: 432-1, $3.95.

■ **Hummels** — Handy pocket guide with **over 2,000 current collector prices** for the most common and most popular Hummels. All the latest releases are included. • **A Hummel encyclopedia** — from Berta Hummel's beginnings to the growth of the Goebel firm, plus a collector's glossary. • **Valuable collector information** on buying, selling, storage, and display. • Pictures for each listing from 1923 to date. • ILLUSTRATED.
2nd Edition, 288 pgs., 4" x 5½", Paperback, ISBN: 435-6, $3.95.

For your convenience use the handy order form.

MINI PRICE GUIDE SERIES

■ **Military Collectibles** — The **indispensable carry along guide** to the fascinating and historical world of **war souvenirs**. • Over **4,000 current prices** for a wide assortment of military objects from all over the world — 19th century to World War II. • **Positive identification** with dates, markings, country of origin, army, and thorough descriptions. • **Valuable collecting tips** — How to build a collection, grading condition, displaying your collection, and glossary of collectors' terms. • ILLUSTRATED.
1st Edition, 240 pgs., 4" x 5½", Paperback, ISBN: 378-3, $2.95.

■ **Paperbacks & Magazines** — Your old paperbacks and magazines could be worth a fortune today! • Over **10,000 values** are given on paperbacks and magazines dating from the 1800's through the 1980's compiled from actual sales between dealers and collectors. • Learn what makes them valuable and why! • ILLUSTRATED.
2nd Edition, 288 pgs., 4" x 5½", Paperback, ISBN: 405-4, $3.95.

■ **Pocket Knives** — A complete price listing of all **Case and Kabar pocket knives** plus **thousands of current values** for all popular collector knives. • **Complete identification** of every knife by manufacturer, pattern, stamping, year of manufacture, length, and handle type. • **Helpful advice** on buying, selling, and caring for your knife collection. • Pocket knife terminology, grading condition, blade patterns, knife collector organizations, counterfeit specimens, and much more. • ILLUSTRATED.
2nd Edition, 288 pgs., 4" x 5½", Paperback, ISBN: 443-7, $3.95.

■ **Scouting Collectibles** — **Attention, Scouts!** Here's your "field guide" to the profitable hobby of scouting memorabilia. • **Price listings for thousands of scouting items** in all categories. • You'll learn about the fascinating history of scouting and the accessories that were in use over the past years including tools, gadgets, badges, and medals. • ILLUSTRATED.
2nd Edition, 288 pgs., 4" x 5½", Paperback, ISBN: 397-X, $3.95.

■ **Sports Collectibles** — Whatever your sport, you will **find it here!** All the popular **collectibles** of baseball, football, basketball, hockey, boxing, hunting, fishing, horse racing, and other top sports. • Over **12,000 current prices** that collectors are actually paying for a host of sports memorabilia. • Old and modern sports collectibles from the 17th to the 20th century. • **The inside facts** on buying from dealers and selling your sports collectibles for maximum prices! • ILLUSTRATED.
1st Edition, 240 pgs., 4" x 5½", Paperback, ISBN: 379-1, $2.95.

■ **Star Trek / Star Wars Collectibles** — The **phenomenal popularity** of these space age collectibles continues to **skyrocket!** • Over **6,000 current values** for every category of Star Trek and Star Wars collector's items. • **Fascinating information** on the history of the television show and the making of the movies. Tips on building and caring for a collection to buying and selling. • **Special sections** on the conventions with a complete calendar of events.
2nd Edition, 288 pgs., 4" x 5½", Paperback, ISBN: 437-2, $3.95.

■ **Toys** — Whether eight to eighty, you are **never too old** to seriously enjoy toy collections. • Over **8,000 current values** for every category of toys from animal-drawn vehicles to rocketships. • **A toy encyclopedia** — histories of the manufacturers, valuable collector information on buying, selling, and grading condition. • ILLUSTRATED.
2nd Edition, 288 pgs., 4" x 5½", Paperback, ISBN: 436-4, $3.95.

For your convenience use the handy order form.

OFFICIAL PRICE GUIDE SERIES

■ **Collector's Journal** — This is the most **valuable** book any collector could own! Use it to record dealers, collectors, clubs, museums, and reference materials. • Special inventory forms allow the recording of individual collectibles in minute detail. • Value development chart provides space for keeping track of investment value. • Vital information is provided on appraisal, insurance, taxes, and buying and selling.
1st Edition, 256 pgs., 5¼" x 7⅜", Paperback, ISBN: 445-3, $4.95.

■ **The Official Encyclopedia of Antiques and Collectibles** — More than 10,000 definitions. • **Plus** – U.S. automobile production figures. • bottle trademarks. • clock chronology. • collector plate backstamps. • pottery and porcelain marks. • U.S. firearm trademarks. • precious metal purity and weight conversion tables. • silversmith's marks. • pewter backstamps. • furniture style charts.
1st Edition, 704 pgs., 5⅜" x 8" Paperback, ISBN: 365-1, $9.95

■ **The Official Guide to Buying and Selling Antiques and Collectibles** — covers every phase of collecting from beginning a collection to its ultimate sale • Examines IN DETAIL the collecting potential of approximately 200 different categories IN ALL PRICE RANGES. • Learn how the collectible market operates and what makes an item valuable. Every possible source of collector's items is explored IN DEPTH.
1st Edition, 608 pgs., 5⅜" x 8", Paperback, ISBN: 369-4, $9.95

■ **Identification Guide to Early American Furniture** — A comprehensive guide to identifying antique American furniture dating from 1603 to the 1840's. • Provides instant access to hundreds of pieces with superb line drawings. • Includes Jacobean, Pilgrim, William and Mary, Queen Anne, Chippendale, and Neo-Classical Revival. • Features the famous cabinetmakers Adam, Hepplewhite, Sheraton, and others. • ILLUSTRATED.
1st Edition, 320 pgs., 4" x 8", Paperback, ISBN: 414-3, $9.95.

IDENTIFICATION GUIDE SERIES

■ **Identification Guide to Glassware** — Over 100 types of glass are completely described. • Hundreds of illustrated marks and line drawings. • Includes Agata, Amberina, Blown, Burmese, Cameo, Carnival, Cranberry, Crown Milano, Custard, Cut, Depression, Durand, Fry, Galle, Kew Blas, Lalique, Loetz, Mercury, Milk, Napoli, Nash, Paperweights, Peach Blow, Pressed, Ruby, Silveria, and dozens more. • ILLUSTRATED.
1st Edition, 320 pgs., 4" x 8", Paperback, ISBN: 413-5, $9.95.

■ **Identification Guide to Gunmarks** — An important "companion" identification guide to both **The Antique and Modern Firearms** and the **Collector Handguns Price Guides.** • Over 1,500 of the most commonly encountered trademarks on modern and antique guns. • Learn which marks are valuable and how to spot fakes and forgeries. • An alphabetical listing of trade names and codes for firearms without trademarks.
1st Edition, 256 pgs., 5⅜" x 8", Paperback, ISBN: 346-5, $6.95.

■ **Identification Guide to Pottery and Porcelain** — Absolutely the most comprehensive guide to identifying pottery and porcelain in print today! • Includes manufacturers in the United States, Austria, Belgium, Denmark, Holland, England, France, Germany, Ireland, Italy, Prussia, Russia, Scotland, Spain, Sweden, and Switzerland. • Complete descriptions of characteristics and all known marks are given for each of the hundreds of individual types listed.
1st Edition, 320 pgs., 4" x 8", Paperback, ISBN: 412-7, $9.95.

■ **Identification Guide to Victorian Furniture** — There is a **tremendous surge of interest** in the ornate furniture of the **Victorian Period.** • Complete descriptions of every piece and hundreds of line drawings make identification quick and easy. • Also contains manufacturers' histories and an extensive furniture glossary. • Includes Victorian, Renaissance Revival, Rococo Revival (Belter), Spool-turned, Cottage, Louis XVI Revival, Arts and Crafts, Wicker, Cast Iron, and Indian Teak.
1st Edition, 320 pgs., 4" x 8", Paperback, ISBN: 415-1, $9.95.

For your convenience use the handy order form.

NUMISMATIC SERIES

■ **1984 Blackbook Price Guide of United States Coins** — *A coin collector's guide to current market values for all U.S. coins from 1616 to date* — over **16,500 prices.** THE OFFICIAL BLACKBOOK OF COINS has gained the reputation as the most reliable, up-to-date guide to U.S. Coin values. This new edition features, an exclusive gold and silver identification guide. Learn how to test, weigh and calculate the value of any item made of gold or silver. Proven professional techniques revealed for the first time. Detecting altered coins section. Take advantage of the current "BUYERS' MARKET" in gold and silver. *ILLUSTRATED.*
$2.95-22nd Edition, 288 pgs., 4" x 5½", Paperback, Order #: 385-6

■ **1984 Blackbook Price Guide of United States Paper Money** — Over **9,000 buying and selling prices** covering U.S. currency from 1861 to date. Every note issued by the U.S. government is listed and priced including many Confederate States notes. Error Notes are described and priced, and there are detailed articles on many phases of the hobby for beginner and advanced collector alike. Comprehensive grading section. *ILLUSTRATED.*
$2.95-16th Edition, 240 pgs., 4" x 5½", Paperback, Order #: 387-2

■ **1984 Blackbook Price Guide of United States Postage Stamps** — *Featuring all U.S. stamps from 1847 to date pictured in full color.* Over **19,000 current selling prices.** General issues, airmails and special delivery. United Nations, first day covers, and more. New listings for the most current commemorative and regular issue stamps, a feature not offered in any other price guide, at any price! Numerous important developments in the fast moving stamp market during the past year are all included in this *NEW REVISED EDITION. ILLUSTRATED.*
$2.95-6th Edition, 240 pgs., 4" x 5½", Paperback, Order #: 386-4

INVESTORS SERIES

■ **Investors Guide to Gold, Silver, Diamonds** — *All you need to know* about making money trading in the precious metals and diamonds markets. This practical, easy-to-read investment guide is for everyone in all income brackets. How to determine authenticity and value of gold, silver, and diamonds. *ILLUSTRATED.*
$6.95-1st Edition, 208 pgs., 5⅜" x 8½", Paperback, Order #: 171-3

■ **Investors Guide to Gold Coins** — *The first complete book* on investing in gold coins. Elcusive price performance charts trace all U.S. gold coins values from **1955 to date.** Forecast price trends and best bets. *ILLUSTRATED.*
$6.95-1st Edition, 288 pgs., 5⅜" x 8½", Paperback, Order #: 300-7

■ **Investors Guide to Silver Coins** — *The most extensive listing* of all U.S. Silver coins. Detailed price performance charts trace actual sales figures from **1955 to date.** Learn how to figure investment profit. *ILLUSTRATED.*
$6.95-1st Edition, 288 pgs., 5⅜" x 8½", Paperback, Order #: 301-5

■ **Investors Guide to Silver Dollars** — Regardless of your income, you can *become a successful silver dollar investor.* Actual sales figures for every U.S. silver dollar **1955 to date.** Comprehensive grading section. *ILLUSTRATED.*
$6.95-1st Edition, 192 pgs., 5⅜" x 8½", Paperback, Order #: 302-3

For your convenience use the handy order form.

FOR IMMEDIATE DELIVERY
VISA & MASTER CARD CUSTOMERS
ORDER TOLL FREE!
1-800-327-1384

This number is for orders only, it is not tied into the customer service or business office. Customers not using charge cards must use mail for ordering since payment is required with the order — sorry no C.O.D.'s. Florida residents call (305) 857-9095 — ask for order department.

OR — SEND ORDERS TO

THE HOUSE OF COLLECTIBLES, ORLANDO CENTRAL PARK
1900 PREMIER ROW, ORLANDO, FL 32809   (305) 857-9095

☐ *Please send me the following price guides—*
☐ *I would like the most current edition of the books listed below.*

☐ 402-X @ 9.95	☐ 393-7 @ 9.95	☐ 409-7 @ 9.95	☐ 388-0 @ 2.95	☐ 413-5 @ 9.95
☐ 417-8 @ 9.95	☐ 395-3 @ 9.95	☐ 407-0 @ 9.95	☐ 432-1 @ 3.95	☐ 346-5 @ 6.95
☐ 420-8 @ 9.95	☐ 411-9 @ 9.95	☐ 418-6 @ 9.95	☐ 435-6 @ 3.95	☐ 412-7 @ 9.95
☐ 381-3 @ 9.95	☐ 433-X @ 9.95	☐ 380-5 @ 9.95	☐ 378-3 @ 3.95	☐ 415-1 @ 9.95
☐ 421-6 @ 9.95	☐ 125-X @ 9.95	☐ 392-9 @ 3.95	☐ 405-4 @ 3.95	☐ 385-6 @ 2.95
☐ 374-0 @ 9.95	☐ 390-2 @ 9.95	☐ 442-9 @ 3.95	☐ 443-7 @ 3.95	☐ 387-2 @ 2.95
☐ 401-1 @ 9.95	☐ 371-6 @ 9.95	☐ 438-0 @ 3.95	☐ 397-X @ 3.95	☐ 386-4 @ 2.95
☐ 399-6 @ 9.95	☐ 398-8 @ 9.95	☐ 440-2 @ 3.95	☐ 379-1 @ 2.95	☐ 171-3 @ 6.95
☐ 383-X @ 9.95	☐ 406-2 @ 9.95	☐ 431-3 @ 3.95	☐ 437-2 @ 3.95	☐ 300-7 @ 6.95
☐ 424-4 @ 9.95	☐ 410-0 @ 9.95	☐ 391-0 @ 2.95	☐ 436-4 @ 3.95	☐ 301-5 @ 6.95
☐ 384-8 @ 9.95	☐ 375-9 @ 9.95	☐ 400-3 @ 2.95	☐ 445-3 @ 4.95	☐ 302-3 @ 6.95
☐ 408-9 @ 9.95	☐ 394-5 @ 9.95	☐ 396-1 @ 2.95	☐ 365-1 @ 9.95	
☐ 367-8 @ 9.95	☐ 403-8 @ 9.95	☐ 382-1 @ 3.95	☐ 369-4 @ 9.95	
☐ 389-9 @ 9.95	☐ 416-X @ 9.95	☐ 434-8 @ 3.95	☐ 414-3 @ 9.95	

POSTAGE & HANDLING RATE CHART

TOTAL ORDER/POSTAGE	TOTAL ORDER/POSTAGE	
0 to $10.00 - **$1.25**	$20.01 to $30.00 - **$2.00**	$50.01 & Over -
$10.01 to $20.00 - **$1.60**	$30.01 to $40.00 - **$2.75**	Add 10% of your total order
	$40.01 to $50.00 - **$3.50**	(Ex. $75.00 x .10 = $7.50)

☐ Check or money order enclosed $_____ (include postage and handling)

☐ Please charge $_____ to my: ☐ MASTERCARD ☐ VISA

Charge Card Customers Not Using Our Toll Free Number Please Fill Out The Information Below.

Account No. (All Digits)_____ Expiration Date_____

Signature_____

NAME (please print)_____ PHONE _____

ADDRESS_____ APT. # _____ (10)

CITY _____ STATE _____ ZIP _____